Amazing Facts III

Trivia
Treasures

Thomas F. Shubnell, Ph.D.

ISBN-13: 978-1530299836

ISBN-10: 1530299837

Cover and interior design by TFS

Please ask your local library to carry my books.

We live in an interconnected world. Many are used to reading quickly, then going back and reading more background information later. I have included some links within the text of this book.

Links are easy enough to overlook while reading, but available for further in depth reading online. For eBook readers, the links are live for easy clicking.

Autohagiography

If you enjoy this, you will also love, Amazing Facts and Bite Sized Brain Food and Amazing Facts II Tons of Trivia. They are collections of thousands of amazing facts about the things you don't know, but want to know, and facts you think you know, but don't. Nestled in among the facts are bite sized tidbits of knowledge you can use to spice up any conversation.

"Bacon Orgazmia" a pandect of porcineology and a homage to the goodness and gallimaufry of all things bacon, including history, types, recipes, events, and more.

"Gracious Me . . . Is Nothing Sacred" is a non-sectarian and hilarious look at all religions from the beginning of time. From Atheism to Zen it truly proves that laughter is good for the soul.

Medical humor abounds in the best selling "Medical Humor - medical nonsense to tickle your funny bone. A great collection of medical funny stuff, including stories, jokes, and hilarious pictures and cartoons.

"Unelectum All" is a reader's digest of politics. It makes the case for change using politicians own words. It begins with early campaign promises and follows with political absurdities that unfold after elections.

A wacky book, "Men vs. Women, a Book of Lists" examines life from a different perspective and tells it all - the differences between the sexes are real and funny.

Even more fun can be found in "The Best of Terrible Tommy and Yucky Chucky," a collection of the best Terrible Tommy and Yucky Chucky jokes of all time.

More hilarious reading can be found in "Giggles, Gags, and Quips, Special Picks" a collection of the best jokes, pictures, billboards, stories, and cartoons.

Relationships can be funny, as shown in "Flowers, Foreplay, Facelifts, and Flatulence" a humorous romp through the four stages of relationships.

Also collect all the "Greatest Jokes of the Century" series of books. 25 wildly funny and hilarious compendiums of the greatest jokes, tidbits, stories, and trivia that are all sure to induce uncontrollable laughter.

"The Art of Installation and the Science of Implementation" is a serious project management primer, including tools and techniques for successful software implementation projects.

Don't forget to collect my Profound Thoughts, a five book series of great wisdom, aphorisms, and quotes from great minds.

All written by Thomas F. Shubnell and available online, your favorite bookstore, or as eBooks.

Table of Contents

Technology Facts

TECHNOLOGY

"Change has never happened this fast before, and it will never be this slow again." Graeme Wood, Social Principal #9, Geek Media, Sept 29, 2009.

Awesome Technology - From the Consumer Electronics Show (CES) comes an awesome speaker. ClearView Audio CLIO is a clear acrylic speaker which pushes sound through the side of the device instead of the rear, like traditional cone speakers.

Edge Motion-driven speakers actuate a thin membrane along the side in a manner that creates an extremely efficient, piston-like motion in front. The resultant speaker system is thin and lightweight with the ability to produce a rich, full sound across the audio range.

Sound Mirrors - Mirrors can actually reflect sound as well as light. Mirrors that reflect sound waves are known as "acoustic mirrors," and were used in Britain during World War I to detect certain sound waves coming from enemy aircraft from 8 to 15 miles away. This was before the development of radar.

Several were built around the coast of Britain, and are still standing today on both the north and south shores of England. They are also called listening stones.

Concrete acoustic mirrors were built on the south and northeast coasts of England between about 1916 and the 1930s. The 'listening ears' were intended to provide early warning of incoming enemy aircraft.

They did work, but the development of faster aircraft made them less useful, as an incoming aircraft would be within sight by the time it had been located. Also, increasing ambient noise made the mirrors more difficult to use successfully, and then radar rendered acoustic detection redundant.

There is also an example of one that is a parabolic sound mirror carved into boulders to dramatically magnify the sound of a nearby stream for listeners. It is inspired by satellite dishes, the seating in choir lofts where curved walls reflect sound, and the antique hand-held sound magnifiers used in the days before hearing aids.

Ultra Thin Circuits - Ultra thin film-like organic transistor integrated circuits are being developed by a research group led by

Professor Takao Someya and Associate Professor Tsuyoshi Sekitani of the University of Tokyo, who run an Exploratory Research for Advanced Technology program sponsored by the Japan Science and Technology Agency, in collaboration with Siegfried Bauer's group at the Johannes Kepler University Linz, Austria.

The circuits are extremely lightweight, flexible, durable and thin, and conform to any surface. They are just 2 microns thick, just 1/5 that of kitchen wrap, and weighing only $3g/m^2$, are 30 times lighter than office paper. They also feature a bend radius of 5 microns, meaning they can be scrunched up into a ball, without breaking. Due to these properties the researchers have dubbed them "imperceptible electronics", which can be placed on any surface and even worn without restricting the users movement.

The integrated circuits are manufactured on rolls of one micron thick plastic film, making them easily scalable and cheap to produce. And if the circuit is placed on a rubber surface it becomes stretchable, able to withstand up to 233% tensile strain, while retaining full functionality.

"This is a very convenient way of making electronics stretchable because you can fabricate high performance devices in a flat state and then just transfer them over to a stretchable substrate and create something that is very compliant and stretchable just by a simple pick and place process."

In the future, the group would like to expand the capabilities of these circuits and open a wide range of new applications, from health monitoring systems, wearable medical instruments, and even robotic skins.

Opt Out - There is a web site that will scare the heck out of you, but will also help you. The ad industry website for opting out of ads from multiple companies goes a long way to keep companies from dropping cookies on your computer, then bombarding you with ads that have become more and more personalized to you. Increasingly, these companies also track your location, contacts, calls, texts, etc., through your smart phone. Check what an app can look at each time before you agree to download. (If it wants access to your contact list, please remove me or change my name to John Doe.) If you like these ads, skip to the next topic.

If you do not like ads, go to the site using the link below and follow the instructions to opt out. These are only the specific companies that target ads to you based on your cookies. Other companies that do not directly target can be eliminated through various add-ons to your

particular browser. In my case, I had only one company showing, although 117 companies were participating. My browser is so locked down, I usually do not see any ads on most pages, but I am vigilant with my lockdown practices. After opting out, a few of them added a preference in my browser to not show me ads.
 http://www.aboutads.info/choices/

My mother used to tell me that too many cookies were not good for me. Now I understand she must have meant both physical and electronic.

Robot Reporting - I love all things tech and I love writing. This program (or app or algorithm) stokes both of my passions. Robots are now writing mainstream media articles. Three minutes after one of the earthquakes hit Southern California a few weeks ago, an article was ready for publication, before reporters were awake or aware of the happenings.

The author was quakebot, a program created two years ago, that reacts to input from devices that report seismic activity. It is called a 'bot', because it reacts to outside stimulus without human intervention. The algorithm adds text to fill in between the 'facts' to create a readable story, suitable for publishing. In this case, it extracted the relevant data from the US Geological Service report, plugged it into a pre-written template, and sent it for publication in the LA Times.

Here is the actual article created: "A shallow magnitude 4.7 earthquake was reported Monday morning five miles from Westwood, California, according to the U.S. Geological Survey. The temblor occurred at 6:25 a.m. Pacific time at a depth of 5.0 miles. According to the USGS, the epicenter was six miles from Beverly Hills, California, seven miles from Universal City, California, seven miles from Santa Monica, California and 348 miles from Sacramento, California. In the past ten days, there have been no earthquakes magnitude 3.0 and greater centered nearby. This information comes from the USGS Earthquake Notification Service and this post was created by an algorithm written by the author."

There are many other examples of 'bot' reporters and one company even has some that scan entire books and publish indexes of words, by topic, and sells the results, in the form of books, on Amazon. *Wow, honest reporting without humans twisting the story to fit the politics. There is hope.*

Google Compare - Here is another great feature of Google that might help improve your health and decrease your waistline.

Google has a nutrition comparison feature that allows you to compare two types of food for nutritional values.

If you want to compare the calories, nutrients, and other values of apples and oranges, type in "compare apples oranges" without the quotes. You will see photos and a chart revealing calories, sodium, vitamins, minerals, etc. It also lists other normal results, like web sites, etc. I also tried "compare banana potato" and found there is only twelve calories difference between them. *Very interesting and useful tool.*

Netflix Facts and Numbers - What is better with pizza than a movie? Netflix was founded in 1997 in Scotts Valley, California by Marc Randolph and Reed Hastings, who previously had worked together. Randolph was a co-founder of a computer mail order company and later was employed by Borland International as vice-president of marketing. Hastings, once a math teacher, had founded Pure Software, which he had recently sold for $700 million. Hastings invested $2.5 million in start up cash for Netflix.

The idea of Netflix came to Hastings when he was forced to pay $40 in overdue fines after returning a rented movie well past its due date.

The Netflix website was launched on August 29, 1997 with only 30 employees and 925 works available for rent and brought a more traditional, online pay-per-rental model (late fees applied). The company offers unlimited vacation time for salaried workers and allows employees to take any amount of their paychecks in stock options.

Netflix introduced the monthly subscription concept in September 1999, and then dropped the single-rental model in 2000. Since that time the company has built its reputation on the business model of flat-fee unlimited rentals without due dates, late fees, shipping and handling fees, or per title rental fees.

Netflix was offered to Blockbuster for $50 million in 2000, but Blockbuster declined.

In 2005, Netflix shipped 1 million DVDs every day.

In February 2007, the company delivered its billionth DVD and began to move away from its original core business model of mailing DVDs by introducing video-on-demand via the Internet.

By 2010, Netflix's streaming business had grown to 14 million subscribers and shifted from the fastest-growing customer of the United States Postal Service's first-class mail service to the largest source of Internet traffic in North America. In November of that year it began offering a standalone streaming service separate from DVD rentals. It launched internationally in 2011.

On January 26, 2012, the company announced it had 24.4 million US subscribers.

Disney and Marvel TV said they will provide Netflix with live action series, beginning in 2015, featuring Daredevil, Jessica Jones, Iron Fist, and Luke Cage, leading up to a miniseries about the Defenders.

Netflix signed an agreement in 2014 with a US Cable company to offer it as a channel on the TV lineup. Users can click on the channel, like any other channel, and have all the Netflix options.

Telling Time - It occurred to me that telling time in sixty second and sixty minute intervals seemed odd, so I looked it up. In the early second millennium B.C., the Babylonians invented their number system, and its influence still affects us to this day. Because of a limited amount of symbols (they only had two, along with their indicator for zero), they had to innovate, creating a system where one column indicated multiples of 1, one column indicated multiples of 60, and one column indicated multiples of 3,600. The columns were separated by a small space.

Once they had their number system in place, the Babylonians began applying it to various aspects of their life, such as the number of degrees in a circle and the number of days in a year. Since their system was much easier to calculate and divide, the Babylonian numbers reigned supreme over those of other nations, remaining the favored system for astronomers up to the 16th century. Eventually, thanks to its divisibility, the base-60 system was applied to the concept of time, giving us the number of minutes in an hour and the number of seconds in a minute.

Bluetooth Symbol - Have you ever wondered how the bluetooth symbol was developed? Look at the top line on your smart phone to see it.

It comes from the Nordic runes for the letters GH and B for Harald 'Bluetooth' Gormson, the king of Denmark and Norway back in the nine hundreds, who turned the Danes to Christianity. The name suggests he had a dark or blue tooth.

Cell Phone Facts - Although Apple iPhone smart phones generally receive the most publicity, they make up just 11.7% of all world-wide smart phones.

Android has 84.7% market share according to Business Insider. The rest, to equal 100% are other brands.

The top 5 countries with the most active cell phones are: China, 1.2 billion; India, 904 million; US, 327 million; Brazil, 276 million; and Russia, 256 million.

A scientific study by the Mayo Clinic in 2005 proved cell phones cause no electromagnetic interference with hospital equipment.

Borrow a Drone - Students at the University of South Florida, US are now able to borrow quadcopter drones from the school library. The university allows students to check out one of the library's two remote control devices for supervised flights. The small white drones come fitted with a video camera. The university says they will be useful for students studying a range of disciplines. Students need to complete a course in drone operation before checking the devices out, and their use is to be monitored by staff members standing over the students' shoulders.

3D Printed Keys - The once almost ubiquitous key kiosks have long since gone and many hardware stores no longer provide the service. Now a company called 'Keys Duplicated' prints keys from photographs. Snap a picture of any key, send it in, and within a few days you will receive a duplicate in the mail. The site suggests to text a link to its page to your phone, or go to keysduplicated.com on your mobile browser. It says it is easier to send a key if you visit the page directly on your mobile phone. No need to download an app.

The charge shows six dollars for the first key and four dollars for the second, with no shipping charges. The company pitches its service to people who need an extra key to their own house. *Practical use for new technology.*

Hologram Shopping - Lowe's may not provide printed 3d keys yet, but it is entering the digital age in a big way. The Lowe's Holoroom is a home improvement simulator which applies augmented reality to provide homeowners an intuitive, immersive experience in the room of their dreams. It was introduced to stores in Toronto during 2014 and equipped with thousands of products to help customers plan a bathroom remodel or refresh project.

Customers begin by choosing their preferred products on a pad device before viewing and experiencing those products in the Holoroom. While in the Holoroom, they can make changes to the room design or finalize their plan. A take-home link allows customers to view a 3-D model of their room at home, and share the model with family and friends by downloading a free app available on smartphones.

The concept is to let customers use a pad to create the room, adding features, textures, tiles, counters, etc., then walk around a physical space set up in the store to view it as if they are in the actual room. They can look down into the sink to see the texture and drain or up to see a light fixture.

Lowes plans to expand additional living spaces in the future, including the kitchen and outdoor living. It is also envisioned to eventually let people do the same thing in their own home, then click to buy everything needed to make that room a reality. *Cool technology, from hammers to holograms. Seems to me this might be a perfect application for an Oculus Rift virtual reality headset device.*

Tricorder Xprize - Qualcomm started a global competition in 2012 that will award ten million US dollars to revolutionize digital healthcare. The idea is to stimulate innovation and integration of precision diagnostic technologies, helping consumers make their own reliable health diagnoses anywhere, anytime.

The device it is seeking will be a tool capable of capturing key health metrics and diagnosing a set of fifteen diseases. Metrics for health could include such elements as blood pressure, respiratory rate, and temperature. Ultimately, this tool will collect large volumes of data from ongoing measurement of health states through a combination of wireless sensors, imaging technologies, and portable, non-invasive laboratory replacements. The only stated limit on form is that the mass of its components together must be no greater than five pounds. The name comes from the medical device used in Star Trek.

This week, August 4 is the qualifying round for review and selection of the ten finalist teams. The final award will be held in January 2016.

Supercomputer TrueNorth - During August 2014, IBM unveiled "TrueNorth". It is the most advanced and powerful computer chip of its kind ever built. This neurosynaptic processor was the first to achieve one million individually programmable neurons, sixteen times more than the then current largest neuromorphic chip. It is designed to mimic the structure of the human brain and is uniquely different from other computer architectures.

TrueNorth is the largest IBM chip ever fabricated, with 5.4 billion transistors at 28nanometers (A human hair is approximately 80,000-100,000 nanometers wide) and it consumes orders of magnitude less power than a typical modern processor. IBM hopes this combination of ultra-efficient power consumption and entirely new system architecture will allow computers to far more accurately emulate the brain.

TrueNorth is composed of 4,096 cores, with each of these modules integrating memory, computation and communication. The cores are able to continue operating when individual cores fail, similar to a biological system.

Smart Phone Tricks - Want to capture something on your phone's screen? Try this

iPhone - Press and hold the Home button along with the Sleep/Wake button. You should hear a shutter click. The screenshot will appear in your Camera Roll or Saved Photos section.

Android - Hold the Power and Volume Down buttons at the same time. The image is saved to the "Captured Images" folder in your Gallery app. That only works in Android 4.0 and higher. For some Samsung Galaxy phones, hold the home and power off buttons at the same time.

Want to increase the font size to something a bit easier to see?

iPhone - Go to Settings>>General>>Accessibility and turn on Bold Text and Larger Text. You can choose either one or both, depending on your preferences. You will need to restart your phone for Bold Text to take effect.

Android - Go to Settings>>Accessibility. Under Vision, tap Font size and set it to Large. Some phones include an even larger 'Huge' option.

Want to have your phone read things out loud?
iPhone - Go to Settings>>General>>Accessibility and turn on VoiceOver. You will need to do some playing around to get used to it. For example you can touch and drag your fingers around the home screen to have it read what's there. Double tap to activate an app, while one tap will give you details about it. VoiceOver will read directions to you in Maps, have your camera tell you how many people are in your shot, and get spoken photo descriptions. You can also hand write notes and letters on the screen and have VoiceOver translate your messages into text for Mail and other apps.

Android - Go to Settings>>Accessibility and tap TalkBack. If you don't see it, you can download it from the Google Play store. Turn it on and your phone will read whatever you touch on the screen and incoming notifications. To perform a regular swipe gesture, you need to use two fingers instead of one. To adjust your TalkBack settings, go to

Settings>>Accessibility and tap Text-to-Speech options. You can adjust the voice engine and speed rate. Then go to Settings and turn on Hands-free mode. This will tell you who is calling or messaging. *(I tried this and it was so irritating, that I shut it off)*

Want to control your phone camera with voice?
Android - Open the camera app and tap the gear to see the settings. Scroll down to Voice control and turn it on. Now you can take pictures with the commands, "Capture," "Shoot," "Smile" and "Cheese." If your phone doesn't have a built-in camera app with this feature, you'll need a third-party app like Say Cheese.

Call Back App - Here is an application that could save your evening or possibly your life. It is based on text messages, works with any cell phone, not just smartphones and it does not rely on an Internet connection. The service is called Kitestring.

A person sends Kitestring a text with time period like '30m'. In 30 minutes, Kitestring will send back a check-up text and you have five minutes to respond with an 'OK'. If you do not reply on time, Kitestring sends an alert to your designated emergency contact. It might be handy to set before blind dates, traveling alone, or for medical situations.

The basic service is free with eight uses per month with one emergency contact. A paid version offers unlimited uses and contacts as well as with a recurring check-in mode and customized response period.

The recurring check-in might be useful for people with medical conditions and/or who live alone. For instance, you can have it check in on you once or twice a day. A pleasant way to be reminded to let someone know you are OK, without the need for a call. *Using this service can mean no call is good news.*

Laptop Tip - Overcharging is not so much of a problem as most modern laptops have circuitry that keeps the battery just under 100% when it is plugged in. That means there is less chance of the battery overheating and catching fire.

However, lithium-ion batteries, like the ones in newer laptops, last longest when they stay between 20% and 80% capacity. When they spend a lot of time above and below those percentages, it shortens the battery's life.

Also, a battery that is charging while the laptop is running will be hotter than usual. That also shortens the overall battery life.

So, if your laptop is always sitting the same place, it is a good idea to unplug it every now and then and let the battery take over. Or you can remove the battery totally and leave it plugged in all the time.

3D Printed Prosthetic Hand - Hayley Fraser, a five-year-old girl from Scotland, recently became the first child in the United Kingdom to be outfitted with a prosthetic limb made using 3D printing technology.

She was born without fingers on her left hand. Her parents, David and Zania Fraser, went online to try and help their daughter who had been turned down by the National Health System. They came across the website of E-nable, a group of volunteers in the United States who design and build prosthetics for children. They made a cast of their daughter's hand and sent it to the group. Professor Flood used the model to print out properly-sized prosthetic components using a 3D printer.

Now, Hayley can manipulate her prosthetic hand's artificial tendons, joints, and fingers by flexing and rotating her wrist. She can hold her teddy, peel a banana, and even paint her nails. Her new bright pink bionic hand was inspired by the movie *Ironman*.

Intel Wearable Awards – Intel's Make It Wearable is a global initiative to inspire ideas and fuel innovation that will evolve personal computing in exciting new ways.

The Development track focuses on concepts that are both excitingly innovative and feasible to execute. They also demonstrate innovative solutions, creative implementation, technical feasibility, intelligent business planning, and potential for long-term success.

Intel is on a mission to identify and support wearable products and/or technology that can go to market in near future. This track features 3 rounds. All submissions are evaluated in round 1 (idea proposal submission), forty advance to round 2, ten advance to round 3, and three winners are chosen. Semifinalists and finalists gain expert support and education aimed at evolving their proposals into fully developed designs and business plans.

Nixie, the Selfie-Taking Drone, won. It is a wristband that unfolds into a remote-controlled flyable camera, and the winner of the US $500,000 prize. Each of the second through tenth place winners took home US $50,000.

In second place was Open Bionics' 3D printed, functioning prosthetic robotic hand.

Third place was won by Team Proglove's "smart glove" for production and manufacturing. It is a sensor-based "smart glove" that can boost productivity for manufacturing jobs. With an embedded Intel Edison module, and an on-board display, ProGlove allows wearers to scan, sense, and record activities.

Computer on a Stick - Intel is coming out with a 'Compute Stick' that is a full personal computer. It is about the size of a USB memory stick. On one end, the device has a full-size HDMI plug which attaches to your TV or monitor. On its side is a microUSB port which plugs into the wall for power using a standard USB cable. A second, full-size USB port allows you to attach peripherals and a microSD card slot provides for memory expansion.

Not to get too technical, but it is a quad-core Atom-powered mini PC with 2GB of RAM, 32GB eMMC storage, running Windows 8.1. The price when it comes out later this spring should be about US $150.

It also has a power button, and in addition to its USB port, it can pair with a keyboard and mouse using Bluetooth. Since Bluetooth sends a signal to about 30 feet, you can sit in your easy chair and have the best of TV and PC on one device, with no extra wires or gadgets. It also supports 802.11n Wi-Fi for connecting to the Internet and your home network. Now you can have a real PC TV with a keyboard, etc. No longer necessary to send YouTube videos from your PC as they are already on the screen. *Am very sure I need one of these and hope by the time it is available I will be able to explain/justify to myself why.*

4K, 8K, LED, OLED, HD, UHD - There are a number of confusing TV terms being thrown around these days to catch our attention and drive us to toss out our relatively new flat screen TVs. I decided to decode a few of the terms so we can make an informed decision - and then rush out to buy something to get the 'first on the block' medal.

4K has about eight million pixels which equates to about four times more than a current 1080p TV. Think of your TV like a grid, with rows and columns. A full HD 1080p image is 1080 rows high and 1920 columns wide. A 4K image almost doubles both those numbers, so you could fit every pixel from your 1080p set onto one quarter of a 4K screen. Recent 4K TVs are the same thickness as a smart phone, less than two tenths of an inch thick.

Since 4K contains four times the information of High Definition (HD or FHD), someone came up with the name Ultra High Definition (UHD). The bad news is the Internet providers have not opened up the pipes enough, so many 4K users see a lag time (that frustrating spinning circle) when watching 4K content. Netflix and Amazon currently charge more for delivering 4K content.

Currently, 1080 resolution comes from the image height, while 4K (3840 x 2160) is derived from image width. If it was described the same way as now, 4K would be 2160p. Seems that was not enough of a difference to command the increased price so they changed the definition to make it seem better to the uninitiated.

8K (7680 x 4320) basically doubles the pixel height and width of 4K to about 32 million pixels. The 8K standard is currently for exhibitions and movie theaters. Since 4K will not become the norm for a few more years, 8K is many years away from the home market.

LED comes from Light Emitting Diode. LED TVs are really LCD TVs, but the difference is how the screen is lit. Traditional LCD TVs use florescent backlights, LED TVs use smaller, more energy-efficient LEDs. LED screens produce great color, but the brightness of the lights can also wash out blacks on the screen.

OLED or Organic Light Emitting Diodes have been around for years, but producing big screens using this technology has proven to be prohibitively expensive until lately. The OLED elements generate their own light so the technology is stunning, with vibrant colors, deep blacks, and bright whites.

3D TV continues to die a slow death, even though some manufacturers are still trying to convince us we need it. Think of 3D as Three Times Dead.

Bottom line, OLED is better than LED, 4K is amazing when you can see 4K content, both 4K and 8K are Ultra High Definition (UHD), both cost twice as much or more than HD, both require faster internet to be useful. Since there is little 4K and no 8K content, people who buy theses TVs are stuck explaining the picture deficiency and Ultra High Cost to guests. When content arrives, these TVs will be awesome and, by then, the price will be much more affordable. Last thing, when it comes to TVs, bigger is better, OLED is much better, 4K is awesome, but too expensive, for now.

IBM Watson Update - During the three years since the *Jeopardy* match on TV, Watson has become 24 times smarter and faster, improved performance by 2,400%, and is 90% smaller. IBM says it has shrunk Watson from the size of a master bedroom to the size of three stacked pizza boxes.

IBM says, "What we believe is happening right now, is that the amount of information being produced in the world is overrunning the ability of humans to consume it. When these kinds of things have happened in history, new tools emerged that helped humans deal with scale, such as in the industrial revolution." "I think as we look at knowledge-based professions today — health care, law, teaching — they're all being overrun with information. It's very difficult for people to keep up — and that leads inventors to come up with ways to help humans deal with that overload."

Zenith Space Command - In 1956, the first widely used TV remote control had four buttons (power, volume, channel up, channel down) but no batteries. Press a button, and a tiny hammer inside the remote would strike an aluminum rod, transmitting an ultrahigh-frequency tone to control the set. They were affectionately known as clickers, because they actually clicked when you pressed the buttons.

Back then they only had a few channels to scroll through, and all TVs were black and white, so it was not a big deal.

I read that you could sometimes drop a coin on it and it would change channels. The Space Command lasted more than 25 years before being replaced by remotes using infrared technology. Before these slick devices, they actually had a remote that was physically wired directly to the TV, and before that they had kids that they would tell to go change the channel, or turn up the volume.

Wallpaper TV - Coming to a wall near you. Many of us are accustomed to watching TV on high-quality flat screens, but now Toshiba has come up with a new solution.

It is a flexible paper that doubles as a TV screen. The paper uses light that has been redirected using a fine grating created by self-assembling nano-particles. In addition to projecting moving and still pictures, the paper could also be used to emit light, eliminating the need for traditional lighting.¶

I won't go into details of the cool OLED technology used, but the basic materials have been around since the 90s. Television wallpaper is currently in the early stages of research and won't be on your wall for quite sometime. *Wow, I don't even have an HDTV yet and they are already on their way out. The speed of technology change is so exciting, I can hardly stand it.*

Light a Picture - This is so ridiculous that I first thought it was an April Fool's joke, but it is not. A group at MIT proposed the idea of a matchstick embedded with a tiny camera and microphone (green half) and micro projector (red half).

A user swipes the red side of the match, physically lighting it on fire. This sets off the camera and microphone to start recording, moving down the length of the match in response to heat. The match stores the image and sound in the middle. When a user lights the other end, a mini projector plays back the video once before burning away (literally). The group has so far designed a prototype, based on two coupled matches synced to a computer webcam and playback program.

Nine Gartner Technology Predictions

Gartner has released its technology predictions for the year.

1. By 2018, twenty percent of all business content, one in five of the documents you read, will be authored by a machine. "Robowriters" are already producing budget reports, sports, and business reports, and this trend is sneaking in without notice.

2. By 2018, six billion connected things will be requesting support. These non-human "things" are customers requesting services and data, and other methods of support.

3. By 2020, autonomous software agents outside of human control will participate in 5% of all economic transactions. Smart algorithms are already beginning to perform transactions without human help.

4. By 2018, more than three million workers globally will be supervised by a robo boss. "The problem with this is that robot bosses don't have human reactions," it said. "The reality is we have to see if robots can get human mannerisms right."

5. By 2018, twenty percent of smart buildings will have experienced digital vandalism. As buildings, both commercial and residential, get smarter and more connected, there is greater potential that these buildings can be attacked. We need to develop a way to detect and correct these intrusions.

6. By 2018, fifty percent of the fastest-growing companies will have less smart employees and more smart machines. Smart systems will be analyzing how a factory is being run, or

deciding whether people are completing a task at an appropriate speed.

7. By 2018, digital assistants will recognize individuals by face and voice. Passwords are unworkable and good ones are hard to memorize. Biometrics have been around for a long time, but will get stronger.

8. By 2018, two million employees will be required to wear health and fitness tracking devices as a condition of employment. One benefit is that insurance costs may be lower for those companies with healthy employees. The use of such devices also raises significant issues about whether an employee keeps a job based on fitness level.

9. By 2020, smart agents will facilitate forty percent of mobile interactions. This is based on the belief that the world is moving to a post-app era, where assistants such as Cortana, Siri, and Google Now act as a type of universal interface.

Top Ten Tech Changes

1. **Farming** is quickly becoming a high-tech job. Farmers are using big-data analytics to better monitor, manage, and understand their outputs.

2. **Energy utility companies** are slow to adopt new technologies, and they have a set business model used for decades. Renewable energy, however, needs advanced battery technology and new storage and transmission systems, so this has to change. It is starting to with the development of microgrids and other smart grid technologies, which are a major part of the future for utilities. The market for smart grid IT will grow to more than $23 billion by 2023.

3. **Electric vehicles** are powered by high-tech batteries, but the technology for them is not yet fully developed. Data analysis is big with EVs too, as most cars are equipped with sensors that track the behavior of the driver so that companies can better understand and develop EV technologies.

4. As **solar panel** prices decrease and more individuals and companies adopt them, the renewable energy industry is finally heading toward the mainstream.

5. There is no industry transforming the future faster than **3D printing**, but the technology is also infiltrating many other ones, like healthcare, manufacturing, and aerospace. It means new tech jobs that revolve around understanding, developing, and monitoring the printers and software development and management.

6. The **healthcare** industry is notorious for developing slowly, but all that is changing with the advent of bioprinting, telemedicine, and big data analytics. There will be IT jobs in hospitals and clinics, software companies, hardware companies, data science companies, and even big tech companies.

7. Technology is changing the way **government** processes work. Cities like Boston and New York are adding social media directors and Chief Digital Officers to promote campaigns, run social media, and get people to interact more with their government. Organizations revamping government websites to make them more efficient.

8. **Technology and computer science education** will be increasingly important as the world works to get more children prepare for the future. Nine out of ten schools in the US do not yet offer computer programming classes.

9. **Toys** are getting smarter. People are building toys that serve a purpose and incorporate robotics, sensors, and computers.

10. Companies are using sensors and data analytics to identify and monitor leaks and **water waste** in the home so that people can better conserve the resource and their money.

Seven Microwave Facts

- A common myth surrounding microwaves is that you cannot put metal in them. The walls of the microwave are metal. You put metal in when you cook things like hot-pockets in those sleeves they come with (lined with aluminum, which heats up and browns the crust via convection). Some even come with a metal rack for double deck cooking.

- A microwave oven's radiation does not cause cancer, because it is not ionizing radiation. Even mice that spent their whole lives exposed to low levels of microwaves at the same frequency as a microwave oven, showed no adverse effects from the microwaves.

- Devices like your wireless router, GPS satellites, Bluetooth devices, and smart phones also likely operate using the same band as your microwave oven. This is also why when you run your microwave, you may notice those wireless devices stop working well when you get too close to the running microwave. Some fractions of the microwaves from the magnetron are escaping and interfering with the signal your devices are using. The amount is too miniscule to be noticed or felt if you stand in front.

- There is nothing special about the material the window of your microwave is made of. It is typically just plastic or glass. What stops the microwaves from cooking you is the metal mesh that is on the inside of the plastic or glass. The holes in the mesh are smaller than the wavelengths of the electromagnetic radiation your microwave is producing. The microwaves bounce off and back into your microwave oven to heat the food.

- Many microwavable foods have a recommendation that you let the food sit for a few minutes before eating it. This is because sometimes the food is very thick and the microwaves may not have managed to penetrate deeply and so the center may not be warm, but is surrounded by a very hot outer layer. By waiting a few minutes, it allows the hot part to warm the center and the overall temperature of the food evens out. This is also why when you click "defrost" on your microwave you hear it periodically kicking on and off. It heats the frozen object for a short period and then lets the heated part warm the inner part by convection.

- Microwaves convert Vitamin B12 to an inactive form, which means about 30-40% of the Vitamin B12 in microwaved foods is not usable by mammals.

- Spinach loses about 77% of its folate when cooked in a normal stove, but retains nearly all of it when cooked in a microwave. In the same way, steamed vegetables, as a rule, tend to retain more of their nutrients in a microwave than when cooked in a traditional oven.

Top Ten Greatest Inventions

According to a survey of 4,000 Brits.

1. Wheel
2. Airplane
3. Light bulb
4. Internet
5. PCs
6. Telephone
7. Penicillin
8. Smart Phone
9. Flushing toilet
10. Combustion engine

Interesting to note that the Smart Phone is before the flushing toilet. Also interesting that TV does not show up in the top 25.

Here is the rest of the list - 11. Contraceptive pill 12. Washing machine 13. Central heating 14. Refrigerator 15. Pain killers 16. Steam engine 17. Freezer 18. Camera 19. Cars 20. Spectacles (glasses) 21. Mobile phones 22. Toilet paper 23. Vacuum cleaner 24. Trains 25. Google.

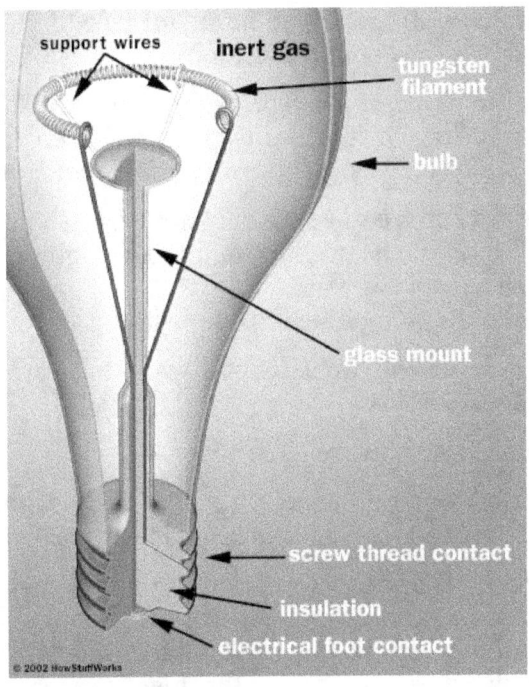

INTERNET AND WWW

Stores Meet Internet - Home improvement giant Lowe's just bought 42,000 handheld point of sales devices for its 1700+ outlets. Its competitor Home Depot spent $64 million placing 30,000+ of its First Phone Motorola mobile devices. Nordstrom's has 6,000 devices. Urban Outfitters and Pacific Sun are following. Mobile and tablet technology is changing the way we shop.

Smaller businesses use Square, a free tiny box like card reader that plugs into smart phones or pads to transform them into registers on the go. In fact, there are a host of other companies offering ways for stores and vendors to capture sales without using a cash register. Great for those who have small stores or do kiosk type shows to now accept credit cards and sales with little expense and no hassle.

Major chains like Whole Foods Market, Gap, Patagonia, Sears, and Kmart are now using mobile devices to email receipts to customers instead of handing them paper. Of course, they are also tacking on email alerts and advertisements, which may explain why only about one third of customers are opting in. Customers can now 'try and buy' in the store and have stuff shipped home for free. Better than lugging it around the mall as they continue shopping.

Amazing how, in a few generations telephones, cash registers, typewriters, incandescent light bulbs, etc., once revolutionary, have become obsolete. For techies in the crowd, the Singularity has begun.

Google Site Search - Did you know that Google has a feature that allows you to search a specific site for information. Here is how it works: To search a single website -
1. Type "site:" into the Google search bar (without the quote marks).

2. Type the name of the website you want to search without the "http://" and the "www."

3. Type the search term you are looking for.

For example, use Google to search my blog for peanuts, you would type this - site:shubsthoughts.blogspot.com peanuts.

Beware Hot Spots - Comcast is doing something different, adding your router output as free WiFi to others passing by. It is also an opt-out solution, which means it is enabled by default and you need to turn it off. It also does not pay you for this use by others.

Comcast is quietly turning on public hotspots in its customers' routers and turning private homes into public hotspots. Other Comcast customers get free Wi-Fi wherever there is a Comcast box and the company gets to build out a private network to compete with telecoms, but using your resources.

Fifty thousand users with basic modems that Comcast cable provides have already been turned into public hotspots in Houston, and there are plans to enable 150,000 more.

It is using your private residence as a corporate resource and using your electricity, your Internet connection, and potentially opening up your private browsing to hackers. Comcast says these two streams are independent, but that has never stopped hackers. There is also nothing to stop someone from downloading illicit material, software, and other junk from your hotspot, implicating you if caught. *Remember, if there is a line out, that means there is also a line in. Caveat Emptor Comcast users.*

Browser Tip - If you accidentally close a tab in either Firefox or Chrome, hold down CTRL and Shift keys then hit the letter t. The tab will come back.

Real Credit Report - Finally, here is a site that provides your actual credit score for free. That is no credit card info required to sign up. No fees. It does ask to link your cards and offers other add ons for fees, but you can get the basic info, including your credit score for free. There are free credit reports from each of the big three, transunion, etc., but they only give transaction info once each six months, and do not provide the credit score.

I never could understand how companies could take my information from wherever they choose, then try to sell that information about me to me. This one is different. CreditKarma.com.

Do Not Call - Go to the website https://www.donotcall.gov/ and enter your landline or cell number. There is an e-mail verification and you are done. You can also call 888-382-1222 from any phone you want on the list. Your number stays on the list until you ask for it to be removed or you give up the number.

If you receive a phone call from someone claiming to work at the Do Not Call Registry or Federal Trade Commission and they offer to sign you up if you provide some personal information, do not respond. This is always a scam.

The Do Not Call list keeps you off of for-profit business call lists, but it can take up to 31 days before it goes into effect. If you receive an unexpected sales call after you registered your number, and you have been on the list for 31 days, you may file a complaint. Go to the donotcall.gov site above or call 888-382-1222. You will be asked to provide the date of the call and the company's name or phone number.

Unfortunately, political organizations, charities, and survey takers are still permitted to call you. Businesses you purchased from or made a payment to in the last 18 months also have a right to call. If you ask them not to, they must honor your request. Political and informational robocalls, such as those from health care providers, banks, and schools, are still allowed.

The fine print on free product offers may say the company may send you telemarketing calls.

In spite of frequent email hoaxes, mobile telephone numbers have never been in any danger of being made public or released to telemarketers. The FTC says that unsolicited telemarketing calls or robocalls to cellphones are illegal. If you get unsolicited marketing calls on your cellphone, tell them you do not want to be contacted and you can file a complaint using the information above.

If you sign up and still receive a telemarketing call, it is most likely the person on the other end is a scammer. Legitimate telemarketers do not want to risk a $16,000 fine for disregarding a number on the list.

Google Tools - Google has a handy feature that allows you to set up a countdown timer. Type in set timer x minutes or hours and it will show a countdown clock. You can continue to surf and an alarm will sound when the time has expired. Handy if you want to limit your activities to a fixed time.

Type "google.com sky" without the quotes, to look around the sky the same way you look at a map of the earth. It shows objects in the sky, such as stars, constellations, planets, the Earth's moon, and other galaxies.

More Google Tips - Google has 12 billion searches per month. Many people try too hard and become frustrated. Using a few tricks makes it much easier to quickly find what you want. *For all of these tips, do not type the quote marks.*

This is very useful for finding one thing, while eliminating something related - to find a sunbird that is not a car, type "sunbird -car" and

Google will eliminate car references or try "beatle -beatles" to get bug info and eliminate the singing group.

Type in a holiday name and it will give you the day and date for the current year.

Put ".." between two numbers and Google will search within that range, as "camera $200..$300" to show cameras within that price range.

To find a definition, type "define:" followed by the word.

If you do not remember a complete headline, book title, song title, etc., fill in the blanks of any search with asterisks (*) and Google will try to complete your search for you.

Search for "Books by" and the name of an author, Google will display all of their works.

If you hit "I'm feeling lucky" without actually typing anything into the search box, you will get a catalog of all the Google doodles.

YouTube Tips - If you are annoyed by the ads when you watch YouTube videos or songs, change "youtube" in the URL to "youtubeskip" (do not use the quote marks) to skip the ads.

To repeat videos or songs without hitting the replay button, type "youtuberepeat" in place of "youtube" in the URL (also without the quotes).

To control volume after you click on a video or song, use the up and down arrow keys on your keyboard. You can use the keyboard spacebar to pause or play. Also use the left and right arrows for rewind and fast forward.

If you cannot seem to get enough of an artist or group, type http://www.youtube.com/disco and it serves up a page where you can search and you can string together a personal playlist.

Internet Radio - Many of us think the radio is for the car, or background music while at home, but do not think of listening to the radio on the Internet. Some internet radio stations require free signup, some do not. Since these are Internet based, they are available on your PC, tablet, smartphone, etc. A few require an app for your phone, but most are just available as a web site.

Following are a few free (most accept donations) stations you can tune into while derping around the net. You can find many more by Googling 'Internet Radio Stations'.

Many genres available, but some have commercials embedded - http://www.internet-radio.com/

Large collection of stations - http://www.sky.fm/

Smartphone favorite - http://www.pandora.com/

Very cool option to check real radio stations that also broadcast live. Check by hometown, country, or genre. http://radio-locator.com/

Was going to add links to specific stations, but thought why limit you to my musical proclivities. Enjoy!

Voicemail Tips - In each of the following, ignore the quote marks as they are used as a separator. You can halt an incoming message by pressing "33". You can still press "4" to replay the message. You can also use "#" so message will be ready to listen to again as a "skipped message" after you heard the rest of your messages. Some carriers allow you to press "7" mid message to eliminate, if not, press "77" to immediately erase.

Some carriers allow you to press "*" to interrupt the recipient's greeting and go right into leaving your voicemail.

Text-to-911 - By the end of 2014, US carriers were required to route all of our emergency texts to 911. The Federal Communications Commission voted 3-2 to require all mobile carriers to route text messages sent to 911, to local emergency response centers, just like phone calls.

The problem is most emergency services agencies are not yet equipped to receive them.

The big four operators had already implemented text-to-911 voluntarily, but many smaller operators had not. In fact, only about 2 percent of 911 response centers were capable of receiving SMS, so most emergency messages were sent into the cloud.

The FCC also now requires messaging apps linked to phone numbers must all support 911. That means an app that works within the phone's SMS client must be able to send 911 texts, but a social messaging app like Facebook Messenger or WhatsApp does not. *Am having difficulty understanding how someone with a phone finds it easier to text than to call, especially when 911 usually requires a series of questions and answers. Thumbs may not be faster than lips, but apps like EVA, SIRI, Skyvi, and Jeannie, etc. might be more linguistically understandable.*

Smart Cards Coming - Beginning in October 2015 in the US, liability for credit card fraud will sit with whichever entity, the issuer or the merchant is using the less secure equipment. A merchant would be penalized if it doesn't have the equipment to accept chip cards and suffers an unauthorized purchase with a card that had a chip in it. The bank would be liable if it doesn't issue chip cards and one of its customers makes an unauthorized transaction with a traditional card at a store that accepts chip cards. *Finally the US is beginning to catch up to the many countries that have had this technology for years.*

Facebook and Messenger - Now that Facebook has decided to separate the messenger service from Facebook it might be time to look at whether you want to use it. It only works for Facebook friends, so you still need another messenger service for non Facebook friends.

The new Messenger allows you to message ONLY your Facebook friends using a Wi-Fi connection or your data plan. It lets you include stickers in your messages and new messages will pop up on your screen while you are using other apps. The app lets you send picture and video messages like other mobile messaging services.

Like Skype, now you can call your Facebook friends all over the world for free using your Wi-Fi connection. Of course Skype does not limit calls to only Facebook friends. Seems silly to add another messenger service that can only access some of your contacts. *Caveat Emptor and absolutely do read the terms of service.*

Yelp Changes - Yelp, the site millions go to for reviews of local eating establishments may be changing, and not for the better. The Ninth Circuit Court of Appeals in San Francisco, said that review site Yelp could manipulate its ratings for money.

So, if a small diner makes a big ad buy on the site, those extra dollars could possibly boost the diner's rating, thus potentially gaining it more customers.

Yelp says that it does not manipulate ratings, despite longtime accusations from business owners. It says it uses an automated process for star ratings on the site. There is no reason to believe that the company is or will be 100 percent fair about business ratings and placement just because it seems like the right thing to do. *Take your Yelp reviews with a grain of salt from now on, as you should have been doing all along.*

Windows Printing Tip - To print a web page, email, or selected text or picture hold down the CTRL key and press the letter p. You can select your PDF printer to create a page to read later.

Read Newspapers Online - I am not a fan of paying for information that should be free on the web, but sometimes there are exceptions. For instance, it you are away from home and wish to keep up with local news, there are ways to get your paper online. Another time might be to look up family historical information that may have been in the paper. Here are a few sites that provide online issues of printed copies.

Newseum – You can find and download front pages of more than 800 newspapers from around the world and it is updated daily. The collection includes small-town and local newspapers as well as globally-distributed big papers. It also maintains an archive of newspaper front pages belonging to dates of significant importance, for example, September 11.

Press Display – Like Newseum, but for a fee, this is where you can find current and past issues of hundreds of newspapers and magazines in full-color, full-page format. Individual issues cost 99¢ each and you may also download them to your PC or mobile device for offline reading.

NewspaperARCHIVE – Billed as the world's largest online archive of historical newspapers published from 1753 on. You can browse newspaper issues by date or find articles that match a particular phrase. NewspaperARCHIVE costs $9.99 a month if you subscribe for a year.

Boston Globe – All issues of The Boston Globe newspaper printed since 1924 are available online. You can access all news articles printed since 1979 for free while the older articles are available at $2.95 for a single article.

Times Machine – This site has archived editions of The New York Times from 1851 through 1922. The issues are identical to the original newspapers, and include all pages including advertisements.

Times Archive – The Times daily paper from the UK offers digital archives of issues from 1785 to 1985 on its website. All pages of the papers are completely scanned, and organized with an index of topics. You can read the articles highlighted on their front page for free while specific papers and articles are available for £4.95/day.

UPS 3D Printing - It has reached a new plateau. UPS is now offering in-store printing of 3D objects for its customers. It is the first nationwide retailer to offer 3D printing services in-store. Other local and regional stores have been set up around the country specifically to offer 3D printing with varying degrees of success, but having a national brand offering the printing service brings a shift from concept to mainstream.

UPS' experiment with in-store 3D printers worked and now has expanded the availability of 3D printing services to over 100 locations across the US, including Hawaii. Customers can print everything from accessories, architecture, functional prototypes, and one-of-a-kind gadgets.

Electronic Swing - Normally, I extremely dislike commercials and mute them at best or change channels. Have heard a few lately that struck my fancy because of the background music. One in particular had a track I remembered, but could not recall the artist. As usual, I scoured the web to find out more information.

If you are reading this on paper, go to YouTube and type in Parov Stelar.

It was Parov Stelar, one of my new besties. His musical style is called Electronic Swing. The first YouTube video I remember from him 'All Night', complete with amazing dancing.

Check 'Booty Swing' for oldies and newbies, Fred Astaire and Ginger Rogers dancing, with samples from 'Oriental Swing' and a rousing live version. *These will get your toes a tappin.*

Internet Time - This is what happens every sixty seconds on the internet.

2,635,217 Google searches

204,709,030 emails sent

1,865 new mobile web users

51,763 app downloads

847 new websites created

200,743 people watching porn

$238,651 is spent on web shopping

$89,300 revenues from products sold on Amazon

778,520,485 Gb of global data transferred

1,875,734 new Facebook likes

159,745 new photos uploaded on Facebook

243,040 new tweets

104 hours of video uploaded on YouTube

2,780,653 YouTube video views

About a million Google searches were completed while you were reading this tidbit.

Ten Web Site Name Origins

Bing, Microsoft's search engine was named "Kumo," during development, but Microsoft went with Bing after focus groups said it reminded them of "the moment of discovery."

Yelp - The "yel" in "Yelp" comes from "yellow," and the "p" comes from "pages." The business listings and ratings site is like an Internet version of the Yellow Pages.

Twitter - It is a microblogging site and users' posts cannot exceed 140 characters. Those short messages reminded company founders of birds chirping or twittering. Individual posts are known as tweets and the logo is a bird.

Wikipedia - "Wiki" is Hawaiian for "quick," and "pedia" comes from "encyclopedia." It is a quick encyclopedia added to and edited by almost anyone.

Skype - The video phone via Internet service got its name from a shortening of the phrase "sky peer-to-peer," as users connect person-to-person via the cloud (Internet).

Etsy - Rob Kalin, founder of the marketplace where users buy and sell vintage and handmade goods, wanted a nonsense word. The online crafts marketplace tried to use a complicated name-generating script that never worked. Rather than fix the kinks, they ran with the program's codename, Etsy and told the media it was an interpretation of the Italian ("oh yes") and Latin ("and if") sayings.

Pinterest - The name is a combination of "pin" and "interest," which reflects how the site functions. It is a social network where users share pictures of things they find interesting by "pinning" them on their pin board.

The Onion - It began as a college newspaper, and founders Tim Keck and Chris Johnson had so little money they ate onion sandwiches. While planning the paper, Keck's uncle saw them eating onion sandwiches and reportedly said, "You should call the newspaper *The Onion.*"

Instagram, Seeking a title that personified the belief of "right here, right now," the folks behind Instagram merged the terms "instant camera" and "telegram" to play off the app's speedy interaction. It took them a week and half to think of something that could be recognized and 'spellable' for bar crowds.

Yahoo - In January 1994, Jerry Yang and David Filo, graduate students at Stanford University, created a hierarchical directory of websites, "Jerry and David's Guide to the World Wide Web." In March of that year, they gave it the name "Yahoo!," for *"Yet Another Hierarchical Officious Oracle."*

As part of an ongoing effort to streamline and focus its business, Yahoo announced that it was retiring its namesake product. During the past few years, Yahoo has shut down more than 60 products and services in a bid to do fewer things better.

The Yahoo Directory (precursor to Google) has escaped previous culls, but has finally been deemed surplus to requirements. It also announced the demise of two other products: Yahoo Education, a portal for education services, and Qwiki, an app for creating short movies from videos on a mobile device.

Email Facts and Tips

Email Study Results - A recent study by USC Viterbi School of Engineering researchers found that speed of email responses depend on a variety of factors including age, platform, volume, and timing.

The paper, "Evolutions of Conversations in the Age of Email Overload," was presented at the World Wide Web Conference. The paper is the largest study of email to date, measuring how the volume of incoming email affects behaviors of recipients and the length of time it takes them to reply to emails. The study was conducted in accordance with privacy standards: individuals opted in to the study, the data was anonymized, and the emails were not read by humans.

The researchers said ninety percent of people respond within a day or two of receiving an email to which they plan to respond. Half of responders will respond in just under an hour.

Age is also an indicator for email response time. Younger people reply faster, but write shorter replies. Teens were the quickest, with an email response time average of 13 minutes. Young adults aged 20-35 years responded on average of 16 minutes of receiving an email. 35 to 50 years tended to respond in 24 minutes, on average. Those over 51 years of age, on average took 47 minutes to respond.

Women typically respond four minutes longer than an email response from a man. The platform also plays a critical role: If someone is working from a laptop, on average it will take them almost twice as long to respond than if using a mobile phone.

Emails with only five words are the most common. More than half the email replies are less than 43 words, and only 30 percent of emails are longer than 100 words.

Younger users can cope with the increased email load more than older email users. When younger users become more overloaded they tend to send shorter and faster replies to cope with the increased load. On the other hand, older people respond to an increased load of emails by replying to a smaller fraction of emails.

People are more active on email during the day than at night. Emails on weekends get shorter replies than weekdays. For a longer reply, email someone in the morning. Researchers found that emails sent in the morning tend to get longer replies than those in the afternoon.

Email Tip - One way to reduce marketing emails is to create a filter. Filter for the word 'unsubscribe' in the body of the email and send the email directly to trash.

Email and Productivity - If you want to be efficient, do not open your email until at least 10am. Do not peek. Do not IM. Do not check Facebook, Google+, LinkedIn, or Twitter, or anyplace else on the web.

Productive people get up and get on with doing the things they have decided are important. Reacting to someone else is not productive, nor is it efficient or effective. It is difficult to read an email without reacting and you are reacting to someone's priority, not yours.

Next, decide the clock time and a certain amount of action time to read and react to email. Quickly scan your inbox and prioritize, file, or delete as necessary. This should take no longer than ten minutes.

Then go back and react to the priority items and attack them. When one hour has elapsed, go back to your priorities.

You might need to get into your email to finish some of your most important to-dos, but can you get 80 or 90 percent done before you go into email and waste your time on other people's priorities Research shows email: Creates stress, can be more addictive than alcohol and tobacco, and checking email frequently is the equivalent of dropping your IQ ten points. It also interrupts your progress. *Happiness is also important, so after you have finished your high priority projects, reward yourself by reading my blog, shubsthoughts.blogspot.com.*

Internet, IP, Web, and URL

The Internet is a collection of computers and cables that form a communications network.

The Web (World Wide Web) is a collection of HTML (web) pages on the Internet. The Web is the user part of the Internet.

The term Interweb is a combination of the words Internet and Web. It is most often used in the context of joking or sarcasm.

A URL (universal resource locator) is synonymous with Internet address. A URL is usually a combination of code and text, such as 'http://www.google.com', but numbers are also allowed. A URL always starts with a protocol prefix like http://, but most browsers will type those characters for you. URLs are internally converted to IP addresses.

IP address (Internet Protocol address), is a unique identifying number given to every device on the Internet. Like a car license plate, an IP address is a special serial number used for identification, such as 208.185.127.40 = www.about.com.

Bottom line, all URLs have an IP address, but not all IP addresses have a URL.

Social Media Explained

Social media is now an essential part of doing business. That does not mean you need to be on every social media platform to get results. Ideally, with one or two focused networks, your message can reach your target audience in no time.

The question is which ones to use and how to maximize your visibility.

If you are clear about your social media goals, it will not be a challenge to determine which channels would work best for your business. Thing to keep in mind when you are deciding - Where are your customers? Before you think of creating your business profile on a site, you need to think: Are my customers here? There is much variation in the demographics of social networks and you need to find out where your customers are so you can reach them effectively.

According to a Pew survey in 2015:

- Facebook has wide, global usage, but fewer young people are staying active.

- Instagram is a favorite among teens and young adults.

- Twitter is home to many information junkies and tech savvy people.

- LinkedIn has higher income, educated professionals.

- Pinterest has a user base which is 80% female dominated, most of whom have a higher income background.

- Google+ is a network with a predominantly older male user base.

- Vine is also a youth oriented platform.

- YouTube has an equal number of men and women, but men are more active users with wider preferences.

Instagram — art, food, retail, lifestyle
Twitter — news, gossip, tech updates
LinkedIn — B2B, recruitment agencies
Pinterest — Retail, DIY, culinary skills, art
YouTube — Luxury products, DIY, Home improvement, music,
Google+ — SEO, IT

Adware, Malware, and Phishing
Also Spyware, Trojan Horse, Virus, and Warez

These terms show up often, especially during the holidays when more people than ever are cruising the web for bargains. Here are a few descriptions to help you understand the lingo.

Adware is typically an application that shows users an excessive amount of advertising in return for providing a service of little value. There is a grey area from most anti-virus companies as to how to handle adware, because so many applications have begun to show ads

Malware generally is an all-encompassing term used to describe any harmful program. This includes spyware, viruses, and phishing scams

Phishing and spyware are closely related. They work by tricking users and sending user information to a third party. A phishing application or website will pretend to be from a trusted source to try and trick a person into entering personal information.

Spyware tries to hide itself from users. It is an application that reads user information and data without the user actually knowing it - and reporting it back to a third party. This includes keystroke loggers to steal passwords or credit card information.

A *trojan horse* is a specific type of virus. The app pretends to be something useful, or helpful, or fun while causing harm or stealing data. This term is often used to describe spyware and phishing attacks as well.

The term *virus* term has mostly been replaced by malware, although there is a subtle difference. Virus typically takes control of the operating system and either damages it, or uses it for its own purposes. An example might be sending emails to everyone in the email address book.

Warez typically refers to pirated or unlicensed software. The files are stolen from the real developers.

Bottom line - Adware is aggravating, but not usually harmful. Phishing and trojan horses wear masks and steal data, while spyware hides itself and steals data. *Malware is the new all-encompassing term, except for Warez. Malware aggravates or steals from us while Warez steals from developers.*

Ten Internet Firsts

Symbolics Inc. registered the first domain name, Symbolics.com, on March 15, 1985, before the real internet was born. Symbolics Inc. grew out of MIT's Artificial Intelligence lab, and was the first company to make workstation computers.

CERN launched very first website on August 6, 1991. It was a simple page, similar to a Word document with black lettering on a white background with blue hyperlinks. It briefly described project W3, better known now as the World Wide Web.

The first picture ever uploaded to the World Wide Web on July 18, 1992 was a picture of the all-girl comedy group Les Horrible Cernettes. The group was made up of administrative assistants and partners of researchers at The European Organization for Nuclear Research.

A little-known band called Severe Tire Damage, played live on the Internet for the first time on June 24, 1993.

YouTube was registered as a domain on February 14, 2005. On April 23, 2005, Chad Hurley, Steve Chen, and Jawed Karim posted the first video called 'Me at the zoo'. The 19-second video features Karim standing in front of elephants at the San Diego Zoo, talking about his interest in "really, really, really long trunks."

Computer-to-computer email started when Bolt Beranek and Newman was hired by the United States Defense Department to work on ARPANET, the precursor to the Internet. Employee Ray Tomlinson started working on an experimental file transfer protocol that could send a message from one computer to another. He also came up with the "@" symbol to connect the user and network, simply because it made the most sense to him. It would include the user's name and the host where it should be sent. In July of 1971 Tomlinson sent the first email to the computer next to his, which read, "QWERTYIOP".

Pierre Omidyar was thinking that the web might make for a great marketplace, specifically utilizing an auction format for fair pricing on items. He launched the website AuctionWeb (which became eBay) on September 3, 1995. The first item to sell was a broken laser pointer, which went for $14.83. He was confused by someone paying for that much for a defective item and discovered the buyer collected broken laser pointers. He thought it was interesting that collectors were so passionate about ordinary items.

The first book sold on Amazon in July of 1995 was Fluid Concepts And Creative Analogies: Computer Models Of The Fundamental Mechanisms Of Thought, by Douglas Hofstadter.

The first Internet single released by a major label happened during 1993, when Geffen Records released the single "Head First" by Aerosmith.

During October 27, 1994, Joe McCambley, who ran a small digital advertising company, created the first banner ad for AT&T. The all-text ad, which said "Have you ever clicked your mouse here?" appeared on Hotwired.com, the first digital magazine. Forty four percent of Hotwired's visitors clicked the ad, and some even shared it with friends.

> *The Internet is what you connect to*
>
> *and*
>
> *the Web is how you view it.*

Today, only about 0.0004 percent of website visitors click on banner ads.

Cisco Internet Predictions

Each year Cisco gets its best and brightest minds together to make some predictions. The following are for the 2015 predictions.

- Annual global IP (internet) traffic will surpass the zettabyte (1000 exabytes) threshold in 2016, and the two zettabyte threshold in 2019.

- Global IP traffic has increased more than fivefold in the past 5 years, and will increase nearly threefold over the next 5 years. Overall, IP traffic will grow at a compound annual growth rate (CAGR) of 23 percent to 2019.

- Content delivery networks will carry 62% of Internet traffic by 2019, up from 39 percent in 2014.

- Over half of all IP traffic will originate with non-PC devices by 2019, up from 40 percent in 2014.

- Personal computer-originated traffic will grow at a CAGR of just 9 percent, while TVs, tablets, smartphones, and machine-to-machine (M2M) modules will have traffic growth rates of 17 percent, 65 percent, 62 percent, and 71 percent, respectively.

- By 2019, Wi-Fi and mobile devices will account for 66 percent of IP traffic and wired devices will account for just 33 percent.

- Global Internet traffic in 2019 will be equivalent to 64 times the volume of the entire global Internet in 2005.

- The number of devices connected to IP networks will be three times the global population in 2019.

- By 2019, global fixed broadband speeds will reach 43 Mbps, up from 20 Mbps in 2014.

- It would take an individual over 5 million years to watch the amount of video that will cross global IP networks each month in 2019. Every second, nearly a million minutes of video content will cross the network by 2019.

Large Data Means?

- ⊙ 1000 **kilobytes** = 1 Megabyte
- ⊙ 1000 **Megabytes** = 1 Gigabyte
- ⊙ 1000 **Gigabytes** = 1 Terabyte
- ⊙ 1000 **Terabytes** = 1 Petabyte
- ⊙ 1000 **Petabytes** = 1 Exabyte
- ⊙ 1000 **Exabytes** = 1 Zettabyte
- ⊙ 1000 **Zettabytes** = 1 Yottabyte
- ⊙ 1000 **Yottabytes** = 1 Bronobyte
- ⊙ 1000 **Bronobytes** = 1 Geopbyte

Wordology

FUN WITH WORDS

In 1828, Noah Webster published his "American Dictionary of the English Language." It was the first dictionary of American English to be published.

Acronyms and Intialisms - Although many believe both are acronyms, there is a difference. An acronym is a pronounceable word that is formed using the first letters of the words in a phrase (sometimes, other parts of the words are also used). Some common acronyms include NASA (National Aeronautical and Space Administration), scuba (Self-Contained Underwater Breathing Apparatus) and laser (Light Amplification by Stimulated Emission of Radiation). WYSIWYG - What You See Is What You Get RAM - Random Access Memory NAFTA - North American Free Trade Agreement WASP - White Anglo Saxon Protestant.

An initialism is formed using the first letters of the words in a phrase -- it is pronounced like a series of letters, not like a word. Some common initialisms include UFO (Unidentified Flying Object) and LOL (Laugh Out Loud). IMHO - In My Humble Opinion.

ROTC - Reserve Officers Training Corps is used both as an acronym and initialism.

Ambulance - The word 'ambulance' derives from the Latin 'ambulare', meaning 'to walk or move about'. This gave rise to the French hôpital (sic) ambulant, meaning mobile hospital. It used to refer to a temporary medical structure that could be easily moved, such as movable army medical hospitals. In English, ambulance first appeared around 1798 and also referred to temporary hospital structures.

Ambulances were first used for emergency transport in 1487 by the Spanish, and civilian variants were put into operation in the 1830s. Mobile medical transport vehicles were also called ambulances in French and were designed to get injured soldiers off the battlefield and to medical aid during battle. One of the first instances of this was during the Crimean War. During the American Civil War they were known as ambulance wagons.

The first known hospital-based ambulance service was based out of Commercial Hospital, Cincinnati, Ohio, US, in 1865.

Anti-Proverbs - also called perverbs (a contraction of perverse proverbs) are permutations of common proverbs. a known saying that has been modified in a way that makes it surprising, confounding or otherwise humorous. There are dozens of ways of altering proverbs, common sayings and phrases. It has been suggested that the original meaning of the term perverb was to describe two proverbs that had been spliced together like a sort of whole-sentence portmanteau. Take the perverb "every dog has a silver lining," a combination of "every dog has its day" and "every cloud has a silver lining." As with the further examples below, you can see that the two hybridized proverbs are not random; rather, they follow a certain format that both have in common:

"Taste makes waist"

"Time flies like the wind, but fruit flies like a banana"

"Nothing succeeds like excess."

"When marriage is outlawed, only outlaws will have in-laws."

"The road to hell is the spice of life."

"If a tree falls in the woods and there is no one to tweet about it, did it really happen."

Anti-proverbs can take other forms beyond this type of splicing, as in "a penny saved is a penny taxed" and "slaughter is the best medicine."

Campus - A campus is traditionally the land on which a college or university and related institutional buildings are situated. It usually includes libraries, lecture halls, residence halls, student centers, etc.

It comes from a Latin word for "field" and was first used to describe the grounds of the College of New Jersey (now Princeton University) during the 18th century. Other American colleges later adopted the word to describe individual fields at their own institutions. A school has multiple spaces, such as a campus, a field, a yard, etc.

Cabo Wabo - Sammy Hagar, lead singer for Van Halen made more money from Cabo Wabo than all record, concert, song royalties, and products combined.

He is the founder of the Cabo Wabo Tequila brand along with Cabo Wabo night clubs and restaurants. In 2007, Hagar sold an eighty percent share of the tequila brand for $80 million and sold the rest three years later. Now he started a new venture with "Sammy's Beach Bar Rum".

Hagar claims he came up with the name after watching a man walk unsteadily along a local beach In Cabo San Lucas after a heavy night's partying. He used Cabo and shortened "wobble" to "wabo" and said the man was doing the Cabo wabo.

Cappuccino - Espresso, hot milk, and steamed milk foam are ingredients for making a cappuccino. Cappuccino comes from German/Austrian 'kapuziner', and is the diminutive form of cappuccio in Italian, meaning 'hood' or something that covers the head, thus 'cappuccino' reads 'small capuchin'. The Capuchin monks of the 16th century, an offshoot of the Franciscan Catholic order wear long and pointy hoods, known as capuche. The monks subsequently received a formal nickname, Capuchin, for their hoods. The color of cappuccino resembles the brown shade of the hoods and thus the naming of the coffee drink.

Cappuccino differs from latte in size. Cappuccino is traditionally small while latte traditionally is large. Latte is often served in a large glass and cappuccino mostly in a cup with a handle. Here is some Java Jive music to listen to while sipping your cappuccino.

Collywobbles - I love words that roll off the tongue and actually sound like what they describe. Collywobble is one of them and means a pain in the abdomen and especially in the stomach; a bellyache. "I awoke this morning with collywobbles, and had to take a small dose of laudanum with the usual consequences of dry throat, intoxicated legs, partial madness and total imbecility..." Robert Louis Stevenson.

Etymologist believe that collywobbles most likely has its origin in cholera morbus, the Latin term for the disease cholera (the symptoms include severe gastrointestinal disturbance). How cholera shifted into collywobbles was probably influenced by the words colic and wobble. *John Chapman is currently suffering from the collywobbles.*

Roughshod - The expression "to run or to ride roughshod" over somebody or something, means to tyrannize or treat harshly. During the 17th century, a "rough-shod" horse had its shoes attached with protruding nail heads to get a better grip on slippery roads.

Punt - A punt is the small indentation on the bottom of wine bottles designed to give the bottle extra strength. It is also known as a kick.

Decimate and Obliterate - The word "decimate" does not mean to destroy something completely and leaving nothing behind. It actually means to destroy a great or large amount, not the entire

48

amount. It also means kill one in ten. Some people tend to use this word in absolute and complete terms, as if there is nothing that can be done, said, or seen after the decimation takes place.

Think of it this way: if a 10-story building gets decimated, then there should still be a story or two left after the decimation. If all ten stories get destroyed, then the building has not been decimated. It has been obliterated.

Smithereen - It is the smallest particle that results from exploding an object. *Yosemite Sam used to threaten to blow Bugs Bunny to smithereens.*

Venomous or Poisonous - Fish, snakes, and spiders are often described as either being venomous or poisonous. The difference is in the delivery system. Those that are venomous inject their target with their toxin through a bite, sting, or sharp body protrusion. Those that are poisonous have toxins that must be swallowed or inhaled in order to be dangerous.

Venomous animals need to get their toxins beneath the skin and then into the bloodstream to be effective. Some have a venomous bite, but are safe to eat. Many caterpillars have defensive venom glands associated with specialized bristles, known as urticating hairs, which can be lethal to humans. There are about six venomous snake and about seven venomous spider fatalities in the US each year. Venoms are usually not lethal if swallowed.

Poisonous fish can be potentially deadly if eaten. Poisons work mostly through the digestive system and mucous membranes of the body. Some poisons can be transferred easily to humans by merely touching or handling.

> If you bite it and you die, it is poisonous.
>
> If it bites you and you die, it is venomous.

The yellow-bellied sea snake has both a venomous bite and poisonous flesh.

There are several types of venom. *Neurotoxins* attack the brain and the nerves. Animals whose bite results in paralysis use this type of venom. *Cytotoxins* are a type of venom that causes the most pain, as this venom attacks cells directly, causing them to rupture and release their contents into the body. *Hemotoxins* attack blood cells directly and most kill red blood cells, which interrupts the flow of oxygen throughout the body. *Not all poisonous or venomous creatures are fatal to humans, but they are all discomforting.*

49

IKEA Naming System - The system was created by dyslexic founder Ingvar Kamprad, who wanted to avoid relying on numbers. Here is the system for naming items:

Upholstered furniture, coffee tables, rattan furniture, bookshelves, media storage, doorknobs: Swedish place names

Beds, wardrobes, hall furniture: Norwegian place names
Dining tables and chairs: Finnish place names

Bookcase ranges: Occupations

Bathroom articles: Scandinavian lakes, rivers, and bays

Chairs, desks: men's names

Fabrics, curtains: women's names

Garden furniture: Swedish islands

Lighting: terms from music, chemistry, meteorology, measures, weights, seasons, months, days, boats, nautical terms

Children's items: mammals, birds, adjectives

Curtain accessories: mathematical and geometrical terms

There are too many more to mention here, but if you want to learn the rest, you can go to http://lar5.com/ikea/ and peruse the IKEA Dictionary.

Double Meaning Animals - We do not often think of the question of which came first, the chicken or the egg, and we ignore how many times we *egg* someone on by calling them *chicken*. Here are a few more ways we use animals in discussions.

Someone tried to *buffalo* me into this.

She double *dog* dared me
and *hound*ed me for no good reason.
I knew it was a bunch of *bull*
and was not *sheep*ish in telling her,
but still, I tried to *ferret* out some information,
because I could not *weasel* out of it.

I also could not *worm* my way out of it.

I was *fishing* for how to begin this
without being a *leech* or trying to *sponge* off of anyone.

Too often we *wolf* down food or just plain *pig* out.

We feel playful and *horse* around or *monkey* around.

When we get caught, it is time to *pony* up.

Children often *ape* their parents and may *parrot* what they say.

When someone *gooses* you, it is time to *duck* out, but most often they just do it as a *lark*.

You probably think it is time for me to *clam* up, but I am not done yet.

I have a few more *squirreled* away, just to *badger* you a bit more.

Luckily there were no *moles* in the crowd to give away my secrets.

Did you ever notice how some people *cat* around,
even the *coyote* ugly ones.

Of course, I am not a social *butterfly*.

Quit *carping*, you know I out *fox*ed you.

I led you down the *rabbit* hole
and *snaked* my way through another post.

I did not *rat* anyone out and am still *crowing* that I managed to finished this even if many think the whole thing is for the *birds*. *(OK, so the egg part was a stretch, but it seemed to work.)*

Porcelain, Fine China, and Bone China - Exported Chinese porcelains were held in such great esteem in Europe that in the English language china became a synonym for porcelain.

Bone china is made from cow bone ash and other ingredients. The addition of animal bone ash gives bone china a warm color, while fine china is a brighter white. Bone china has a translucent quality compared to fine china. Fine china is made the same way, replacing bone with kaolin clay.

Spone china - American artist Charles Krafft replaced cow bone ash with human bone ash, retrieved from a crematorium.

Porcelain is fired at a higher temperature and is much harder. Porcelain gets its name from old Italian porcellana (cowrie shell) because of its resemblance to the translucent surface of the shell. The raw materials are finely ground, cleaned, formed in a mold, and then fired.

If the temperature is high the finished product is more durable and known as porcelain. If it is fired at a lower temperature it becomes fine china. Fine china is much softer than porcelain, making it suitable for plates and cups. Porcelain is strong enough and durable enough for a wide range of products, such as electrical insulators and toilets. *Bottom line, all china is porcelain, but not all porcelain is china.*

Orchid - Take a look at certain orchids' roots, and you will notice that they look like testicles. The word, introduced in 1845 for the flower comes from the Greek orchis, which literally translates as "testicle." Speakers of Middle English in the 1300s came up with a different word, inspired by the same description. They called the flower ballockwort from ballocks, or testicles, which evolved from beallucas, the Old English word for balls.

Bang for Your Buck - 'Bang for your buck' means 'value for the money spent' or 'excitement for the money spent' and is based on the slang meaning of bang (excitement) and buck (money).

Finland had one of the highest-ranked education system for many years, but came in #2 in 2013, behind to Japan. The UK #3 in 2013; Canada #7; Estonia #17 and the United States #18, out of 200 countries considered.

Japan spends an average of $10,596 per student and Finland $10,157. The US spends $15,172 per student, the highest of any country and 2.5 times more per student than #17 ranked Estonia. *The US does not appear to be getting a bang for its bucks.*

Crumb - Bread crust surrounds the inner part of bread, which is called the crumb. As pieces of the crumb break off they are called crumbs.

Lunatic - Lunatic literally means 'moon-sick' in Old English, or 'affected with periodic insanity, dependent on the changes of the moon'. It stems from the Old French 'lunatique'. *Maybe more sun is why we feel better in the spring.*

Minced Oath - No, it is not a spicy oath. 'Bye George, by George we'll miss ya!' The minced oath, "by George" where one letter - 'g' word is substituted for another 'g' word. In this case, the second George is substituted for God, because some people did not believe in God. The use of George came into use around the turn of the 20th century and usually meant great or OK, as in 'everything is George'.

Gray vs. Grey - The spelling depends on what part of the world you are in. In Britain, Canada, Australia, Ireland, New Zealand, and South Africa, the spelling is commonly 'grey'. In the United States, the preferred spelling is 'gray', although 'grey' is also accepted. Gray became the preferred spelling in America during the early 1800s.

Octothorpe - The proper name for the symbol **#** we call 'pound sign' or 'hash tag'.

Small Fry - Seahorses are one of very few species where the male 'gives birth'. The female deposits her eggs in a brood pouch located on her mate's belly. He fertilizes them internally and carries them until they hatch, which can be anywhere from 9 to 45 days based on species and water temperature. A single male may carry hundreds of eggs in his pouch. Baby sea horses are called fry (singular and plural). Baby big-belly seahorses, aside from being too small to exhibit their distinct characteristic round bellies, are exact miniature replicas of their parents. The picture shows how small a fry is.

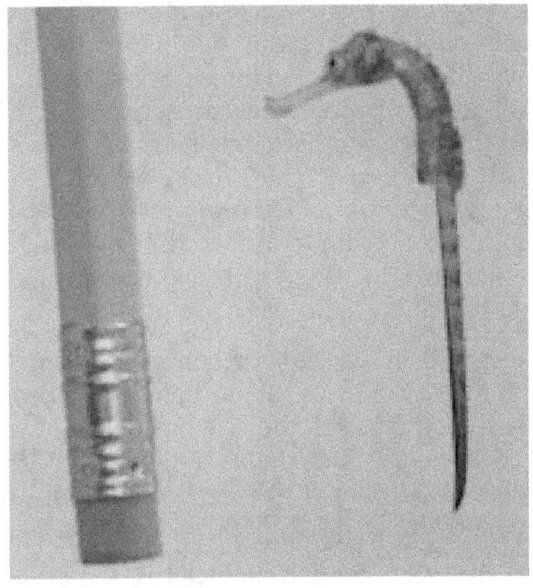

When baby seahorses are first born, the fry will gulp air at the surface to help fill their swim bladder. Their diet is usually live brine shrimp called Artemia. Seahorses live among coral reefs and sea grass beds.

Hay and Straw - Hay is a crop that is grown specifically for the purpose of creating a nutrient-rich food for livestock. Straw is a byproduct of different crops. Straw is more often used for bedding, a compost pile, fuel for burning, etc.

When farmers plant a hay field, the field is harvested before the grains go to seed. This keeps valuable nutrients in the stalks and makes for a much more well-rounded diet for horses and other forms of livestock. Straw, on the other hand, is a byproduct of other types of grain crops. When crops like wheat, barley, and oats are harvested for their seed, the stalks are left behind. These stalks, which have been drained of most of their nutrients during the process of seed production, are harvested and baled to create straw.

There are different types of hay, and have different nutritional values and usages. Alfalfa, red clover, timothy, Bermuda grass, and tall fescue are all types of hay grown as feed crops for animals from horses to rabbits. The nutrient value of the hay is also dependent on when it is harvested. Early maturity harvests will contain more of their nutrients than hay that is harvested closer to seed production. For horses, the type of horse and dietary needs will mean a difference in the type, quantity, and quality of hay that is used.

Straw can be made from a variety of grain crops, and regardless of where it comes from, its purposes are generally the same. Some farmers will leave the stalks behind after harvesting seeds, tilling them back into the soil and returning what nutrients are left. Straw is often used as bedding for large animals, but it also has non-farming uses. Straw is a highly valuable renewable energy source, and burning straw can be used to generate power. Many power plants in the UK fuel thousands of homes by burning straw. A single power plant in East Anglia burns about 210,000 tons of straw a year, and that provides enough energy to run about 80,000 homes.

A bale of straw can also be used for composting into gardens or in place of dirt. Recent attempts at bringing a bit of home-grown vegetables and country living to the city have yielded some surprising results. A bale of straw can be used as a planting medium for garden vegetables. A wet bale of straw will decay from the inside out, providing a fertile bed for crops from potatoes to herbs.

Lb - Did you ever wonder why we use the Lb abbreviation for pound? Lb is an abbreviation of the Latin word libra. The primary meaning of libra was balance or scales (as in the astrological sign), but it also stood for the ancient Roman unit of measure libra pondo, meaning "a pound by weight." The word "pound" in English comes from the pondo part of the libra pondo, but the abbreviation comes from the libra. The libra is also why the symbol for the British pound is £, an L with a line through it. The Italian lira also used that symbol (with two lines through it), the word "lira" itself being a shortened version of libra.

"Ounce" is related to the Latin uncia, the name for both the Roman ounce and inch units of measurement. The word came into English from Anglo-Norman French, where it was unce or ounce, but the abbreviation was borrowed from Medieval Italian, where the word was onza. These days the Italian word is oncia, and the area once covered by the Roman Empire has long since switched to the metric system.

Perfect Storm - It is actually a cliché and will not go away as most clichés usually do. One would naturally think a perfect storm is about weather, but it is seldom used to discuss weather. In fact, it was used for a few hundred years before a Texas weather bureau first used in 1936: "The weather bureau describes the disturbance as 'the perfect storm' of its type. Seven factors were involved in the chain of circumstances that led to the flood."

A meteorologist with the National Weather Service said "I haven't used it once after 30 years in the Weather Service and am proud to say I've never used 'Storm of the Century,' either." Major weeknight network newscasts (NBC, ABC, CBS) used it a total of 32 times in the past year; USA Today used it 22 times, and the New York Times used it 57 times, all discussing non-weather related items.

Current usage describes a perfect storm as a confluence of circumstances that tend to exaggerate a situation, such as:

May was another perfect-storm month for the NBA.

A strong showing by Tiger Woods was a perfect storm of scoring conditions.

Budget cuts led to a perfect storm of unintended consequences.

The confluence of the Internet, TiVo, cable TV, and DVDs, means we are looking at a perfect storm.

The economic disaster was caused by a perfect storm of real-estate headaches.

About the recently fired Catholic bishop - 'Bishop Bling' was a perfect storm.

At the end of the day, I guess a perfect storm is better than using 'at the end of the day'.

Lemniscate - In geometry, the lemniscate of Bernoulli is a plane curve defined from two given points. It is also generally called the infinity symbol.

Lemniscate comes from a Latin word lēmniscātus that means decorated with, or hanging ribbons, an origin that is reflected in the symbol's shape. It is pronounced Lemm nis kit.

Seminar - From the mid-15 century, "plot where plants are raised from seeds," from Latin seminarium "plant nursery, seed plot," figuratively, "breeding ground," from seminarius of seed, from semen (genitive seminis). It is also a school for training priests and commonly used for any school (especially academies for young ladies) from 1580s to 1930s. *Also commonly used today to describe where business people go to waste time and money.*

Ultimate and Penultimate - When 'ultimate' it is used as an adjective it describes something that is the best, highest, or the most extreme example. As a noun the word ultimate means the final or last in a series or the best, greatest, and most extreme.

Penultimate means the second-to-last item in a series of things. It does not signify a large or vast number of variables, or the abundance of something. It is one.

To clarify, Chapter 14 in a 15-chapter book is the penultimate chapter and the ultimate chapter would be the 15th chapter, not necessarily the best or most exciting.

Advesperate - to grow dark, to become night. On Halloween we wait for the day to advesperate.

Idiot, Imbecile, Moron - We often hear these words during an election cycle. Each of these words has a different meaning. The medical definitions have been mostly abandoned and the words are now used more in a pejorative sense, rather than diagnostic.

In psychology, an idiot has the least intelligence on the IQ scale, equivalent to someone who is mentally challenged. Idiot derives from the ancient Greek, 'idio', meaning "person lacking professional skill" or "mentally deficient person incapable of ordinary reasoning." Those who have an IQ between 0 and 25 are considered idiots.

From Middle French imbécile, from Latin imbēcillus meaning weak or feeble, literally "without a staff." An imbecile is considered equivalent to moderate retardation or moderately mentally challenged. People with IQs between 26 and 50 are considered imbeciles.

The word 'moron' was coined in 1910 by psychologist Henry H. Goddard and derived from the ancient Greek word 'moros', which meant 'dull'. Those who have an IQ between 51 and 70 are considered morons. A moron is the highest level of intelligence for someone who is mildly mentally challenged.

These terms were popular in psychology as associated with intelligence on an IQ test until the 1960s. They were then replaced with the terms mild retardation, moderate retardation, severe retardation, and profound retardation. Other factors are now used in diagnosing these levels of mental deficiency.

Retarded comes from the Latin 'retardare', which means "to make slow, delay, keep back, or hinder." The term retarded was used to replace the terms idiot, moron, and imbecile as these terms gradually became thought of as derogatory. Now 'retarded' is considered a derogatory term.

Many old words seem to pop up around election time as politicians seek to differentiate themselves, while preaching the same drivel. Even 'politician' used to be a good word, which has now become thought of as derogatory.

Handicap - The word handicap is known to originate from the old English trading game Hand-in-cap. The game was based on trading possessions, and proceedings would take place with the help of an umpire. The umpire had a responsibility to decide if the items were valued the same, and if not, he had to decide what the difference was. The two players then put the money in a cap. They had to place their hands in the cap and subsequently remove them either holding money or not, to show if they had accepted the terms of the deal.

Other uses for the word handicap include a condition that markedly restricts a person's ability to function physically, mentally, or socially. The word also means a disadvantage imposed on a superior competitor in sports such as golf, horse racing, and competitive sailing in order to make the chance of winning more equal.

Napkin - When eating bacon with your fingers, you need a napkin. The word comes from Middle English, borrowing the French nappe, a cloth covering for a table and adding kin, the diminutive suffix. The English word napkin means, "A usually square piece of cloth, paper, etc., used at a meal to wipe the fingers and lips, and to protect the clothes"

That same "nappe," led to the English "apron," which was originally "napron." Through a linguistic process the initial "n" of "napron" in the phrase "a napron" shifted and produced "an apron."

The use of paper napkins is documented in ancient China, where paper was invented in the 2nd century BC. In Roman times, each guest supplied his own mappa and, on departure it was filled with delicacies leftover from the feast. German-speaking people were reputed to be such neat diners that they seldom used a napkin.

In the United Kingdom and Canada both terms, serviette and napkin, are used. In Australia, 'serviette' generally refers to the paper variety and napkin refers to the cloth variety.

There is no relation to taking a nap or snooze during the day, that 'nap' comes from the Old English word 'hnappian', meaning "to doze or sleep lightly."

Homogamy, Hypergamy, and Hypogamy - This is a marriage between individuals who are, in some culturally important way, similar to each other. Homogamy may be based on socioeconomic status, class, gender, ethnicity, or religion. Concerning age homogamy, there is an old maxim, "Never date anyone under half your age plus seven." This rule of thumb is sometimes used to judge whether the age differences in potential intimate relationships are socially acceptable within a Western-oriented culture. Homogamy can also refer to the socialization customs of a particular group; such that people who are similar in religion, class, gender, or culture tend to socialize with one another.

Hypergamy, or marrying up, is the practice of marrying someone wealthier, or of higher caste or status than oneself. The term is not gender specific, but it is generally used by social scientists to refer to women marrying higher-status men, rather than to men marrying higher-status women.

Hypogamy typically refers to instances of marrying a person of lower social class or status. *So, this hypergamist and hypogamist got married and lived happily ever after.*

Pipsqueaks, Plonkers, and Whizz-bangs - World War I, soldiers in the trenches gave cute names to the artillery shells that were constantly killing and maiming their friends and comrades. Some of these names, like 'whizz-bang', 'plonker' and 'pipsqueak' describe some of the lethal devices.

> **Oche** is the line behind which darts players must stand while tossing.
> (pronounced O Kee)

Another war term from the time is strafe, as in The German phrase "Gott strafe England!" (God punish England!) was widely used in German propaganda. The word strafe then entered the English language, meaning punish, bombard, or reprimand. Strafe definition later narrowed to refer to attacking with machine-gun fire from low-flying aircraft.

Briffits and Dustups - Briffits are the clouds left behind when comic-strip characters speed off. They are most often found in the comic strips with hites, which are the horizontal lines streaking between a cartoon character and the briffit to represent speed.

Dustups are the clouds that obscure comic-strip fights.

Things that look like clouds, but are not, include various fumetti, such as word balloons and thought balloons (cumulus fumetti).

Incidentally, although storytelling with pictures and words had been around for hundreds of years and, until recently it was generally believed that the first comic was the Yellow Kid in 1896. However, Rodolphe Töpffer is considered the father of the modern comic strips. His illustrated stories of Histoire de M. Vieux Bois (1827), was first published in the USA in 1842 as The Adventures of Obadiah Oldbuck.

Capons, Chickens, Cockerels, Hens, and Roosters - A *capon* is a rooster or cockerel that has been castrated. This culinary practice existed in ancient China and Europe. Romans castrated roosters to double their size. Capon meat is more moist, tender, and flavorful than that of a cockerel or a hen and is less gamey tasting.

Chickens are a domesticated fowl, bred primarily as a source of food, including meat and eggs. In the UK and Ireland adult male chickens over the age of 12 months are primarily known as cocks. In the US, Australia, and Canada they are more commonly called *roosters*. Males less than a year old are *cockerels*.

Hens are female chickens over a year old and younger females are called pullets. In the egg-laying industry, a pullet becomes a hen when she begins to lay eggs at 16 to 20 weeks of age. Chicken eggs vary in color depending on the hen, ranging from bright white to shades of brown, blue, green, and purple.

Here is a quick summary. Roosters generally crow and hens generally cluck. All capons, cockerals, hens, and roosters are chicken. All capons, cockerals, and roosters are male. All hens and pullets are female. All cocks are not chicken, but also the male of other species, such as cock sparrows. "Roosting" is the action of perching to sleep and is done by both chicken sexes.

During the course of the 2014 Super Bowl, American consumers devoured a total of 1.25 billion chicken wingettes and drumettes (the wing tips were sent to Asia). There is a chicken sound app for smartphones that can be used as a ringtone, or just to irritate those around you.

Coupes, Flutes, and Tulips - During the 19th century, champagne glasses were wide and shallow, not at all like the flutes we use today. They were called 'coupes' and legend has it that they were modeled after the shape of Marie Antoinette's left breast.

The coupe eventually gave way to the 'flute', the tall, narrow glasses, which most of us currently drink our bubbly. The flute both displays and preserves champagne bubbles, and makes it easier to drink.

 Many champagne lovers say the 'tulip' is the true way to enjoy the beverage. The glass is tall, but curves outward to within a couple inches from the mouth, then curves inward to the mouth. This design allows a little more space for swirling, and focuses the aromatics.

Goodbye - The customs of English speakers and many English words are based on religion, often without most people being aware of the fact. In this vein, our most common phrase to bid someone farewell is 'goodbye'. While it seems like a mundane, secular word, goodbye is actually a contraction of the phrase "God be with ye," an expression that dates back to the 14th century.

Tips, Tipsy, Tipple, and Wingtips - The etymology of these words is a bit different than the generally accepted (although incorrect) stories that they come from acronyms.

Tip does not come from 'to insure prompt service'. It dates back to the 1600s and meant to give a small present of money. It was also used in thieves jargon about the same time, meaning 'to give, hand, or pass'. The meaning 'give a gratuity to' is first documented in the early 1700s. The incorrect acronym story came from an editorial in "Life" magazine from July 15, 1946, claiming the restaurant server's word tip "probably comes from a London coffeehouse custom of two centuries ago when the words 'To Insure Promptness' were written on notes to the waiter, with coins attached.

Tipsy comes from another definition of tip, from the 1300s meaning 'to knock down, topple, or knock askew'. Possibly from Scandinavian tippa 'to tip, dump'. Tipsy-cake from the 1800s was stale cake saturated with wine or liquor.

Tipple dates back to the 1500s, meaning 'sell alcoholic liquor by retail'. It is possibly from a Scandinavian source tipla 'to drink slowly or in small quantities'. The meaning of 'drink (alcoholic beverage) too much' is found in the 1550s. A tippler is a seller of alcoholic liquors.

Wingtips are totally unrelated to the above discussion, except that many businessmen who wear these shoes with a back-curving toe cap suggestive of a bird's wingtip often tipple after work and are tipsy by the time they go home.

Shmoo - The origin of the word comes from Al Capp and his cartoon Lil Abner. A Shmoo is a cuddly creature that desires nothing more than to be a boon to mankind.

Shmoos are the world's most amiable creatures, supplying all man's needs. However, they reproduce so prodigiously they threaten to wreck the economy.

They require no sustenance other than air, have no bones, and reproduce asexually and prolifically. Shmoon (plural) are delicious to eat, are eager to be eaten, and taste like chicken. Nogoodniks are anti-Shmoo. They are Shmoo-shaped, but colored sickly green with yellow teeth, red eyes, and often had five-o'clock shadow, chomp stogies, and devour their friendly Shmoo cousins.

Since then, the word schmoo now has taken on other meanings. In socioeconomics, a shmoo refers to any generic kind of good that reproduces itself.

In microbiology, the cellular bulge produced by a haploid yeast cell towards a cell of the opposite mating type during the mating of yeast is referred to as a shmoo, due to its structural resemblance to the cartoon character.

In the field of particle physics, shmoo refers to a high energy survey instrument. Over one hundred white shmoo detectors were at one time sprinkled around the accelerator beamstop area and adjacent mesa to capture subatomic cosmic ray particles emitted from the Cygnus constellation. The detectors housed scintillators and photomultipliers in an array that gave the detector its distinctive shmoo shape.

In electrical engineering, a shmoo plot is the technical term used for the graphic pattern of test circuits. The term 'to shmoo means to run the test. *Incidentally, there is no relationship between schmoo and schmooze.*

A Few Drinking Terms - Two old words that I miss are - GROG-BLOSSOM, A word from the 18th century for the dilation of blood vessels caused by long-term overconsumption of the drink in an alcoholic's nose.

CRAPULENCE, This word, from the Latin root crapula, arose in the 18th century. It denoted intestinal and cranial distress arising from intemperance and debauchery. *Put another way: If you get drunk, expect crapulence.*

Crocodility - I love the way that word rolls off the tongue. Crocodility is an ancient word for fallacious reasoning.

See if you can follow this paradox. A crocodile snatches a young boy from a riverbank. His mother pleads with the crocodile to return him, to which the crocodile replies that he will only return the boy safely if the mother can guess correctly whether or not he will return the boy.

There is no problem if the mother guesses that the crocodile will return him. If she is right, he is returned; if she is wrong, the crocodile keeps him. If she answers that the crocodile will not return him, however, we end up with a paradox: if she is right and the crocodile never intended to return her child, then the crocodile has to return him, but in doing so breaks his word and contradicts the mother's answer. On the other hand, if she is wrong and the crocodile actually did intend to return the boy, the crocodile must then keep him even though he intended not to, thereby also breaking his word.

The paradox is such an enduring logic problem that in the Middle Ages the word "crocodilite" came to be used to refer to any similarly brain-twisting dilemma where you admit something that is later used against you.

Crumpet, Muffin, and Pikelete - Most websites and cookbooks agree that crumpets and English muffins are different, although they all disagree exactly how.

Crumpets and English muffins are both griddle cakes - meaning they were originally made on the stove top in a cast-iron griddle pan. They are both round and generally biscuit-sized. They both have a spongy texture full of nooks and crannies for absorbing melted butter and other toppings. They are also both considered to be a breakfast, brunch, or tea food, but not the kind of bread you would serve with dinner.

Crumpets are always made with milk, but English muffins are not.

Crumpet batter is a loose batter. English muffins are usually made from more firm dough.

Crumpets are made only using baking soda. English muffins are usually made with yeast or sourdough.

Crumpets are cooked only on one side, so the bottom is flat and toasted while the top is speckled with holes. English muffins are more bread-like and toasted on both sides.

Crumpets are served whole with jam and butter spread on top. English muffins are usually split before coating and serving.

A regional variation of the crumpet is the pikelet, whose name comes from the Welsh bara piglydd or "pitchy [dark or sticky] bread", later shortened simply to piglydd. This spread initially to the West Midlands, where it became anglicized as "pikelet", and subsequently to Cheshire, Lancashire, Yorkshire, and other areas of the north. The main distinguishing feature of the Welsh or West Midlands' pikelet is that it was traditionally cooked without a ring, with an end result rather flatter or thinner than a crumpet.

Idioms - Here are a few idioms that have preserved words that we no longer use by themselves. They are almost exclusively used in context, rather than stand-alone.

Eke is usually used as to 'eke out a living'. It comes from an old verb meaning to add, supplement, or grow. It is also the same word that gave us "eke-name" for additional name, which became "nickname."

Dint comes from the Old English where it originally referred to a blow struck with a sword or other weapon. It is now used as "by dint of something" where 'something' can stand for charisma, hard work, or anything you can use to accomplish something else.

Deserts, as in 'just deserts' comes from an Old French word for 'deserve', and it was used in English from the 13th century to mean that which is deserved. When you get your just deserts, you get your due.

Kith, as in 'kith and kin' comes from an Old English word referring to knowledge or acquaintance. The expression "kith and kin" originally meant your country and your family, but later came to have the wider sense of friends and family.

Fro, as in 'to and fro' comes from the old English way of pronouncing from.

Umbrage, as in 'take umbrage' comes from the French ombrage (shade, shadow), and it was once used to talk about shade from the sun. It took on various figurative meanings having to do with doubt and suspicion or the giving and taking of offense. To give umbrage was to offend someone, to 'throw shade'.

Shrift, as in 'short shrift' came from the practice of allowing a little time for the condemned to make a confession before being executed. *In that context, shorter was never better.*

Dull, Bland, and Boring - Elizabeth Leighton of Aberfeldy, Scotland proposed a pairing of the Scottish town of Dull while passing through Boring, Oregon on a cycling holiday. Boring has a population of 12,000. Dull has a population of about 84.

During 2013, Dull entered into another partnership with the Australian town Bland. Seems the residents of Bland Shire in New South Wales want to cash in on humorous publicity by creating a trinity with Dull and Boring. Bland has a population of about 6,000.

Dull's name is thought to have come from the Gaelic word for meadow, but others have speculated it could be connected to the Gaelic word "dul" meaning snare. Bland was named after William Bland, the first person in the Australian Medical Association and was transported to Australia as a convict after he killed a man in a duel in Bombay. Boring was named after one of its first residents, W.H. Boring, a farmer and Union veteran who moved to Oregon after the Civil War.

Berserk, Pea, and Edit - A back-formation is a word created by removing an element from an existing word. It can change the word's meaning or the part of speech.

Berserk is a back-formation from berserker, one of a band of ancient Norse warriors legendary for their savagery and reckless frenzy in battle.

Pea and plural peas are a back-formation of Middle English 'pease', which was a mass noun in wide use, like oatmeal.

Edit is a back formation of editor. Editor was in use for almost 150 years before edit. Edit arose because the word 'editor' sounds as if it should mean 'one who edits'.

Bums, Hobos, Tramps, Vagrants, and Vagabonds - Hobo, tramp, and bum are all terms for a person who is homeless and without a steady job. While most folks use these words interchangeably, there is a slight difference between the three. A hobo

64

is someone who travels from place to place looking for work, a tramp is someone who travels, but avoids work whenever possible, and a bum does not care to work or travel.

While no one is quite sure how the word "hobo" developed, it seems to have originated in the American West after the US Civil War, when many discharged veterans were looking for employment. The hobo population also increased during the Great Depression, as unemployed men took to train-hopping with the hopes of finding better prospects on the road. Although "hobo" is a slang word, its meaning was well known by the late 19th century and Funk and Wagnall's even listed "hobo" in the 1893 edition of its dictionary. It was derived from the term hoe-boy meaning "farmhand", or a greeting such as "Ho, boy!". Bill Bryson suggests in Made in America, 1998 that it could either come from the railroad greeting, "Ho, beau!" or a syllabic abbreviation of homeward bound.

The British Hobo Museum exhibits hobo history and lore. Initially just a "Hobo Convention" museum, in the late 1990s it evolved into the Hobo History Museum.

The word "tramp" comes from a Middle English verb meaning to "walk with heavy footsteps," and, like "hobo," it also became widely used after the Civil War. It initially referred to migrant workers searching for permanent work, but it was later used to designate those who "prefer the transient way of life." In Britain the term was widely used to refer to vagrants in the early Victorian period. It is also used for a sexually promiscuous woman.

Lately, the word is experiencing a bit of resurgence as many wanderers have adopted the title to more clearly differentiate their way of life from hobos. Some, for example, intentionally avoid participating in the economic system and therefore take pride in their 'tramp' status and may even view themselves as superior to hobos.

A vagrant could be described as being "a person without a settled home or regular work who wanders from place to place and lives by begging." Both "vagrant" and "vagabond" derive from Latin word vagari "wander." The term "vagabond" is derived from Latin vagabundus. In Middle English, "vagabond" originally denoted a criminal.

Panhandling is a solicitation made in person for immediate donation of money or other gratuity. Bottom line, most bums, tramps, and vagrants, but only some hobos panhandle.

All politicians and some other groups and individuals engage in panhandling or public fundraising for many causes and charities.

Lector - The word 'lector' usually makes us think of university lecturers and public speakers, but in the 1900s, a lector was actually a form of entertainment. A factory lector was employed to entertain workers in cigar factories by reading out loud, usually newspapers and sometimes novels. The profession started in Cuba, later becoming more prominent in New York and Florida.

Gnurr is the official name of the lint that collects at the bottom of your pockets.

Life in a cigar factory was mostly manual labor, such as rolling cigars by hand, so the lectors proved to be good for the morale of workers. The employees would pool money together to help pay the lector's salary. Lectors had a huge influence on the workers, providing an education for them through their reading. Lectors were eventually replaced by radios during the 1920's.

Moms and Dads - A word extremely similar to "mom" occurs in almost every language on Earth and they are surprisingly similar across nearly all of the most commonly spoken languages. For example, if you wanted to address your mother in Dutch you would say "moeder", in Germany "mutter", in Italy "madre". Here are a few more:

Chinese: Mãma
Hindi: Mam
Afrikaans: Ma
Swahili: Mama
French: Mère, Maman
Irish: Máthair
Italian: Madre, Mamma
Norwegian: Madre
Spanish: Madre, Mamá, Mami
Ukrainian: Mati
Romanian: Mama, Maica
Russian: Mat'
Welsh: Mam
Yiddish: Muter

The word "Papa" is present in several languages including Russian, Hindi, Spanish, and English, while slight variations appear in German (Papi), Icelandic (Pabbi), Swedish (Pappa) and a number of other languages. In Turkish, Greek, Swahili, Malay and several other languages the word for dad is "Baba" or a variation of it.

It has been observed that babies, regardless of where in the world they are born, naturally learn to make the same few sounds as they begin to learn to speak. It has also been noted that during the babbling stage, babies will create what is known as "protowords" by combining combinations of consonants and vowels. These protowords are consistent across different cultures. The words babies make in this early babbling stage tend to use the softer contestants like B, P and M, often leading to the creation of otherwise non-words like baba, papa, and mama by the children.

It is theorized that since these are often the first sounds babies are able to make consistently, parents tended to use them to refer to themselves, which explains why words like "mama", "papa," "dada", "tata" and "baba" are present in so many languages as a way of addressing parents.

These sounds are usually less complex to say than parent's real names. Popular belief among many is the gibberish phrase da-da may have transposed to the use of the word Dad. Aroana tadi, Aztec tahtil, ta, Basque aita (father) and aitatxo (dad) and aitaita (grandfather), Czech, Irish and Latin daid, German Vati, Greek tata, Inca tayta, Inuit ataatak, Hungarian atya, Polish tatus, Quechua tayta, Rumanian tata, Russian dyadya, Sanskrit Tatah, Sumerian ada, Tagalog tatay, Turkish ata, Welsh tad.

Old English fæder, Proto-Germanic fader, Old Saxon fadar, Old Frisian feder, Dutch vader, Old Norse faðir, Old High German fatar, German vater, Greek pater, Latin pater, Old Persian pita. *Seems children are very intelligent. They teach us to use the names they give us.*

Fog, Smog, Vog, Haze, and Mist - This time of year we see many of these weather conditions and some people can get a bit foggy about the definitions.

Mist and fog are caused by water droplets in the air, and the only difference is how far you can see. The airline industry's definition of fog uses the guideline of not being able to see more than 1,000 meters (3,280 ft), although the civilian definition of fog is when visibility is less than 200 meters (650 ft). If you can see farther than that, it is considered mist. Different types of fog include Valley fog, Upslope fog, and coastal fog. Also, evaporation fog causes freezing fog.

Haze is the reflection of sunlight off air pollution. Some naturally occurring sources of haze include smoke particles from fires. Most haze is air pollution, carried by the wind often hundreds of miles from where it originated.

> **Vinculum** is the line between two numbers in a fraction.

Smog was first used in London during the early 1900s to describe the combination of smoke and fog. It occurs when pollution causes low-lying ozone. When certain pollutants enter the air, such as nitrogen oxides, they react with the sunlight to form ozone. Major smog occurrences often are linked to heavy motor vehicle traffic, high temperatures, sunshine, and calm winds. During 1952, weather conditions led to massive smog descending on and gathering over London. Visibility was less than 30 centimeters (12 in), the air was black with coal and pollution, and the usually bustling city came to a standstill. By the time the smog cleared, 4,000 people died from exposure to the pollution, and another 8,000 died during the following weeks.

Vog only happens when a nearby volcano is releasing sulfur dioxide into the air to react with what is already there. When a volcano erupts, or begins to erupt, it releases sulfur dioxide, which then reacts with other gases already in the air. When lava reaches the sea, it also reacts with the water to produce other chemicals like hydrogen sulfide. The resulting "fog" is called vog and can mean anything from severely reduced visibility to adding a mild, blue-grey tint to the landscape.

Hair of the Dog - The expression, "hair of the dog that bit you" refers to an old method of treating a rabid dog bite by placing hair from the same dog on the wound. We now use it to acknowledge the practice of soothing a hangover by ingesting the same substance that caused the problem. The earliest known reference to the phrase "hair of the dog" in connection with drunkenness is found in a text from ancient Ugarit dating from the mid to late second millennium.

This metaphor first surfaced in a 1546 collection of English colloquial sayings: "What how fellow, thou knave, I pray thee let me and my fellow have a haire of the dog that bit us last night. And bitten were we bothe to the braine aright."

Applied to drinks, it means, if overnight you have indulged too freely, take a glass of the same drink to soothe the nerves. "If this dog do you bite, soon as out of your bed, take a hair of the tail the next day." Aristophanes used the Latin 'similia similibus curantur' (like cures like) and it exists today as the basic postulate of classical homeopathy.

During the 1930s, cocktails known as Corpse Revivers were served in hotels.

The Hungarian translation to English is, "(You may cure) the dog's bite with its fur," but has evolved into a short phrase "kutyaharapást szőrével" that is used frequently in other contexts when one is trying to express that the solution to a problem is more of the problem.

Among the Irish and Mexicans, the phrase "the cure, or "curarse la cruda" in Spanish is often used. In Costa Rica the same expression is used but it refers to a pig as in: hair of the same pig.

In some Slavic languages (Polish, Bosnian, Croatian, Serbian, Slovenian and Russian) hair of the dog is called "a wedge" (klin), as in dislodging a stuck wedge with another one, which is used figuratively with regard to alcohol and in other contexts. The proper Russian term is – опохмелка "after being drunk", which indicates a process of drinking to decrease effects of drinking the night before.

In German, drinking alcohol the next morning to relieve the symptoms is sometimes described as ein Konterbier trinken "having a counter-beer." In Austria people have a reparatur-seidl "repair-beer." In Portuguese people speak of uma rebatida "a hit," meaning to strike away the hangover with more alcohol. *There is a new Belgian beer called Snuffles and it is brewed exclusively for dogs. Maybe a new term, 'Hair of the Human' will come into vogue.*

Fat Free and Free Range - When the dangers of saturated and trans fat became popular headlines, the market was flooded with products that touted their **fat-free** status. They sometimes contained nearly as many calories as full-fat versions. "Just because it says it's fat-free, doesn't mean you get a free ride," says Bonnie Taub-Dix. "Packages could say it is fat free, but be loaded with sugar, and sugar-free products could be loaded with fat." Check the label for calorie content, and compare it to the full-fat version.

Although a food label may say **free range** chicken, it does not mean the chicken is out prancing in the wide open farmer's field. The US Department of Agriculture does define the words free range, but there are no requirements for the amount, duration, and quality of outdoor access. "What it's supposed to mean is that they are out running in a field," says Bonnie Taub-Dix, nutrition expert and author of Read It, Before You Eat It. "But what it really means is they just have exposure to the outdoors."

      Brumal, Hibernal, and Hiemal - I am officially tired of brumal, hibernal, and hiemal weather.

brumal - adj. wintry
hibernal - adj. of, pertaining to, or proper to winter
hiemal - adj. of or relating to winter

In 380 AD, the church issued a law specifically forbidding anyone to read the Bible while naked.

People had been trying to emulate the innocence of Adam and Eve by taking their clothes off before services.

WHAT'S IN A NAME

Sports Jerseys - Jersey is a crown dependency island of the UK where the people have been knitting great wool sweaters for centuries. These tight knit warm sweaters were initially used as an inner layer by rural seamen before evolving into common outerwear. Jersey sweaters spread about the UK and northern Europe as the country's trading industry rose in prominence during the late 17th and early 18th centuries. Their popularity gained so much, the name "jersey" became synonymous with "sweater" in countries as far away as the United States during the 1850s. When American football developed, players needed strong, insular uniforms, and thick wool jerseys did the job.

Athletic jerseys bore increasingly little resemblance to their bulky ancestral tops. Just as the name had become a synonym for sweater, it soon became a synonym for athletic uniform. Lightweight baseball shirts were often called "jerseys" despite being generally made of flannel and incorporating short sleeves, buttons, and collars. Canadian hockey sweaters also were called jerseys. Americans used jerseys when playing football, then baseball, then hockey.

Origin of Crest Toothpaste - The major ingredient in Crest was discovered by accident when a student left a sample in the furnace too long and when discovered, found that it made it possible to mix the ingredient with fluoride. At first it used stannous fluoride, marketed as 'Fluoristan' (this was also the original brand name it was sold as. Later it changed from 'Fluoristan' to 'Crest with Fluoristan'). The composition of the toothpaste was developed by Drs. Muhler, Harry Day, and William H. Nebergall at Indiana University, and was patented by Nebergall.

Procter & Gamble paid royalties from use of the patent and thus financed a new dental research institute at the university. The active ingredient of Crest was changed in 1981 to sodium monofluorophosphate, or 'Fluoristat'. Today Crest toothpastes use sodium fluoride, or 'Dentifrice with Fluoristat'. Recently introduced Crest Pro-Health, uses stannous fluoride again and an abrasive whitener together called 'Polyfluorite'.

Old Spice - The first Old Spice® product, called Early American Old Spice for women, was introduced in 1937, and was followed by Old Spice for men in 1938. The Old Spice products were manufactured by the Shulton Company, founded in 1934 by William Lightfoot Schultz.

Early American Old Spice was developed around a colonial theme. When Old Spice was introduced, Schultz was interested in maintaining a colonial framework for those products and chose a nautical theme for Old Spice. Thus, colonial sailing ships were used as a trademark. Through continuous use and advertising, the various ships have become a valuable trademark identifying the Old Spice product for men.

The original ships used on the packaging were the Grand Turk and the Friendship. Other ships used on Old Spice packaging include the Wesley, Salem, Birmingham, and Hamilton.

Procter & Gamble purchased the Old Spice fragrances, skin care, antiperspirant, and deodorant products from the Shulton Company in June 1990.

Special Olympics and Paralympics - The Paralympics are held following the respective Olympic Games. The Summer Games of 1988 held in Seoul was the first time the term 'Paralympic' became official. Many confuse Paralympics with Special Olympics.

Special Olympics and Paralympics are two separate organizations recognized by the International Olympic Committee. Both focus on sports for athletes with disabilities and both are run by international non-profit organizations. Special Olympics and Paralympics differ in three main areas: disability categories of the athletes, criteria and philosophy of athletes participation, and organizational structure.

Special Olympics welcomes all athletes, 8 and older, with intellectual disabilities of all ability levels, to train and compete in 30 Olympic-type sports. To be eligible, athletes must have an intellectual disability; a cognitive delay, or a development disability. They may also have a physical disability. Paralympics welcomes athletes from six main disability categories: amputee, cerebral palsy, intellectual disability, visually impaired, spinal injuries, and Les Autres (includes conditions that do not fall into the other categories).

Special Olympics believes deeply in the power of sports to help all who participate to fulfill their potential and does not exclude any athlete based upon qualifying scores, but divisions the athletes based on scores for fair competition against others of like ability. Special Olympics believes athletes' excellence is personal achievement and reaching one's maximum potential.

To participate in the Paralympic Games, athletes must fulfill certain criteria and meet certain qualifying standards in order to be eligible. These criteria and standards are sports-specific.

Paralympics focuses on highest qualified based on performance. Special Olympics focuses on all ability levels and is committed to inclusion, acceptance, and dignity for all.

Whipping Boy - This term is still used, but did you know there really were whipping boys? Whipping boys were created, because of the divine right of kings, which stated that kings were appointed by God, and implied that no one but the king was worthy of punishing the king's son. Tutors to young princes found it difficult to enforce rules or learning.

A whipping boy was a young boy who was assigned to a young prince and was punished when the prince misbehaved or fell behind in his schooling. The idea was that seeing a friend being whipped or beaten for something that he had done wrong would be likely to ensure that the prince would not make the same mistake again. Whipping boys were established in the English court during monarchies of the 15th and 16th centuries.

Digitalis - The first known heart medicine was discovered in an English garden. In 1799, physician John Ferriar noted the effect of dried leaves of the common plant, digitalis purpurea, on heart action. The scientific name means "finger-like" and refers to the ease with which a flower of digitalis purpurea can be fitted over a human fingertip. The term digitalis is also used for drug preparations that contain cardiac glycosides, particularly one called digoxin, extracted from various plants of this genus. Digoxin was approved for heart failure in 1998. Also, a group of medicines extracted from foxglove plants are called Digitalin.

Once the usefulness of digitalis in regulating the human pulse was understood, it was employed for a variety of purposes, including the treatment of epilepsy and other seizure disorders, but is now considered to be inappropriate treatment. The most common prescription form of this medication is called digoxin. Digitoxin is another form of digitalis.

Paisley - The distinctive paisley or boteh pattern is originally from Persia through India, and has been in use in the Middle East and Asia since 200 AD. When its European popularity boomed and imports could not keep up with the demand, various cities produced their own, including the town of Paisley in Scotland. It is also called

Palme in France, Bota in Netherlands, Bootar in India, and Peizuli in Japan.

Richter Scale - The Richter Magnitude Scale, often shortened to Richter scale, was developed to assign a single number to quantify the energy that is released during an earthquake. It was developed in 1935 by Charles Francis Richter in partnership with Beno Gutenberg, both from the California Institute of Technology. The scale was originally intended to be used in a particular study area in California.

The scale is a base-10 logarithmic scale. The magnitude is defined as the logarithm of the ratio of the amplitude of waves measured by a seismograph to an arbitrary small amplitude. An earthquake that measures 5.0 on the Richter scale has a shaking amplitude 10 times larger than one that measures 4.0.

Since the 1970s, Richter scale use has mostly been replaced by the Moment Magnitude Scale (MMS) in many countries. However, the Richter scale is still widely used in Russia and other European countries. The MMS was developed in the 1970s to succeed Richter magnitude scale. Even though the formulae are different, the new scale retains the continuum of magnitude values defined by the older one.

The MMS is now the scale used to estimate magnitudes for all modern large earthquakes by the US Geological Survey. Earthquake measurements under the Moment Magnitude Scale in the United States are still usually erroneously referred to as being quoted on the Richter scale by the general public and the media, due to their familiarity with the old Richter scale name vs. the newer MMS.

Meringue - The name meringue came from a pastry chef named Gasparini in the Swiss town of Merhrinyghen. In 1720, Gasparini created a small pastry of dried egg foam and sugar from which the simplified meringue evolved. Its fame spread and Marie Antoinette is said to have prepared the sweet with her own hands at the Trianon in France.

Rugby - According to legend, this sport was invented when a pupil at Rugby School in England picked up the ball and ran with it during a soccer game. The first written rules for the game originated at the school in 1845.

Bacardi Bats - Bacardi Limited is the largest privately held, family-owned spirits company in the world. It has a portfolio of more than 200 brands and labels. Rum drinkers have likely noticed the bat symbol on Bacardi products.

The Bacardi brothers purchased their first distillery in Cuba which had a tin roof and fruit bats lived in the rafters. Bats in Cuba are considered a symbol of good health, good fortune, and family unity. That is why it is used as the symbol.

When you see Ron Bacardi, it is not the owner's name, ron means rum in Spanish.

Brand Names - Many words we use are really patented or trademarked names owned by specific companies. Here are a few of names that have become more-or-less generic, but are still owned.

Breathalyzer, Bubble Wrap, ChapStick, Crock Pot, Dumpster, Jacuzzi, Jet Ski, Kleenex, Ouija Board, Ping Pong, Popsicle, Rollerblade, Seeing Eye Dog, Styrofoam, Taser, Velcro, Zamboni

Sherry - This fortified wine is named for the Anglican version of its town of origin, Jerez de la Frontera in Spain. Like champagne, sherry is a Protected Designation of Origin, and only wine from that area of Spain can be labeled sherry in Europe.

Bronx - A seventeenth century Scandinavian man by the name of Jonas Bronck immigrated in 1639 to New Amsterdam (now New York), which was right next to the Bronx River, that was later named after him.

Jonas owned a 680 acre farm called 'Bronck's Land' and the river abutting it 'Bronck's River'. Various people owned this property and kept the name, until Colonel Lewis Morris acquired it and renamed it the 'Manor of Morrisania'. The river next to it continued to be called Bronck's River. From the river's name, the modern-day name of 'Bronx' extended to the region directly around it.

The spelling change happened around the same time there was a big push for the simplification of English, such as the names of the Boston Red Sox and the Chicago White Sox, from 'Socks'.

Spumoni - Spumoni originated in Naples and is the ancestor of Neapolitan ice cream. Spumoni ice cream, like Neapolitan ice cream is a molded Italian ice cream made with layers of different colors and flavors. The difference is that Spumoni usually also contains candied fruits and nuts. The name Spumone comes from spuma or 'foam'. The plural form is spumoni.

Typically it is of three flavors, with a fruit/nut layer between them. The ice cream layers are often mixed with whipped cream. Cherry, pistachio, and either chocolate or vanilla are the typical flavors of the ice cream layers, and the fruit/nut layer often contains cherry bits, causing the traditional red/pink, green, and brown color combination. It is popular in places with large Italian immigrant populations such as the United States and Argentina. August 21 is National Spumoni Day in the United States. November 13 is National Spumoni Day in Canada.

Welsh Rarebit - It is cheese on toast with added ingredients. When it was devised in the 18th century, the English (by then well-established in their teasing of the Welsh) jokingly called it Welsh Rabbit - as a Welshman, supposedly too poor to have meat, had to eat cheese instead.

The earliest reference can be traced to 1725 and the diary of a poet called John Byrom who wrote, "I did not eat of cold beef, but of Welsh rabbit and stewed cheese."

Sixty years later, the rarebit popped up in Francis Grose's Classical Dictionary of the Vulgar Tongue: "A Welsh rabbit is bread and cheese roasted, i.e. a Welsh rare bit."

Lego - Danish carpenter Ole Kirk Christiansen, the founder of Lego, asked his staff to come up with a name for his growing toy company. The two names that ended up being finalists were 'Legio' and 'Lego'. The first was a reference to a legion as in a Legion of toys. The second was made from a contraction of "leg godt", which is a Danish phrase meaning 'play well'. Lego is also a Latin word meaning 'to gather or collect'.

Pabst Blue Ribbon - On September 19, 2014, Oasis Beverages announced it acquired the Pabst Brewing Company. Pabst owns Pabst Blue Ribbon, Old Milwaukee, Schlitz, Ballantine India Pale Ale, and Colt 45. Oasis has brewing operations in Ukraine, Belarus, and Kazakhstan. *Maybe they will change it to Pabst red ribbon.*

Viagra - The official name is Sildenafil Citrate. Pharmaceutical chemists at Pfizer's research facility in Kent, England originally conceived it as a treatment for hypertension, angina, and other symptoms of heart disease. Clinical trials during 1991 and 1992 revealed the drug was not great at treating what it was supposed to treat, but eighty percent of male test subjects were experiencing a side effect of erections.

It was finally approved by the US FDA in 1998 and the drug took US markets by storm as a treatment for penile dysfunction and became an overnight success. It and female Viagra now raise over two billion dollars a year.

Starbucks - Starbucks is named for Captain Ahab's first mate, Starbuck in the 1851 novel *Moby-Dick*. The founders had considered naming it Pequod's, after Ahab's ship.

Coffee related and true - The first webcam watched a coffee pot. It allowed researchers at Cambridge to monitor the coffee pot without leaving their desks. *Well, call me Ishmael.*

Harvard - Harvard was founded mainly by a bequest from John Harvard, along with his extensive library in 1636. The iconic statue of him is really not him, because they could not find a real picture of him so the artist had another person sit in. That guy was a student, Sherman Hoar.

Santa Fe - "Santa" can also mean holy, and "fe" means faith, so Santa Fe = holy faith. The full name of the New Mexico state capital is "Villa Real de la Santa Fe de San Francisco de Asis," or "Royal Village of the Holy Faith of St. Francis of Assisi."

Budapest - Óbuda united with Buda and Pest in 1873. Budapest is the capital and largest city of Hungary.

Pest is the eastern, mostly flat part of Budapest, Hungary, comprising about two thirds of the city's territory. It is separated from Buda by the Danube River. In colloquial Hungarian, "Pest" is often used for the whole capital of Budapest. *Harry Houdini was from Pest.*

Buda is the former capital of the Kingdom of Hungary and the western part of Budapest. Buda comprises about one-third of Budapest's complete territory and is mostly wooded and hilly. Buda Castle is the historical castle and palace complex of the Hungarian kings in Budapest, and was first completed in 1265.

Obuda means old Buda and it is located on the western side of the city. It has a sculpture in the town square of people waiting for the rain to stop.

Sony, Combine the Latin term for sound 'sonus' with the American slang for bright youngster 'sonny' and you have the name for the electronics business. Founder Akio Morita believed 'Sony' was a way of letting the public know they "were sonny boys working in sound and vision" in the industry at the time. It is also an easy pronunciation in all languages.

Microsoft - Paul Allen not Bill Gates, came up with the name for their billion-dollar PC dynasty. He found inspiration from the creation of MICROprocessors and saw the future of computers in SOFTware, leading to the blend of terms.

Ig Nobel Awards

On September 18, 2014 the 24th annual Ig Nobel, pronounced 'ig no bell' Prize ceremony was held at Harvard. Each winner did something that makes people laugh then think. Winners traveled to the ceremony from around the world at their own expense to receive their prize from a group of amused Nobel Laureates. On lucky person won a date with a Nobel laureate. Real Nobel Laureates hand out prizes.

The awards ceremony is traditionally closed with the words: "If you didn't win a prize, and especially if you did, better luck next year!"

The "Stinker" is the official mascot of the Ig Nobel Awards.

The Physics prize went to a team that measured the amount of friction between a shoe and a banana skin and then a banana skin and the floor, when a person steps on a banana skin that is on the floor.

The Neuroscience prize went to a team that attempted to dissect the inner workings of the brains of people who see Jesus in their toast.

The Economics prize went to the Italian government's National Institute of Statistics, for taking the lead in fulfilling the European Union mandate for each country to increase the official size of its national economy by including revenues from prostitution, illegal drug sales, smuggling, and all other unlawful financial transactions between willing participants.

The Biology prize went to a team that discovered when dogs poop and pee, they tend to align their body axis with Earth's north-south geomagnetic field lines.

The Public Health prize went to a team that investigated whether it is mentally hazardous for a human being to own a cat.

The Arctic Science prize went to a team that observed how reindeer behave upon seeing humans disguised as polar bears.

The Medicine prize went to a team that was able to treat "uncontrollable" nosebleeds using strips of cured pork. A team at the Detroit Medical Center decided to try the folk remedy as a last resort after failed attempts to stop an uncontrollable nosebleed in a 4-year-old who suffers from Glanzmann thrombasthenia, a rare condition in which blood does not properly clot. They stuffed strips of cured pork into the child's nostrils twice, and the hemorrhaging ceased. They reported the clotting factors in pork and the high level of salt pulls in a lot of fluid from the nose. *Ah, they may never stop finding new uses for bacon.*

Real People Facts

Aerosmith - These rock legends have been entertaining folks for three decades, but the band's biggest money maker is from the Guitar Hero: Aerosmith rhythm action game.

The royalties the band earns from the game dwarfs anything they ever earned from any of their other albums, concerts, or other merchandise. So, the band earned more money from people pretending to play their music than actually playing it themselves.

Larry, Moe, and Curly - When it comes to laughter, these three were in the front of the pack. Their antics spanned generations of slapstick aficionados. For the Three Stooges fans in the bunch, just received the following. My niece, Kalyn turned me on to a Kickstarter to produce a history of the Three Stooges. Also the fans home page http://www.threestooges.com

Top Five Lead Singers Net Worth -
1: Paul McCartney – $800 Million (The Beatles, etc.)
2: Bono – $600 Million (U2)
3: Jimmy Buffett – $400 Million (Solo)
4: Elton John – $320 Million (Solo)
5: Mick Jagger – $315 Million (The Rolling Stones)

Procter and Gamble - William Procter was a candle maker from England, and James Gamble was a soap maker from Ireland. They settled in Cincinnati and met when they married sisters, Olivia and Elizabeth Norris. They began business as Procter and Gamble, October 31, 1837. Their first product was a floating soap called Ivory.

During the 1920s and 1930s, the company sponsored a number of radio programs. *As a result, these shows often became known as 'soap operas'.*

How Tall are Hollywood Stars - We have all heard Hollywood stars are shorter than they appear on film. Here is a list that proves it to be true.

Snooki is 4'8"

Paula Abdul 5'0"

Reese Witherspoon, Lady Gaga 5'1"

Salma Hayek, Hillary Duff, and Prince 5'2"

Martin Scorsese, Paul Simon 5'3"

Seth Green, Michael J. Fox, Emilio Estevez 5'4"

Dustin Hoffman, Bruno Mars, Daniel Radcliffe, Scott Cann 5'5"

Jon Stewart, Jack Black, Cheech Marin 5'6"

Robert Downey Jr. (5'7" or 5'8"), Tom Cruise, Martin Sheen, Ben Stiller 5'7"

Chuck Norris Belts - Carlos Ray "Chuck" Norris, born March 10, 1940, is the first Westerner in history to be awarded an 8th degree Black Belt (Grand Master) in Taekwondo. He also has 10th degree black belt in Chun Kuk Do (he is founder of this school); 9th degree black belt in Tang Soo Do and BJJ; and brown belts in Brazilian Jiu-Jitsu and Judo. In 2005, Norris founded the World Combat League, a full-contact, team-based martial arts competition.

Writer's Worth - The top famous authors are worth much more than we might expect. J.K. Rowling went from rags to riches and was worth over 1 billion dollars in 2011. Other wealthy authors include Danielle Steel ($610 million), Stephen King ($400 million), Tom Clancy ($300 million), James Patterson ($250 million), John Grisham ($200 million), Barbara Taylor Bradford ($200 million), Nora Roberts ($150 million), Stephenie Meyer ($125 million), and Dan Brown ($100 million). *That is something to write home about.*

Billionaires and Millionaires - In 2013, the world had about 2,170 billionaires. Women make up 8.5% of those. Ten of America's 43 self-made billionaires dropped out of college.

Sheldon Adelson dropped out of City College of New York ($36.4 billion)

Paul Allen dropped out of Washington State ($16.2 billion)

Andy Beal dropped out of Baylor University ($11.1 billion)

Michael Dell dropped out of University of Texas ($15.3 billion)

Larry Ellison dropped out of University of Chicago ($52 billion)

Bill Gates dropped out of Harvard ($81.6 billion)

Jan Koum dropped out of San Jose State University ($7.5 billion)

Jack Taylor dropped out of Washington University ($11.4 billion)

Mark Zuckerberg dropped out of Harvard ($33.1 billion)

Four of the youngest billionaires in the world are connected to Facebook (Dustin Moskovitz, Sean Parker, Eduardo Severin, and Mark Zuckerberg,).

America's youngest self-made female billionaire is 30 years old and a college dropout.

New York has the largest number of billionaires, with 96, Hong Kong has 75, Moscow 74, and London 67.

Carlo Slim Helu, a Mexican billionaire worth $69 billion, is considered to be the first world's richest man from a developing nation. He has lived in the same modest home for the past 30 years. His wealth is equal to 5% of Mexico's economic output.

Millionaires

❖ The average millionaire goes bankrupt at least 3.5 times.

❖ In the United States, approximately 7% of households are millionaires.

❖ A 2010 study shows that millionaires pay approximately 40% of all taxes in the United States.

❖ According to the book The Millionaire Next Door, only 20% of millionaires inherited their wealth. The other 80% earned it on their own.

❖ Half of all millionaires are self employed or own their own business.

❖ Eighteen percent of millionaires have Master's degrees, eight percent have law degrees, six percent have medical degrees, and six percent have PhDs.

❖ Those with Russian ancestry have the highest concentration of millionaire households in America, with $1.1 trillion, or nearly 5% of all the personal wealth in America. The Scottish rank second, Hungarians rank third, and English ancestry groups rank fourth.

❖ A pentamillionaire is someone with the net worth of $5 million. A decamillionare has a net worth of $10 million. A hectamillionaire has a net worth of $100 million.

❖ The number of US millionaires is 6.9 million individuals in 2014. China has 3.6 million and Japan 1.1 million.

❖ On average, millionaires are 61 years old with $3.05 million in assets.

❖ Twenty percent of millionaires are retirees.

❖ In 2008, there were 10 million people around the world who were classified as millionaires in US dollars.

❖ There were 418,000 millionaires in Canada in 2014.

Top five countries with highest percent of millionaires.

Rank, Country, % Population with Millionaire Status, Total Number of Millionaires
#1 Singapore 17.1% 188,000
#2 Qatar 14.3% 47,000
#3 Kuwait 11.8% 63,000
#4 Switzerland 9.5% 322,000
#5 Hong Kong 8.8% 212,000

Actor's Net Worth - We all have heard that actors make a bunch of money, but here are a few that are outrageously wealthy. Julia Louis-Dreyfus (from Seinfeld fame) is worth 2.9 billion dollars, most of it from the family business started by her grandfather. The Louis Dreyfus Group is one of the world's largest commodities trading and merchandising firms.

Jerry Seinfeld made his money the hard way and is worth over 800 million dollars. He is followed by Tom Hanks ($350 million), Johnny Depp ($350 million), Tyler Perry ($350 million), Harrison Ford ($200 million), Leonardo DiCaprio ($200 million), Will Smith ($188 million), John Travolta ($160 million), Brad Pitt ($150 million), Julia Roberts ($140 million), Ben Stiller ($120 million), Denzel Washington ($120 million), and Redneck Jeff Foxworthy ($100 million).

Charlie Chaplin, Composer - Last week was listening to one of my favorite singers, Judith Durham, singing 'This is My Song', and found the composer was Charlie Chaplin, the movie comedian. He composed many tunes for his movies, including 'Smile', covered by Nat King Cole. The lyrics of both are especially tender. Chaplin was the only known person who wrote, directed, acted, and scored a motion picture.

Dale Carnegie - His teachings never go out of style. Here are a few worth adopting.

- Become genuinely interested in other people.

- Smile.

- Remember that a person's name is, to that person, the sweetest and most important sound in any language.

- Be a good listener. Encourage others to talk about themselves.

- Talk in terms of the other person's interest.

- Make the other person feel important – and do it sincerely.

J.K. Rowling - In 2004, she became the first person to become a billionaire by writing books. *I plan to be the second, as long as I can hang on for about 500 more years.*

Joseph Lister - The idea of clean operating rooms did not exist until Joseph Lister began his practice of antisepsis in the 1860's. He introduced washing surgical instruments in carbolic acid, and keeping the operating area clean and sterile. He used it on the incision wound, dressings, and instruments. It was a revolutionary change for hospitals. Lister discovered that the infections in wounds which caused so many surgical deaths were not caused by the miasma in the air, but by something entirely different.

In his article in The Lancet of 21 September 1867 and his book 'Antiseptic Principle of the Practice of Surgery' he explained the cause was microorganisms that traveled from the surgeon's hands onto the wound. Because of his miraculous results in operative and post-operative infection, Lister is considered to be one of the founders of modern surgery.

In 1893 Dr. J.C. Bloodgood (his real name) insisted on surgical glove use by his entire surgical team. This was followed by W. Steward Halstead's adoption of surgical gloves at Johns Hopkins that gained national exposure. Halstead is generally credited with the glove's discovery, which is not true.

Listerine was formulated by Dr. Joseph Lawrence and Jordan Wheat Lambert in St. Louis, Missouri, in 1879. Joseph Lister had nothing to do with it, other than his name.

Horsepower and Watts - Although he was not first to use the horsepower name, James Watt was the first to apply specific measurement to it. During the 1780s, after making a vastly superior steam engine to the common Newcomen steam engine, Watt was looking for a way to market his invention, advertising the fact that his engine was superior and used about 75% less fuel than a similarly powered Newcomen.

He came up with a new unit of measurement that those in need of his engine understood, horse power, referring to powerful draft horses. He calculated how much power a typical draft horse could generate and figured out a typical draft horse could do about 32,400 foot-pounds of work per minute and maintain that power rate for a full workday. He then rounded up, going with 33,000 foot-pounds per minute for 1 horsepower. By overestimating what a horse could do he made sure that his product would always over deliver what he said when trying to get people to buy it.

Watt's engine was revolutionary and played a huge role in the Industrial Revolution. His unit of measure of an engine's power became popular. Today the SI (international system of units) unit of power, the Watt, which was named in homage to James Watt, has widely come to replace horsepower in most applications.

James Watt:

• radically improved the steam engine, starting the industrial revolution.

• continued to produce a stream of new ideas and inventions, which eventually resulted in an engine that needed 80% less fuel than earlier engines.

• invented high pressure steam engines capable of even higher efficiencies, but the technology of the time was not capable of operating them safely.

• introduced the word horsepower to describe an engine's power output. We now generally use watts to measure power, although engine power is still often rated in horsepower.

• was the first person to propose that water was made of hydrogen combined with oxygen.

• independently discovered the scientific concept of latent heat.

• invented the world's first copying machine – similar in function to a photocopier – to make copies of correspondence, pages of books, and pictures.

Names and Initials - You may have wondered about some famous person's initials.

- E. E. Cummings - The famous poet's initials stood for Edward Estlin Cummings

- E.B. White - Writer and author of English Language Style Guide, Elwyn Brooks White

- H.P. Lovecraft - Horror author, Howard Phillips Lovecraft

- H.G. Wells - "war of the worlds", "time machine", etc., Herbert George Wells

- J.K. Rowling - The "K" in J.K. Rowling is not her name. Joanne Rowling does not have a middle name, but her publishers wanted to add another initial to her name for her books. She settled on Kathleen, the name of her favorite grandmother.

- J.R.R. Tolkien - "Hobbit", lord of rings series, etc., John Ronald Reuel Tolkien.

Satchmo - Louis Armstrong had many nicknames as a child, all of which referred to the size of his mouth: "Gatemouth," "Dippermouth," and "Satchelmouth." During a visit to Great Britain, Louis was met by Percy Brooks, the editor of Melody Maker magazine, who greeted him by saying, "Hello, Satchmo!" (He contracted "Satchelmouth" into "Satchmo.") Louis loved the new name and adopted it for his own. It provides the title to Louis's second autobiography, is inscribed on at least two of his trumpets, and was on his stationery.

Dalai Lama - This title as first given to the third Dalai Lama, Sonam Gyatso, by Altan Khan. In order to help secure his rule in Mongolia, Altan Khan agreed to let Sonam Gyatso convert Mongolia to Buddhism.

Gyatso then proclaimed that Altan Khan was, in fact, the reincarnated of the great Khublai Khan, former ruler of China and Mongolia and grandson of Ghengis Khan, helping legitimize Altan Khan's rule. The fourth Dalai Lama, Yonten Gyatso, the only Dalai Lama to be born outside of Tibet to date was the great grandson of Altan Khan.

The title Dalai Lama literally means 'The Ocean Lama' with the 'lama' coming from the Tibetan 'blama', meaning guru, mentor, teacher, wise-one." So, it could be interpreted as 'Ocean of Wisdom'.

"Man surprised me most about humanity, because he sacrifices his health in order to make money. Then he sacrifices money to recuperate his health and then he is so anxious about the future that he does not enjoy the present; the result being that he does not live in the present or the future; he lives as if he is never going to die, and then dies having never really lived." ~Dalai Lama

The current Dalai Lama, Lhamo Dondrub is the fourteenth Dali Lama and he may be the last.

Nine Names for Benjamin Franklin

Franklin was prolific, regardless of which name he used.

Richard Saunders - He used this name for his Poor Richard's Almanac, which ran annually from 1732 to 1758. The Richard character brought humor to what was otherwise a serious resource in the almanac. During the years of publication the unnecessary character gradually disappeared.

Silence Dogood - When Benjamin was 16-years-old, he wanted to write for his brother James' newspaper, The New England Courant, but James would not allow it. Ben contributed to the paper as a middle-aged widow named Silence Dogood whose witty and satirical letters covered a range of topics from courtship to education. Fifteen Dogood letters were published, resulting in the amusement of Courant readers and several marriage proposals for the pretend widow, Mrs. Dogood.

Anthony Afterwit - Mr. Afterwit, a gentleman, wrote humorous letters about married life that appeared in Franklin's own Pennsylvania Gazette.

Polly Baker - Polly Baker was a pseudonym Franklin used to examine colonial society's unequal treatment of women. She was pretend punished by society for having children out of wedlock while the fathers of the children went unpunished.

Alice Addertongue - Alice is another middle-aged widow who wrote a gossip column for Franklin's Gazette in the form of scandalous stories about prominent members of society.

Caelia Shortface and *Martha Careful* - These pseudonyms were used by Franklin to settle a personal dispute. They wrote letters mocking Franklin's former employer, Samuel Keimer, who had stolen some of Franklin's publishing ideas. Shortface and Careful's letters were published in The American Weekly Mercury, a publication by a Keimer rival.

Busy Body - Also published in The American Weekly Mercury, Miss Body's letters were gossip stories about local businessmen.

Benevolous Benevolous - He wrote letters to British newspapers while Franklin was in London. The primary focus of the letters was to correct negative statements made about Americans in the British press.

Food Facts, Factoids, and Trivia

The Truth About Egg Color - Americans eggs tend to have bright yellow yolks, because of what they feed the hens. Egg yolk color is almost entirely influenced by its diet. If you feed yellow corn it shows and if you feed birds white corn, the egg yolks are whiter. In South America, hens that peck at red annatto seeds lay eggs with yolks ranging from pink to orange to deep reddish.

The yellow color in egg yolks, as well yellowish chicken skin and fat, comes from pigments found in plants.

In most parts of the world, diners prefer their yolks with a bit more color so commercial feeds often contain lutein as an additive, although yellow maize, soybeans, carrots, and alfalfa powder will also add the color.

Many egg eaters assume that darker yolks are a sign of higher nutritional value. That is not true. Although chicken feed does influence the nutritional value of birds and their eggs, researchers say yolk color does not tell you anything about nutritional value. *When it comes to taste, slap a few eggs next to a huge hunk of bacon and the taste becomes awesome, regardless of yolk color.*

Banana Food Hack - Take two to four ripe bananas, peel them and let them sit in the freezer for an hour, then slice them up toss into a blender. You will get a smooth and tasty treat that is good for you. If you feel the need to punch up the taste, add two tablespoons of peanut butter, or chocolate chips, or bacon bits.

Chocoholics Rejoice - Everyone knows the importance of eating vegetables and chocolate is a vegetable. Chocolate is made from cacao beans and sugar. Beans are vegetables. Sugar is derived from either sugar cane or sugar beets. Both are plants in the vegetable category.

Chocolate candy bars contain milk, which is dairy. Therefore, chocolate candy bars are a health food.

Chocolate covered raisins, cherries, orange slices and strawberries all count as fruit and fruits are good for your health.

Eat a chocolate bar before each meal. It will take the edge off your appetite, and you will eat less at meals.

Chocolate has many preservatives. Preservatives make you look younger.

A box of chocolates can provide your total daily intake of calories in one place. *Am just trying to help.*

Herbs and Spices - Herbs are only obtained from the leafy part of a plant while spices can come from any other part of the plant. A single plant can be the source of both an herb and a spice, or more than one spice.

The coriander plant is an example of a plant that produces both an herb and a spice. The leafy green part is known as coriander leaf (typically known as cilantro in the Americas), while the dried seeds are sold whole or ground as coriander.

Nutmeg and mace, both spices, are derived from the seed of the fruit of the myristica fragrans, or nutmeg tree. The seed has a waxy red outer layer (called the "aril") which is carefully removed, dried, and ground to make mace. The rest of the seed is then dried and sold whole or ground to be used as nutmeg.

Culinary herbs are the leafy portions of a plant that die down after each growing season and can be used as dried or fresh. Examples include basil, bay leaves, parsley, cilantro, mint, rosemary, and thyme.

Spices have a much broader spectrum of origin and can be utilized from any other part of a plant such as the roots, bark, flowers, fruit, and seeds. Examples come from berries (peppercorns), roots (ginger), seeds (nutmeg), flower buds (cloves) or the stamen of flowers (saffron). Spices are always used in dried form and have also traditionally been used as a preservative. Archaeologists have found evidence in Egyptian tombs of spices used for embalming, dating back to 3000 B.C.

Allspice is not a combination of anything. It is the dried unripe fruit of Pimenta dioica tree. The name allspice was coined by the English, who thought it combined the flavor of cinnamon, nutmeg, and cloves.

Black pepper is a flowering vine, cultivated for its fruit, which is dried and used as a spice and seasoning. *Salt is neither an herb nor a spice, because it is an inorganic mineral.*

Knife Tips - I hesitated to add these tips as most seemed obvious, but after talking to a few friends, decided they are worth mentioning. These tips are for cutting knives, not table knives. Most people have their favorite few knives used for almost all cutting tasks. Two things cause the most damage to knives, moisture and improper use.

- Keep it dry. After using your knife, rinse and dry to keep rust from beginning to form (yes, even on stainless).

- Do not put good knives in the dishwasher, wash and dry by hand.

- Do not let knives air dry.

- Store in a way that the blades of knifes do not touch anything which could dull them.

- Use food knives for food only. Keep other knives for other purposes.

- Sharpen twice a year. Use a wet sharpening stone or a honing steel (instrument for repairing cutting edge).

- Use wood cutting board to reduce blade dulling. (Keep peroxide handy in a spray bottle and spray the board after rinsing, to prevent germs).

Chopsticks Facts - Chopsticks were created about 5,000 years ago in China. The earliest versions were used for cooking and were most likely made from twigs. They began being used as table implements about 500 A.D.

The table knife's decline in popularity in these regions at this time can also be attributed to the teachings of Confucius, who was a vegetarian. He believed that knives were not appropriate to eat with. Confucius supposedly said, "The honorable and upright man keeps well away from both the slaughterhouse and the kitchen and he allows no knives on his table."

Chopsticks later migrated to Japan and Korea. One distinct difference between Japanese and Chinese chopsticks was that the former were made from a single piece of bamboo that were joined at the base.

While the early chopsticks were more often than not made of some cheap material, such as bamboo, later silver chopsticks were sometimes used during Chinese dynastic times in order to prevent food poisoning. It changes color if touched by garlic, onion, or rotten eggs, which release hydrogen sulfide that reacts with the silver causing it to change color.

Arousal Ice Cream - Not a joke. Ice cream maker Charlie Harry Francis of 'Lick Me I'm Delicious' has a new flavor called the Arousal. The flavor combines two key ingredients, Champagne and Viagra. It is dosed with 25mgs of Viagra and is flavored with bubbly champagne. The upside down cone presentation says it all.

Other flavors from Charlie include Chocolate Rhubarb Macaroon, Glow in the Dark Ice Cream, and Salted Whiskey Caramel Cupcake, and more. There is a Facebook page and the official website boasts, "We specialize in making the most delicious incredible frozen treats your mouth will have the pleasure of melting." *Yes, he is serious and he obviously loves his job.*

Nuts to Food Allergies - Food allergies are less common in underdeveloped countries. Proponents of the hygiene hypothesis say that the relatively low incidence of childhood infections in developed countries contributes to an increased incidence of allergic diseases.

Harvard Medical School asserts that recent increases in peanut allergies, and the measures taken in response, show elements of mass psychogenic illness - hysterical reactions grossly out of proportion to the level of danger.

Only 150 people (children and adults) die each year in the US from all food allergies combined. The US Centers for Disease Control and Prevention officially documents 13 deaths (including six adults) due to peanuts between 1996 and 2006. *Peanuts are legumes, not true nuts.*

Four percent of adults and four percent of children have food allergies. Less than one percent (0.6) of people in the US have a peanut allergy. In France, the rate of peanut allergy is between .3 percent and .75 percent, Denmark is .2 to .4 percent; and Israel about .04 percent.

The exact cause of someone developing a peanut allergy is unknown.

Smelling the aroma of peanuts cannot cause an allergic reaction.

Highly refined peanut oil is purified, refined, bleached, and deodorized, which removes the allergic proteins from the oil.

A recent study showed 26.6% of children with a peanut or tree nut allergy outgrew their allergies, at an average age of 5.4 years old. Black children were less likely to outgrow their allergy than white children and boys were more likely to outgrow their allergy than girls.

The American Academy of Pediatrics used to instruct parents to avoid peanut use until their kids reached age 3, but that has been rescinded. A British study has found that consuming peanuts in infancy lowers the risk that a child will develop peanut allergies.

Headlines most often ignore that people who are allergic to peanuts are also often allergic to one or more tree nuts (almonds, walnuts, pecans, cashews, pistachios, etc.).

A new study shows increased peanut consumption by pregnant mothers who were not nut allergic was associated with lower risk of peanut allergy in their offspring.

Origin of Popcorn - The Aztecs inadvertently introduced popcorn to the world as a result of the Spanish invasion. When Columbus first interacted with the Arawak tribe, he was given a popcorn corsage. Believed to be a key component in the foundation of their empire, popcorn played a large role in Aztec culture. It was often made into necklaces or headdresses, and it was commonly used to decorate religious statues. One Aztec ritual involved throwing a whole ear of un-popped popcorn into a fire as a sacrifice to the gods. They referred to the kernels which came out as 'hailstones'.

Some archaeologists believe that popcorn was actually the first form of corn ever cultivated, with evidence of its existence dating to the Anasazi tribe of Utah, who arose around 350 B.C. Using seed selection, an agricultural process to determine the healthiest future crop, Native Americans are thought to have developed the crop almost 5,000 years ago.

Summer Tip - Put pineapple chunks or grapes on skewers and freeze for a tasty and refreshing summer treat.

Watermelon - Some of the earliest references to the cultivation of watermelons are found in Egyptian hieroglyphics dating back more than 5,000 years. Cultures across Africa, India, and the Mediterranean all have records referring to the watermelon. David Livingstone confirmed the origin of the watermelon, when he found wild watermelon fields in Africa.

Watermelons thrive in dry areas, and they have long served a very important purpose beyond just being a healthy part of a meal. Watermelons are about 92 percent water, and in many dry areas of Africa, the fruit has long been tapped and used as a water source for both people and animals. Evidence has even been found that they were carried by explorers as a sort of natural water bottle.

Another advantage of watermelons is that there is no waste as all of the fruit can be eaten. Aside from the juicy flesh, the seeds can be roasted and the rind can be made into preserves. The sweet juice from a watermelon is used for making beer in Russia, and it can also be used as a base for syrups.

Fresh vs. Frozen Food - In two recent studies from Britain, researchers purchased a half dozen different kinds of fruit and vegetables, all of which came in two varieties: fresh and frozen. After buying them and then having them chill out in either a fridge or freezer for three days, researchers conducted 40 tests to compare their nutritional content.

Turns out the frozen varieties were richer in health-boosting vitamins and antioxidants. In fact, frozen broccoli had four times more beta-carotene than its fresh counterpart, while frozen carrots had three times more lutein and double the beta-carotene as well as greater levels of vitamin C and polyphenols. Raspberries and peas performed about the same, whether they were fresh or frozen.

While it is true that foods gradually lose nutrients as they move through the supply chain, that chain is far longer for fresh produce. Fruits and vegetables are regularly held in storage for up to a month before you ever see them. Plus, according to study author Graham Bonwick Ph.D., a professor of applied biology at the University of Chester, once they hit your refrigerator, the nutritional loss escalates. It is probably due to the plant's continuing metabolic activity and how cells react to oxygen and exposure to artificial dark-light cycles.

A recent study from Rice University and the University of California at Davis found that the fluorescent lights of supermarkets and the constant darkness of your refrigerator affects fruit and vegetable circadian clocks so that they excrete fewer glucosinolates, compounds with cancer-fighting properties.

"Produce's degradation reactions are very much slowed by lowering the temperature to freezing levels," Bonwick says. "Furthermore, when you freeze produce, the water present in the cells of the food is locked up as ice, slowing or preventing these processes that require the presence of free water." Since produce in the freezer section was frozen solid almost immediately after being picked, it is preserved at its nutritional peak.

Orange - The color orange may have been named for the fruit, but the irony is that oranges usually are not the color orange. The color orange wasn't defined until 1542, when it was cobbled together from words that had previously been used to refer to the fruit. Its first form was the Arabic word naranj and the Persian narang, which were both derived from a Sanskrit word, naranga.

Most oranges that come from their native tropical countries are not orange. In their natural, ripe state, in the warmer countries where they are grown, the outside of the orange is full of chlorophyll, making it green. In colder areas, the chlorophyll is killed by the cold weather, and similar to the leaves on a deciduous tree, the orange color of the flesh inside emerges through the green.

It is actually the green oranges that are ripe, and those that turn orange are on their way from their peak ripeness. Many people in the

United States and Europe think of green fruit as being unripe, so some orange crops are turned orange unnaturally, exposed to flash freezing or ethylene gas to eliminate the chlorophyll in the skins.

Jalapeños - While known in its native Mexico as huachinango or chile gordo, to the rest of the world Jalapeños get their name from the town of Xalapa or Jalapa.

German Beer - Food website Chefkoch.de claimed at a rate of one per day, trying every German beer would take more than 13 years. Trying Bavaria's 4,000 types would take almost 11 years.

Mason Jar Cooking - Mason jars have been around for years and only recently have folks begun to use them for cooking things in a microwave. Taking soup to work and heating in a mason jar is an old standby for office workers, but have you thought of doing this for the family?

Many other things can be cooked in mason jars for individual servings and no mess. It works for mac and cheese (with bacon bits of course). Try cobblers and pies, just be sure to put the fruits on the bottom and dough on top. Same trick for pizza, put the dough on top, so it can rise.

Have not tried this, but will do so soon. The recipe calls for putting fruit in the bottom of a small mason jar and filling it halfway with pancake mix (the mix rises from cooking), or dropping in some chocolate chips on top of the mix, then microwaving for 60 - 90 seconds. Great way to make individual pancakes quickly and with less dirty pans. A side benefit of Mason jar cooking is strict portion control, which is good if you are trying to watch your weight.

Salisbury Steak - This dish was created by and named after James Salisbury in 1886 as a treatment for many afflictions such as gout, bronchitis, and tuberculosis. He believed that well-done ground beef should be eaten three times a day and a glass of hot water be taken before and after each meal.

Lobsters Colors - Before you cook a lobster it looks grey-blue, and when you cook it, it turns pink. It does not really change color, the red pigment is already there, but is surrounded by the grey and blue pigments. When those pigments are heated they are destroyed. The red pigments take the heat and remain.

White Meat, Dark Meat - White meat is white because of the chicken's lack of exercise. White muscle is suitable only for short, ineffectual bursts of activity such as, for chickens, flying.

Dark meat, which avian myologists (bird muscle scientists) refer to as "red muscle," is used for sustained activity, mainly walking. The dark color comes from a chemical compound in the muscle called myoglobin, which plays a key role in oxygen transport. That's why the chicken's leg meat and thigh meat are dark and its breast meat (primary flight muscle) is white.

Other birds, such as ducks and geese, have red muscle (dark meat) throughout.

Guarana - This is a climbing plant in the maple family, native to the Amazon basin and especially common in Brazil. Guarana features large leaves and clusters of flowers, and is best known for its fruit, which is about the size of a coffee bean. As a dietary supplement, guarana is an effective stimulant and its seeds contain about twice the concentration of caffeine found in coffee beans (about 2–4.5% caffeine in guarana seeds compared to 1–2% for coffee beans). As with other plants producing caffeine, the high concentration of caffeine is a defensive toxin that repels herbivores from the berry and its seeds.

If you look at the contents of any energy drink, chances are that guarana is listed as one of the main ingredients. European missionaries in 17th-century Brazil recorded the native people's use of the berry, noting that it not only gave them energy, but allowed them to go for days without feeling hungry. It became a colonial trading commodity that was said to help protect the body from illness, but too much of it was known to cause insomnia.

The caffeine that is found in the guarana berry is thought to be different from the caffeine found in coffee. Guarana contains chemical components called tannins, which are thought to produce a longer-lasting effect than caffeine from other sources. For centuries, guarana berry seeds have been powdered or smoked in a long process that is done by hand. Drinking properly prepared guarana can be central to formal occasions and gatherings, where groups of people pass around a calabash bowl.

Two Summer Ice Cream Tips - Ice cream two ways - one is to slice it for serving the other is to put the whole carton in a large freezer bag and it will not freeze so hard, so it is easier to extract.

Reheat Crunchy Fried Foods - Few foods are as good the next day when you reheat them, especially fried foods. If you want to get your French fries or fried chicken crispy again after they spent a night in the refrigerator, wrap them in aluminum foil and stick them in the broiler. The top-down heat on oil-soaked food makes these leftovers become crunchy again.

Nutella Facts - Nutella is a great tasting spread. The chocolaty nut spread was thought of as a great substitute for peanut butter, but a recent study found out it is not much different.

One tablespoon of Nutella contains 100 calories, 6 grams of fat, and 11 grams of sugar. One tablespoon of Peanut butter has 94 calories, 8 grams of fat, 1.48 grams sugar. *Generic cake frosting has 75 calories, 3 grams of fat, and 7.5 grams of sugar.*

Origin of Scotch Eggs - Scotch eggs are hard-boiled eggs wrapped in sausage meat, dipped in breadcrumbs, and deep-fried. According to food historian Alan Davidson, the Scotch egg originated in India and was brought back by returning soldiers of the British Empire.

It is a descendent of the Indian dish nargisi kofta, which consists of eggs covered in minced lamb and cooked in curried tomatoes.

The first written reference to Scotch eggs, with the recommendation that they be eaten hot with gravy, was in the 'Cook And Housewife's Manual' in 1910.

Chicken McNugget Ingredients - These tasty little nuggets are said to have a worldwide flavor. Now we know why. Abu Dhabi did some checking and found out the chicken is from Brazil, bread crumbs are from the United Kingdom, and wheat is imported from Canada, Australia, Pakistan and Paraguay.

Emulsifiers come from Spain, Germany supplies salt and stabilizers, India supplies spices, flavor enhancers, and vegetable protein, while China produces dextrin for enhancing crispness. All this is cooked up in vegetable fat processed in the UAE, but made from canola seeds imported from Canada. *Who said we do not have a world economy.*

More McDonald's Facts - Thirty Three percent of all french fries sold in the US are from McDonald's. It will buy 54 million pounds of fresh apples this year. One in eight working people are work at or have worked at a McDonald's. More than 50,000 students from all over the world have earned a "Bachelor of Hamburgerology" at McDonald's "Hamburger University," in Illinois. China has a wedding package for couples who wish to be married at a McDonald's. It has sold over 100 Billion hamburgers. I could not find out how many of those were bacon burgers. *I am getting hungry.*

Grinders, Heros, Hoagies, and Subs - The Grinder arose in New England and was likely named after the dockworkers whose jobs involved much noisy grinding to repair and refurbish the ships. However, some attribute the name to the amount of chewing and grinding it takes to work through the crusty Italian bread and meats on the typical sandwich.

The Hero can contain an infinite number of combinations of meats, cheeses, condiments, vegetables, and pickled things. Many believe the Hero Sandwich was named by food columnist, Clementine Paddleworth in the 1930s relating to the Submarine sandwich, when she noted, "You had to be a hero to eat it." The Oxford English Dictionary credits the naming to armored car guards.

Hoagie is what the folks in Philadelphia call it. Most claim that the name came originally from Al De Palma who thought that a person "had to be a hog" to eat such a large sandwich. When he opened his own sandwich place during the Great Depression, Al called his big subs 'hoggies'. It is assumed that the strong Philadelphia accent changed the pronunciation, and eventually, the spelling.

The Submarine sandwich originated in several different Italian American communities in the Northeastern United States from the late 19th century. *So, all Grinders, Heros, Hoagies, and many other regional names for these great sandwiches are Subs and all Subs are sandwiches, but not all sandwiches are Subs.*

Fast Food Surprise - Many of us suffer (not me) the guilty pleasures of enjoying fast food. Some try to make up for it by buying the wonderfully healthy salads that have been added to the menus for those trying to watch diets. However, many fail to watch the real facts. For men, you can feel vindicated that meat is better for us.

Wendy's Mandarin Chicken Salad has more fat, sugar, carbs, and total calories than a quarter pound Wendy's Double Stack cheeseburger.

McDonald's Double Cheeseburger has less calories, less sugar, less sodium than the Asian Chicken Salad w/Crispy Chicken and Newman's Own (Low Fat) Sesame Ginger Dressing.

Taco Bell Fiesta Taco Salad has more calories, more carbs, more sugar, and more fat than a chicken grilled stuffed burrito.

Wendy's Garden Sensations Mandarin Chicken Salad has more sugar than 8 ounce Coke.

Burger King's Tendercrisp salad has 210 more calories than a Whopper Jr.

Three Quick Food Hacks - Put a few of those small ketchup packs in the freezer. They stay soft and can be used for small bruises or bumps.

Use the microwave to soften some chocolate in an ice cube tray, then add strawberries for an easy and clean way to make chocolate covered strawberries with no mess (not as pretty, but taste just as good).

If you mix a tablespoon of vanilla extract to a gallon of paint, the smell will be much more pleasant and it will not change the color of the paint.

Avocado - The original name for avocado is Ahuacatl, an Aztec word which means testicle. The avocado tree is originated from Central America and Mexico. The plant is cultivated in countries with very warm or hot climates. The fruit, when ripened, is very tasty and is used in many savory dishes. It can also be used as an aphrodisiac to stimulate the sex drive.

The fruit consists 67% fat and mostly made up of oleic acid and monounsaturated fat. An oil is extracted from the fat found in this fruit, and can be used in cosmetics, lubricants, and cooking oil. Avocado oil is also used in the manufacturing of numerous skin-care products.

Vodka Pie Crust - Use vodka instead of water when baking your next Holiday pie. Vodka is only 60% water, so it forms less gluten, which makes for a more tender crust.

Oatmeal, Porridge, Gruel, and Spurtles - Oats taken from the farmer's field are sieved in a rotating drum to remove impurities like seeds, stalks, sticks, and stones. Then they are put into a rotating drum to remove the husk. Finally, the oats are heat dried to reduce the moisture content before being ground or crushed to produce fine oatmeal.

Oatmeal is a product made by processing oats. In North America, oatmeal means any crushed oats, rolled oats, or cut oats used in recipes such as oatmeal cookies. It is also a name for a breakfast cereal made by cooking the oats. *All oatmeal is porridge, but not all porridge is oatmeal.*

Porridge made from oatmeal is also called oatmeal or oatmeal cereal. Porridge can be made with oats, rice, barley, cornmeal, brown rice, or basically any grain that is cooked, usually in water or milk. Similar dishes made with other grains or legumes often have other names, such as groat, polenta, grits, owsianka, or kasha.

Since porridge was used as prison food for inmates in the British prison system, 'doing porridge' became a slang term for a sentence in prison.

Gruel is similar to porridge, but is made without milk and has a very thin consistency.

Bonus - Pease porridge made from dried peas is another traditional English and Scottish porridge. It inspired the Mother Goose rhyme "pease porridge hot, pease porridge cold, pease porridge in the pot, nine days old.

A *spurtle* is a Scottish kitchen tool used for stirring porridge.

Searing Meat - A 19th century German chemist Justus von Liebig was one of the first people to propose that by applying very high temperatures to meat you would create a 'sealed' layer of cooked meat through which liquid inside the meat could not escape.

Liebig's experiment compared the liquid and nutrients from a piece of meat submerged in cold water which was gradually heated in that water and simmered in the cooking liquid with a dry piece of meat applied to an extremely hot surface. Liebig thought that searing meat "sealed in juices," because the resulting meat was juicier than the meat that was essentially boiled to death.

However, in the book On Food and Cooking, Harold McGee makes a direct comparison between a seared piece of meat and an un-seared piece, both cooked with identical methods. The result was that the seared piece of meat actually retained fewer juices than the un-seared piece, and at the very least the searing did nothing to preserve the moisture inside the meat. This debate still continues. Many people think that searing meat does result in moister meat, while others dispute it.

In reality, the best thing about searing meat is that when applied to high heat, the surface of the meat undergoes the Maillard Reaction, which results in some delicious browning on the surface of the meat. Bottom line; sear your steaks, not because it locks in juices, but because it is tastier.

Expired Milk Dates - That date on the carton of milk could mean very different things depending on what US state you are in. Some states require a sell by date, which indicates the last day a store can legally sell the milk. It is calculated to give the consumer a reasonable amount of time to enjoy. Other states have a use by date that indicates the date milk is believed to be at peak flavor. For instance, milk cartons in Montana are labeled with a sell by date 12 days after pasteurization, Washington requires a use by date that is 21 days after pasteurization.

While the pasteurization of milk kills most of the harmful bacteria, precautions always need to be made by the consumer to keep the milk from going bad. One way to keep milk as fresh as possible is to keep it on a shelf, never in the door of your fridge, where temperature fluctuates the most.

> Whole milk's expiration date is
> five days after the "sell-by" date.

Depending on whom you ask, the refrigerator temperature should be 34-38 °F or 38-40 °F. Warmer temperatures give bacteria more of a chance to develop.

One rule of thumb is that if you are properly refrigerating it, whole milk's expiration date is five days after the "sell-by" date. If it is non-fat, skim, or reduced fat, you will have a bit less time. Ultra pasteurized milk has a longer shelf life than other types of milk and can be left in the pantry until opened, and then it must be chilled.

Top Three Markups - According to Reader's Digest, here are the largest markups for the things we buy.

Bottled water: 4,000 percent markup - *Come on, it's just water.*

Text messages: 6,000 percent markup. A typical text message costs you 20 cents and the phone company 0.3 cents to transmit.

Movie theater popcorn: 1,275 percent markup - *Lots of greasy phony butter and salt make up for it.*

Milking It - For years I have been buying milk in half gallons. That way, I use it up before it goes bad. Last year I noticed the gallon size was a few cents cheaper than a half gallon. The spread continued to increase. Last week, the gallon size was less than half the cost of the half gallon. This means I can buy a gallon and throw half of it away and still come out ahead (not that I plan to do it.) Not sure what has prompted this change, but is something to watch for the next time you are shopping. The store is my local Walmart. *A trick my mother taught me is to put the remaining milk in the freezer if you are planning to be away for a while. Freezing does not harm the milk or make it taste any different. However, it may take 24 hours or more to completely thaw.*

Dirty Dishes - A change in dishwasher detergents that became final in 2010 may cause some changes in your kitchen. The new formulas lack phosphates, chemicals that are bad for the environment, but good for cleaning. Check the package and try something new for a change. Your old cleaner may not have been reformulated to replace the cleaning power of the old ingredients. Does your old cleaner seem as effective as it used to? Do you seem to use more to get those dirty dishes clean?

Consumer Reports, in September 2010, generally scored tablets and packets higher than cheaper powders and gels, but it said new products are still evolving. Rinse aids help, and are often combined with detergents in the newer products. *If you spot spots, it's time to change.*

Wine is Better Than Exercise - A recent study found that a glass of red wine is the equivalent to an hour at the gym. Also, drinking red wine could help burn fat says another study.

The health benefits of red wine have been well documented. Studies have revealed that those who drink a glass of red wine a day are less likely to develop dementia or cancer, that it is good for your heart, it is anti-aging and can regulate blood sugar.

Research conducted by the University of Alberta in Canada has found that health benefits in resveratrol, a compound found in red wine, are similar to those we get from exercise. Resveratrol was seen to improve physical performance, heart function and muscle strength in the same way as they are improved after a gym session. Other sources of resveratrol are blueberries, peanut butter, red grapes, and dark chocolate.

Salt Facts

Kosher Salt - Kosher salt is not Kosher, does not come from the Dead Sea, is not necessarily blessed by a rabbi, and may contain additives, although it is usually free from iodine.

Kosher salt refers to any coarse-grain salt that is used to make meat kosher. Kosher salt usually is mineral salt, which may mined anywhere. A rabbi does not "bless" the salt to make it Kosher (although Morton's Coarse Kosher Salt in the past has claimed to be packaged under Rabbinical supervision). As with any other salt, some commercial Kosher salt, uses anti-caking additives to make it free-flowing.

More About Salt - Salt is a terrific flavor enhancer, helping to reduce bitterness and acidity, and bringing out other flavors in food.

Adding salt to bread dough controls the action of the yeast and improves the flavor. Bread made without salt will have a coarser texture and a blander flavor than bread made with salt.

Try sprinkling salt on citrus fruit, melons, tomatoes, and even in wine to enhance flavor.

Adding a little salt balances the flavor of sweets like cakes, cookies, and candies.

Boiling eggs in salted water makes them easier to peel.

Adding a pinch of salt to cream or egg whites before they are whipped increases their volume and serves as a stabilizer.

Salt is a mineral, so it can be stored indefinitely without going stale. It will not taste any fresher if you grind it with a salt mill.

Salt has been used for millennia as a preservative for meats, fish, cheese, and other foods. It works by absorbing moisture from the cells of bacteria and mold through osmosis, which kills them or leaves them unable to reproduce.

Salting slices of eggplants helps draw out the bitter juices.

Another Salt Study - Adding to the library of salt studies is yet a new one which again finds that salt is not that bad and that too little salt may be as bad for us as too much salt. The same can be said for calories or carbohydrates.

> Too little salt may be as bad for us as too much salt. The same can be said for calories or carbohydrates.

More than 100,000 people from the general public in 17 countries were observed for nearly four years and sodium levels were determined from urine tests. The researchers found people who consume 3 to 6 grams of sodium a day (salt contains about 39% sodium by weight) had the lowest risk of heart problems or death from any cause. About three-fourths of the world's population is in the ideal range, including the US, which averages 4 grams a day salt consumption.

The study published in the New England Journal of Medicine suggests the US's daily consumption of about 3,400 milligrams is not only perfectly fine, but may be healthier than abstaining. It suggests eaters should shoot for between 3,000 and 6,000 mg of salt each day. Dr.

Suzanne Oparil, a cardiologist at the University of Alabama, Birmingham, who wrote an editorial accompanying the publication, added, "Japan, one of the highest salt consumers, has one of the longest lifespans."

Table salt also contains iodine, and desiccants to keep it from clumping. Sodium is essential for human nutrition, but too much sodium or too little sodium raises health risks. Sodium levels generally correlate with the risk of high blood pressure, but correlation (are related) is not causality (one causes the other). Chlorine is also important to overall health. Our bodies, like salt water swimming pools, separate sodium from chlorine for use.

Potassium, found in vegetables and fruits appears to lower blood pressure and heart risks, and offsets sodium's effect. Potatoes, bananas, avocados, leafy greens, nuts, apricots, salmon, and mushrooms are high in potassium.

Determining that worldwide deaths are caused by one ingredient, without relation to complete diet, or other factors, is like saying global warming is caused only by CO_2, or that drinking only diet soda makes us fat.

As with all studies, results 'should be taken with a grain of salt'. Reducing or increasing one item from the panoply of food we ingest is interesting fodder for highly funded studies, but taking results too seriously can be hazardous to our health.

Salt Tips - If you do not use milk for a while, it goes bad. Add a pinch of salt to a gallon of milk to keep it from spoiling as fast.

Salt reduces bitterness. It is the sodium ion that interferes with the transduction mechanism of bitter taste. Add a small pinch of salt to tonic and it will reduce the bitterness.

Apples, pears, and potatoes dropped in cold, lightly salted water after they are peeled will not brown.

Salt can deodorize thermos bottles and jugs, decanters and other closed containers.

Sprinkle a little salt in the pan before frying fish to prevent sticking.

To prevent mold on cheese, wrap it in a cloth dampened with saltwater before refrigerating.

Spread salt between patio bricks, then sprinkle with water to kill and prevent weeds.

Perky Coffee - To perk up your morning cup of Joe, toss a dash of salt into the uncooked grounds to reduce bitterness. We are all aware of the health benefits of cinnamon; toss some cinnamon into the uncooked grounds to add a subtle flavor that is also good for you.

Five Super Spices

Very interesting that many spices, which have been around for years are only recently 'discovered' to have beneficial health properties. Here are a few.

Cayenne pepper has been used as a healing spice for hundreds of years. Capsaicin, which gives the spice its kick, can boost metabolism, helping to burn extra calories, and increase enzyme production. It is thought to act as an anti-inflammatory and is so powerful that capsaicin can be found as the active ingredient in both over the counter and prescription ointments for arthritis and muscle pain. It can be used to stop nosebleeds by mixing one half teaspoon of cayenne pepper into a glass of warm water and drink it. Cayenne has the ability to ease upset stomach, ulcers, sore throats, spasmodic and irritating coughs, and diarrhea. It can ease the digestive tract by increasing gastric juices. It is also good to put out in the yard to keep away squirrels and rabbits.

Cinnamon, according the American Diabetes Association, regular consumption of between one and six grams of cinnamon helps reduce blood glucose, triglyceride, and total cholesterol levels in people with type 2 diabetes. It can also help manage short-term spikes in blood sugar. That makes it good to add to high carbohydrate foods such as oatmeal and rice pudding, which tend to spike blood sugar levels. It also contains strong antiviral, antibacterial, and antifungal properties making it an excellent addition when trying to fight a cold. Try sprinkling some in your coffee or even using it in a face mask combined with a little coconut oil to help fight acne. Sprinkle some on cookies or doughnuts for an extra beneficial kick.

Clove is usually the spice we think of to kill pain and sooth toothaches. Gently bite on a whole clove to release the oils and move them around to a sore tooth. Clove tea can help reduce, or even prevent, colds while also working as a natural expectorant to get rid of excess phlegm. Cloves used to be put in cigarettes, but are now outlawed in the US. Cloves stuck in oranges have been long used to add a pleasant odor to a room and are often used for decorative aromatherapy. In Chinese medicine, cloves are considered acrid, warm, and aromatic, entering the kidney, spleen, and stomach and their ability to warm the middle, also to treat hiccoughs. Other findings concluded that cloves can also boost insulin function in the body.

Curcumin was first isolated a few hundred years ago and numerous therapeutic activities have been assigned to turmeric for a wide variety of diseases and conditions, including those of the skin, pulmonary, and gastrointestinal systems, aches, pains, wounds, sprains, and liver disorders. Extensive recent research has proven that most of these activities are due to curcumin. Curcumin has been shown to exhibit antioxidant, anti-inflammatory, antiviral, antibacterial, antifungal, and anticancer activities and has a potential against various malignant diseases, diabetes, allergies, arthritis, Alzheimer's disease, and other chronic illnesses. Turmeric is the name of the spice we use that is derived from the plant Curcuma longa, is a gold-colored spice is commonly used in India for health care, for the preservation of food, and as a yellow dye for textiles.

Ginger is best known to help soothe a queasy stomach and help reduce pain and inflammation. It is also useful for arthritis, migraines, or menstrual cramps. It might also help reduce pain. Fresh ginger is more potent than the powdered variety and can be added to herbal teas, baked goods, and added to fruit or vegetable juices.

Twelve Sandwich Origins

The Earl of Sandwich is purportedly the first to put a slab of meat between two slices of bread.

The existence of the *club sandwich* comes from a cook named Danny Mears, who worked at the Saratoga Club House in Saratoga Springs, N.Y. during the 1800s.

During the 1920s, Reuben Kulakofsky, who was playing poker at the Blackstone Hotel in Omaha, Nebraska, ordered a sandwich with corned beef and sauerkraut. Bernard Schimme made the sandwich by draining the sauerkraut and mixing it with Thousand Island dressing then layering it with corned beef and Swiss cheese on dark rye bread. He then grilled the sandwich and served it with it a sliced kosher dill pickle and potato chips. Thus became the first *Reuben sandwich.*

A French myth says *croque monsieur* was accidentally discovered in 1910 when some French workers left their lunch pails full of cheese and ham sandwiches too close to a hot radiator. The sandwich was originally made with ham and Gruyère cheese, later evolving into other variations like the the *croque madame, the croque Provencal, the croque tartiflette, and the Monte Cristo* (*my favorite*).

The *grilled cheese* sandwich was first widely eaten as a cheap meal during the US Great Depression, when cheese and bread were some of the least expensive food items.

In 1901, Julia David Chandler published the first known recipe for a *peanut butter and jelly sandwich*. Peanut butter is not widely consumed in Europe and is almost never mixed with jelly. In the US peanut butter and jelly sandwiches are a staple.

Joe Lorenza added cheese to a popular chopped steak sandwich creating the *Philly Cheesesteak sandwich* during the 1940s.

The *bacon chip butty* is made with handfuls of French fries and large pieces of crispy bacon between two slices of soft buttered bread. It was originally considered a working-class meal and was served in English pubs. *Yum!*

The most likely story of the origin of the New Orleans *po' boy* belongs to Clovis and Benjamin Martin, who had a restaurant on St. Claude Avenue during the 1920s. When streetcar drivers went on strike in 1929, the brothers created an inexpensive sandwich consisting of gravy and bits of roast beef on French bread that they served unemployed workers out of the back of their restaurant. A worker would come to get one and the restaurant employees would yell, "Here comes another poor boy." which eventually transferred to the name of the sandwich, po' boy.

Leftovers

Some foods taste better the second time than when first cooked. Many people say leftover pasta tastes great. Now an experiment has shown that it also might be better for us.

Pasta is a form of carbohydrate and like all carbohydrates it gets broken down in our gut and then absorbed as simple sugars, which in turn makes your blood glucose quickly rise. In response to a surge in blood glucose our bodies produce a rush of insulin to get our blood glucose back down to normal as swiftly as possible, because persistently high levels of glucose in the blood are extremely unhealthy.

A rapid rise in blood glucose, followed by a rapid fall, can often make a person feel hungry again quite soon after a meal. It is true of sugary sweets and cakes and also true for things like pasta, potatoes, white rice, and white bread. That is why dieticians emphasize the importance of eating foods that are rich in fiber, as these foods produce a much more gradual rise and fall in blood sugars.

Cooking pasta and then cooling it down changes the structure of the pasta, turning it into something that is called 'resistant starch'. It is called that because once pasta, potatoes or other starchy food is cooked and cooled it becomes resistant to the normal enzymes that break carbohydrates down and release glucose, which causes a blood sugar surge.

According to Dr. Denise Robertson, from the University of Surrey, if you cook and cool pasta then your body will treat it much more like fiber, creating a smaller glucose peak. You will also absorb fewer calories.

A study was conducted and volunteers had three days of testing, spread out over several weeks. On each occasion they had to eat pasta on an empty stomach. The volunteers were randomized to eating either hot, cold, or reheated pasta on different days.

On one day they ate the pasta, freshly cooked and hot with a plain sauce of tomatoes and garlic. On another day they had to eat it cold with the same sauce, but after it had been chilled overnight. On a third day they ate the pasta with sauce after it had been chilled and then reheated.

On each of the days they also gave blood samples every 15 minutes for two hours, to see what happened to their blood glucose as the pasta was slowly digested. Eating cold pasta led to a smaller spike in blood glucose and insulin than eating freshly boiled pasta.

Cooking, cooling, and then reheating the pasta had an even smaller effect on blood glucose. It reduced the rise in blood glucose by 50%.

We can convert a carb-loaded meal into a more healthy fiber-loaded one without changing a single ingredient, just the temperature. Pasta leftovers appear be healthier than the original meal.

Eleven Coconut Facts

There are more than 1,300 kinds of coconut, and they can be separated into two main genetic origins: the Pacific Ocean and the

Indian Ocean. There are also over a thousand uses for coconut and its tree.

Coconut water is a workable short-term substitute for human blood plasma and was positively tested as emergency intravenous fluid as far back as the 1950s. Coconut water is also low in calories, carbohydrates, and sugars, and almost completely fat-free. In addition, it is high in ascorbic acid, B vitamins, and proteins.

The soft meat inside the coconut helps to restore oxidative tissue damage and contains a source of healthy fats, proteins, vitamins, and minerals.

Gas mask manufacturers in the US developed the use of steam-activated coconut char, obtained by burning coconut husks as an important component in gas mask production. They found that masks using coconut carbon were superior at filtering noxious substances. Coconut carbon is still an important ingredient in cleaning up radiation and was heavily used in the cleanup project at the Fukushima nuclear plant.

Coconut lumber is a good building material, a fossil fuel alternative, and coconut trees can produce oil in workable quantities.

In the Philippines, sap from an unopened coconut flower is distilled into a potent drink called lambanog. It is 80 to 90 proof, but is organic and chemical-free. Lambanog is traditionally homemade, but some commercial distilleries have introduced several flavors into the market, such as mango, bubblegum, and blueberry.

Coconut armor consisted of a cap, body armor, back plate, leggings, and a close-fitting jacket. A high collar in the back protected the warrior from stones thrown from his own side.

Coconut butter is the flesh of the coconut which has been ground into butter. It is creamier than the oil, and makes a great dairy-free spread.

Coconut oil is an edible oil extracted from the meat of mature coconuts. Use coconut oil to remove heavy makeup. Rub into your skin, leave it on for a few minutes, and wipe it all off with a warm cloth. Treat dry, flaky cuticles by rubbing coconut oil into your nail beds. Use your fingers to massage some oil into the area and it will moisturize your hands.

Use coconut oil to lubricate a squeaky hinge.

Coconut meat can be eaten raw, cooked, or as a preserve. You can top salads with shredded or grated, lightly toasted coconut meat. You can use a blender to make it into smoothies. Coconut meat is high in fiber, polyphenols, and phytosterols, and can decrease the levels of LDL cholesterol.

Eleven More Uses for Butter

Butter has many more uses than just for sandwiches and sautéing.

- If you have anything sticky on your hands, like glue, tar, or paint, rub with butter, then wash with soap and water.

- Gum in hair comes off easier if rubbed with butter.

- Tree sap on a car comes off easier if rubbed with butter before washing.

- Cutting things like marshmallows, pies, toffee, dates is easier if you slice the knife through butter first so it does not stick.

- Butter works like oil to shine shoes, baseball gloves, etc. Just put some on a cotton swab and rub in.

- Large pills can go down a bit easier if rubbed with a bit of butter before swallowing.

- Butter works like expensive skin oils to soften cuticles and nails and to soften dry skin. it can also be used in a pinch to replace shaving lotion.

- Rubbing butter on hard cheese helps keep down mold if you rub it on the cut edge before wrapping.

- Dingy dusty holiday candles can be brought back to life by rubbing with butter. It cleans and brings back the shine.

- Difficult to remove rings slide off easy if you apply butter first.

- After handling and cleaning fish, rub some butter on your hands before washing with soap and water to remove the smell. *(Butter is not good to rub on burns, use an ice cube instead.)*

Top Eight Fruit Savers

1. Keep broccoli, celery, and lettuce their crispiest by wrapping them in foil before storing them in the refrigerator. Celery will stay crisp for four weeks or more,

lettuce heads up to six weeks, and broccoli up to seven weeks.

2. To store carrots, cut off the greens and place them in a plastic bag before sticking them in your crisper drawer. Carrots will keep for up to two weeks. BTW - Carrots do not improve your eyesight and will not help you see better at night.

3. Cherries should be refrigerated in a plastic bag, but not washed until ready to eat, because moisture hastens mold where stems meets the fruit.

4. In warm weather, avocados will ripen fast, but do not store avocados in the refrigerator unless they are cut, otherwise the cold will turn them black inside. To keep them at their most palatable state, spritz a bit of lemon or lime juice, or another acidic agent, and place in an air-tight container or tightly covered clear plastic wrap.

5. Apples are a year-round delight, but some of the most flavorful kinds (e.g. Gala, Ginger Gold, Pink Lady) make their appearance during the summer. During the warmer months, apples should be stored in the fridge, while in the fall; they can be stored on the counter. When storing apples in the fridge, drape a damp paper towel over the container of apples instead of a top. Do not put them in a drawer or air-tight container. Both the cold temperature and the moisture will help them stay their freshest for up to several weeks.

6. What's a summer BBQ without some grilled corn? When storing corn, keep the husks on, but cut away the shank (worms love this part). Put your corn in a plastic bag and place it in your refrigerator's crisper. The corn will remain at its freshest for two days. The corn will begin to dry out after day two, but will still remain edible.

7. Melons will keep for about ten days in cold temperature, but are most flavorful at room temperature. Take your melon out of the fridge and allow it to warm for about thirty minutes before serving.

8. Peaches and nectarines should be bought firm, and stored at room temperature. Do not put in the fridge before ripe, as chilling before ripe will make them mealy and flavorless.

They should keep for a few days before they begin to lose their flavor.

Eight More Egg Facts

We all know dinosaurs laid eggs. Ostriches and turkeys also lay eggs, but the ones we eat most often are chicken eggs.

> Eggs take about 24 to 26 hours to form inside a hen.

> An average hen can lay 250 to 270 eggs per year.

> In China, approximately 390 billion eggs are produced a year, while the US produces about 75 billion eggs a year.

> An egg shell is made of calcium carbonate and makes up 9-12 percent of an egg's total weight. It contains pores that allow oxygen in and carbon dioxide and moisture out.

> The blood sometimes seen in an egg comes from the rupture of small blood vessels in the yolk. It does not indicate the egg is unsafe to eat.

> An average person consumes 173 eggs a year (less than one chicken lays).

> The world record for eating hard-boiled eggs is 65 in 6 minutes 40 seconds, by Sonya Thomas in 2003. *She would have eaten more but they ran out of eggs.*

> Here is the big answer to the big question of which came first, the chicken or the egg. *The egg came first, because dinosaurs laid eggs before chickens evolved.*

And More Egg Facts - In modern hen houses, computers control the lighting, which triggers egg laying. Most eggs are laid between 7 and 11 a.m. A hen requires about 24 to 26 hours to produce an egg.

Egg size and grade are not related. Size is determined by weight per dozen. Younger hens tend to lay smaller eggs. The size increases as the hen grows older and bigger. Grade refers to the quality of the shell, white and yolk.

Dates on egg cartons reflect food quality, not food safety. An 'expiration' or 'sell-by' date on an egg carton tells the grocer to pull the eggs if they have not sold by that time. A 'best-by' or 'use-by' date tells you that your eggs will still be of high quality if you use them by that date.

You can keep fresh, uncooked eggs in the shell, refrigerated in their cartons for at least three weeks after you bring them home, with insignificant quality loss. Properly handled and stored, eggs rarely spoil. If you keep them long enough, eggs are more likely to dry up. Eggs age more in one day at room temperature than they will in one week in the refrigerator.

The chef's hat, called a toque, is said to have a pleat for each of the many ways you can cook eggs.

Even More Egg Facts - Hens lay eggs whether they have mated with a rooster or not. Eggs produced without help from a rooster will never become a chicken.

A hen must mate with a rooster in order for her egg to contain both the male and female genetic material necessary to create an embryo inside the egg. An egg laid after mating may or may not become a chicken.

Chickens develop only from eggs that have been incubated (heated). When a fertile egg is incubated under precise, steady temperatures and humidity levels for 21 days, a chick may be developed.

A fertile egg that is never incubated will never contain an embryo and will never look like anything other than common breakfast food. There is no harm and no difference between fertilized and unfertilized eggs, unless the fertilized eggs have been properly incubated. There is no difference in look, taste, or nutritional value between fertilized and unfertilized eggs. *All foods, including eggs go well with bacon.*

Twelve Types of Eggs

There are many more types than the typical eggs we generally eat for breakfast. I found a few to be interesting.

Shark eggs are strangely shaped eggs, sometimes called a mermaid's purse. These consist of an egg case in a thin capsule made of collagen. They often are square or rectangular with stringy or pointy corner horns, but can come in a variety of odd shapes. Shark eggs can wash up on the beach and are often hand-sized, although the largest recorded was over six feet (2m) long. Female sharks lay fertilized eggs onto the sea floor where they stay until they hatch, with no attention from their mother. Some shark eggs contain several baby sharks which cannibalize each other before hatching to ensure that only the strongest survives.

Octopus eggs are soft, translucent and often stuck on overhangs of rock or coral. The females lay hundreds of thousands of eggs at a time and will stay to guard them against hungry predators until they hatch. This often takes so long that she begins to starve and some octopuses will eat their own arms to survive. Once hatched, they feed on microscopic organisms like plankton until they grow large enough to live on the sea floor as adults.

Fish eggs are released as unfertilized eggs until and the male injects them with sperm. In some species, the male and female might never meet each other. Most have nothing more to do with the eggs and leave them to develop on their own. Millions of soft eggs are laid at once, so hungry predators will usually not destroy all of them before they hatch. Some eggs are laid on secure surfaces like rocks whereas others drift freely in the water, sometimes for up to hundreds of kilometers.

Bird and Reptile eggs are internally fertilized eggs and most are protected until they hatch. Bird egg shells are made from calcium carbonate, which is also the major component of sea shells and pearls. For camouflage, some egg shells are colored or patterned with various other chemicals.

Dinosaur eggs sometimes contain fossilized baby dinosaurs inside. Dinosaur eggs have many shapes, such as elongated spheres or teardrops. Some dinosaurs laid many eggs in a nest and protected them while others laid eggs indiscriminately before abandoning them. There are many types of dinosaur eggs, with the largest being over 23 inches (60cm) long and 7.8 inches (20cm) wide.

Sponge, Jelly, and Coral eggs are similar to most fish eggs. They do not have males and females. Instead, simple male and female organs both occur on a single creature, which release eggs and sperm into the water. Some reproduce asexually without male and female organs, by simply releasing some of their cells to grow directly into new individuals without needing to be fertilized.

Insect eggs are formed from stored sperm from a single mating, which is also used for subsequent fertilization. Insects will lay many eggs at once, and sometimes construct extravagant nests or nurseries for them. Some eggs are laid in water and the newborn insects spend the first portion of their life aquatically, before emerging into the air. Many insects will care for their eggs after they are laid, with some ants and termites even controlling the humidity and pH for them.

Amphibian eggs are often laid in water, surrounded by a gel to keep them all together. When they hatch, the offspring are called 'tadpoles' and have gills, but no legs. They swim around like fish, although initially they also lack a mouth and live directly off the yolk left over from their egg by absorbing it through their skin. Eventually, tadpoles grow mouths, legs, lungs, lose their tail, and become fully adult. Some frogs carry their eggs to protect them.

Platypus eggs are an anomaly as platypuses are mammals. They are warm-blooded, have hair, and produce milk. While the egg is still inside a mother, she supplies it with nutrition from her own body, similar to other mammals. Monotreme eggs are small, white, and spherical. They are laid in small numbers and are fastidiously cared for by their mother in her burrow until 4 to 6 months after hatching. Platypuses do not have nipples to produce milk. They sweat milk, which their newly-hatched young drink.

FDA Terms Defined

Although the FDA has definitions for terms like reduced sugar, no added sugar, and sugar free, companies sometimes come up with marketing lingo that has no official meaning. One of those terms is **lightly sweetened**, which is not defined by the FDA. "Whether Kellogg's Frosted Mini-Wheats Bite Size is "lightly sweetened" should be determined by federal rules, not the marketing executives of a manufacturer," according to a CSPI report from 2010.

Cholesterol free does not mean no cholesterol. Cholesterol-free products must contain less than 2 mg per serving while **low-cholesterol** products contain 20 mg or less per serving. Foods that say reduced or less cholesterol need to have at least 25% less than comparable products. Cholesterol is made by the liver, so only animal products like meat, dairy, eggs, and butter can contain it. If a plant-based product, such as corn oil touts its cholesterol-free status, there is no benefit compared to other vegetable oils, which also do not contain it.

Sugar free does not mean a product has fewer calories than the regular version; in fact it may have more calories. (Food makers are supposed to tell us if a product is not low-cal). Sugar-free products have less than 0.5 grams of sugars per serving, but they still contain calories and carbohydrates from other sources. These products often contain sugar alcohols, which are lower in calories (roughly 2 calories per gram, compared to 4 per gram for sugar). We need to compare labels to see if the sugar-free version is any better than the regular version. (Common sugar alcohols are mannitol, xylitol, or sorbitol).

Products that say **trans fat free** or **no trans fat** can contain less than 0.5 grams per serving. If a product says zero trans fat on it, it may not be zero. If you have two servings, then you may get a good amount added to your diet. Check for words on the ingredient list such as hydrogenated oils and shortening, which mean trans fat is still present.

Gluten is a protein found in grains like wheat or rye and can cause problems for those with celiac disease or gluten intolerance. **Gluten-free** products are becoming easier to find, which is great for those with Celiac's Disease (less than 1% of the population). For the other 99% of us there is no advantage to buying them. In fact, gluten-free whole grains may have less fiber than the regular version. Unless you have metabolic problems, gluten-free products do not help you lose weight and are not necessarily good for you, but because it is a buzz word, companies put it on packages.

More Egg Facts

Eggs contain very little saturated fat (1.5 grams per large egg) and no trans fat. A medium egg contains about 63 calories and a large about 74 calories.

The nutrients in eggs can play a role in weight management, muscle strength, healthy pregnancy, brain function, eye health, and more.

Egg yolks are a great source of choline, an essential nutrient. Two eggs provide about 250 milligrams of choline. Choline also aids the brain function by maintaining the structure of brain cell membranes, and is a key component of the neuro-transmitter that helps relay messages from the brain through nerves to the muscles.

Lutein and zeaxanthin, two antioxidants found in egg yolks, help prevent macular degeneration, a leading cause of age-related blindness and may even reduce the risk of cardiovascular disease.

Eggs have the highest nutritional quality protein of all food sources. Protein is a source of energy, but its main role in the body is growth and repair. It helps in the formation of muscles, hair, nails, skin and organs, such as the heart, kidneys and liver.

Vitamins and minerals in eggs include:
Biotin - helps cell metabolism and the utilization of fats, proteins, and carbohydrates
Calcium - for building and maintain bones and teeth
Cephalin - a phosphorus-containing lipid found in tissues
Folate - for growth
Iodine - to ensure proper function of the thyroid gland
Iron - to produce hemoglobin, which carries oxygen around our bodies maintenance of healthy cells
Lecithin - contains acetylcholine which has been proven to help brain function
Pantothenic acid (Vitamin B5) - releases energy from our food for our body to use
Phosphorous - helps build strong bones and teeth
Selenium - antioxidant that protects our body and immune system
Thiamine - to turn carbohydrates into energy our body can use

> Eliminating eggs from your diet, because you are concerned about cholesterol is of no value and you lose the dietary benefits.

Vitamin A (retinal) - for growth and eye health
Vitamin B12 (riboflavin) - for brain and nervous system functions and blood formation
Vitamin D - important in bone health
Vitamin E - antioxidant to protect our bodies against disease
Zinc - helps in growth, wound healing, blood formation and maintenance of tissues.

Eliminating eggs from your diet, because you are concerned about cholesterol is of no value and you lose the dietary benefits. Harvard Medical School and Mayo clinic agree that even though yolks contain cholesterol, very little of it actually makes it into your bloodstream, where it matters.

Top Ten Pistachio Facts

Pistachio seeds were a common food as early as 6750 BC. Remains of the Atlantic pistachio and pistachio seed along with nut-cracking tools were discovered by archaeologists at the Gesher Benot Ya'aqov site in Israel's Hula Valley, dated to 780,000 years ago. The seed, commonly thought of as a nut, is a culinary nut, not a botanical nut. When they split open while on the tree, there is an audible pop.

The United States is currently the world leader in pistachio (Pistacia vera) production and second is Iran. Exports more than doubled during the past six years from 100 million pounds to almost 270 million pounds. China is the largest importer of pistachios.

One ounce of pistachios provides:
- More dietary fiber than 1/2 cup of cooked broccoli
- Six grams of protein – the same amount as 1 ounce of soybeans
- Seven grams of monounsaturated and four grams of polyunsaturated fats, which are considered heart healthy
- Less than 2 grams of saturated fat
- As much potassium as 1/2 of a large banana.

- Pistachios contain more potassium than any other nut.

- They contain only three to four calories each.

- Pistachios help maintain healthy blood glucose control, and tend to minimize a rise in blood glucose levels when added to certain high carbohydrate meals.

- Pistachios have four hundred times the amount of vitamin A as almonds.

- Pistachio trees, a member of the cashew family, take from five to seven years to produce nuts and are biennial bearers, with a heavy crop one year and a smaller crop the next.

- California, Arizona, and New Mexico represent 100 percent of the US commercial pistachio production.

- Eating pistachios may help lower cholesterol and reduce the risk of cancer. Pistachios are an excellent source of phytosterols, plant compounds that have been found to decrease levels of LDL (bad cholesterol), and they are packed with cancer-fighting antioxidants (including the carotenoids beta-carotene and lutein, which gives the pistachio kernel its distinct green color.

- Red pistachios do not exist in nature. Pistachio importers used to dye the nuts red to hide blemishes resulting from traditional harvesting methods.

Twelve Pizza Facts

1. Ancient Greeks and Egyptians covered flat-breads with toppings and are considered the real originators of the tasty dish.

2. Modern Pizza originated in 1738 in Naples, Italy when people covered focaccia (Italian bread with olive oil and herbs) with tomatoes. Cheese was added as a topping about a hundred years later.

3. Frozen pizzas were introduced during the 1950s.

4. The first online pizza purchase was from Pizza Hut in 1994.

5. Ninety-three percent of Americans eat pizza at least once a month.

6. Saturday night is the biggest night of the week for eating pizza worldwide.

7. More pizza is consumed during the week of the Super Bowl than any other time of the year.

8. In 2001, Pizza Hut paid the Russians one million US dollars to deliver a six inch pizza to the international space station.

9. Thin crust pizza remains the most popular crust across the world. More than 61 percent of all pizza orders are for thin crust.

10. Some popular pizza toppings in Japan are squid and Mayo Jaga (mayonnaise, potato, and bacon).

11. The world's largest pizza was constructed during 2012 in Italy. It contained 19,800 pounds of flour, 10,000 pounds of tomato sauce, 8,800 pounds of mozzarella cheese, 1,488 pounds of margarine, 551 pounds of rock salt, 220 pounds of lettuce and 55 pounds of vinegar. It weighed 51,257 pounds, and took 48 hours to cook. *(According to the World Record Academy)*

12. Over five billion pizzas are sold worldwide each year.

Five Food Hacks

To cook potatoes evenly, drop in cool water, not hot. Hot water will make the outsides mushy and not cook the insides evenly. Allowing to water to warm up with the potatoes cooks the outside and inside evenly. Potatoes are more dense than veggies.

Heat the pan before cooking veggies. Preheating the pan and using a bit of olive oil keeps the veggies from sticking and helps them evenly brown without making them mushy.

Meat should never be tossed into a cold pan, in the oven, or on the stovetop.

Slicing onions vertically is to slice along with the fibers of the onion. When you slice with the fibers, the onion pieces hold up a bit better as they cook. If you do not want them to retain the shape, cut along the side like circles or dice them and they will be more mushy.

Cakes should be light and airy and one way to help is to alternately mix in dry and wet ingredients. It is bubbles, unpopped and whole, that give an open crumb in cakes. When you are beating sugar into softened butter or when you are beating eggs into a froth, you are making bubbles. Adding dry ingredients keeps the bubbles from popping and makes for a light, airy cake. Dump and stir is better for more dense things, like brownies.

Monosodium Glutamate Facts

Monosodium glutamate (MSG) has been used to enhance the flavor of food for more than 100 years. It was originally synthesized by Japanese biochemist Kikunae Ikeda in 1908 after he realized that the Japanese broth called dashi (a basic stock made with seaweed and dried fish) had a meaty flavor that had not yet been identified. He called this flavor umami, which can be translate as "delicious taste" and set about synthesizing the main source of it. The basic sensory function of MSG is attributed to its ability to enhance savory taste-active compounds when added in the proper concentration.

MSG, which first hit the market in 1909, is today created by bacterial fermentation in a process similar to that used in making yogurt.

Monosodium glutamate added to foods produces a flavoring similar to the glutamate that occurs naturally in foods. It acts as a flavor enhancer and adds a fifth taste, called umami, which is best described as a savory, broth-like, or meaty taste.

In the European Union, monosodium glutamate is classified as a food additive (E621) and regulations are in place to determine how and when it can be added to foods. Typically, monosodium glutamate is added to savory prepared and processed foods such as frozen foods, spice mixes, canned and dry soups, salad dressings and meat or fish-based products. In some countries, it is used as a table-top seasoning.

The US Food and Drug Administration has given MSG its generally recognized as safe (GRAS) designation. While a popular belief holds that large doses of MSG can cause headaches and other feelings of discomfort, in controlled studies scientists have been unable to consistently trigger reactions. MSG has been used for more than 100 years to season food, with a number of studies conducted on its safety. International and national bodies governing food additives currently consider MSG safe for human consumption as a flavor enhancer.

> Scientific studies have not shown any direct link between monosodium glutamate and adverse reactions in humans.

MSG contains about one third of the sodium of table salt and is used in smaller amounts.

Children metabolize glutamate in the same way that adults do and monosodium glutamate is safe for children. In fact, human breast milk contains ten times more glutamate than cow's milk.

When added to food, MSG provides an umami-rich flavor boost that regular table salt doesn't, even though MSG contains two thirds less sodium than table salt. Many people cook with it regularly (one kind is sold under the brand name Accent). While it does not have much of a flavor on its own, when added to other foods it blends, balances, and rounds out the other flavors that are present.

MSG does not occur naturally in whole foods, so you do not have to worry about it in fruits and vegetables.

The human body also produces glutamate and it plays an essential role in normal body functioning.

Types and Names of Bacon Sandwiches

A bacon sandwich (known in parts of the United Kingdom and New Zealand as a bacon butty or bacon sarnie, in Ireland as a rasher sandwich, and as a bacon sanger in Australia and parts of Scotland is a sandwich of cooked bacon between bread that is usually spread with butter or margarine, and may be seasoned with ketchup or brown sauce. It is generally served hot. The BLT is a popular variant of the bacon sandwich with the additional ingredients of lettuce and tomato, but served cold. It is also called piece 'n bacon, bacon cob (made with bread roll rather than slice), grilled bacon and cheese.

A *Fool's Gold Loaf*, mostly in Colorado, US consists of a single warmed, hollowed-out loaf of bread filled with one jar of creamy peanut butter, one jar of grape jelly, and a pound of bacon.

Bacon Gerber in Saint Louis, Missouri, US half section of Italian or French bread with garlic butter, containing ham, provolone cheese, topped with paprika, then toasted.

Hot Brown in Louisville, Kentucky, US open-faced with turkey and bacon, topped with Mornay sauce, and baked or broiled.

Bacon sandwiches are an all-day favorite throughout the United Kingdom. They are often served in greasy spoons, and are sometimes recommended as a hangover cure. Australian hamburger shops sell a bacon sandwich, which is made much like a traditional Australian hamburger with fried bacon, fried onions, lettuce, tomato, tinned beetroot, and barbecue sauce or tomato sauce. In some places the sandwich is made from bread toasted on only one side and other establishments serve it on the same roll as used for hamburgers. In Toronto, Canada, peameal bacon (rolled cured and trimmed boneless loin in dried and ground yellow peas) is served on a Kaiser roll.

Irish formula - Place at least three carefully chosen bacon rashers on grill pan. Insert grill pan under grill (broiler). Cook until sizzling, then turn over (the rashers, not the pan), and cook other side until sizzling.

In the meantime, cut two hunks of Kelly's small loaf. Butter liberally with real butter (none of that low cal crap). According to taste, apply your chosen sauce to the bread. Evenly spread the rashers (still sizzling) onto the bread. Apply the upper part of the sandwich. Turn off the TV and the radio. Tell the wife / girlfriend / dog etc to go away. Enjoy!

Perfect Bacon Sandwich - Experts at Leeds University discovered the secret to the ideal sandwich, after four researchers at the Department of Food Science spent more than 1,000 hours testing 700 variations of a traditional bacon sandwich. They tried different types and cuts of bacon, cooking techniques, types of oil and a range of cooking times at different temperatures. They found that two or three back bacon rashers should be cooked under a preheated oven grill (broiler) for seven minutes at about 240C (475F). The bacon should then be placed between two slices of farmhouse bread, 1cm to 2cm thick. They concluded that is not only the taste and smell of bacon that consumers find most attractive, but that texture and how crispy and crunchy rashers are. *Side note - A rasher of bacon can also be used to mean a "portion" or "serving" of bacon, not just a single slice. Also, streaky bacon is the British term for American style bacon.*

Twelve Turkey Facts

Here are a few tidbits to digest along with your turkey leftovers.

1. Turkeys have been roaming North and South America for over ten million years.

2. Over short flights, a wild turkey can top out at about 55 miles per hour (89 km/h). Domestic turkeys cannot fly because they are too heavy.

3. The largest turkey on record weighed 86 pounds.

4. Turkeys (and many birds) ingest small stones that go into a part of their stomachs called the gizzard, which helps the turkey break down food. This process is necessary because turkeys, like all birds, do not have teeth.

5. Turkeys have two stomachs: the glandular stomach that softens the food with gastric juices and the gizzard that grinds it up for the intestines or the first stomach, if needed.

6. The feces of male turkeys are J-shaped, and also straighter and larger than a female's, which look more spiral shaped.

7. There is a festival honoring turkeys, the Eldon, Missouri Turkey Festival which is held each October. It includes a turkey egg toss, turkey calling seminars and a 5-K turkey trot.

8. Wild turkeys prefer to sleep in trees, because their eyesight is so poor.

9. The tops of male turkeys are not only colorful, but highly variable. Males normally have almost no feathers on their heads, but when it comes time to breed, the colors can change between red, white, and blue.

10. Male turkeys gobble, female turkeys do not gobble, they make a clicking noise.

11. Mature turkeys have about 3,500 feathers at maturity.

12. The red bumps on a turkey's head are called caruncles.

Benefits of Dark Chocolate

It is fitting that we look at some of the positive benefits of dark chocolate. I

Dark chocolate is in the top 10 dietary sources of antioxidants, along with seasonings like cloves, mint, anise, cacao powder, black chokeberry, and black elderberry, according to the European Journal of Clinical Nutrition. Dark chocolate is also rich in bioactive flavanols and theobromine. These have good effects on the cells of our hearts and blood vessels.

The Journal of the American Heart Association research showed that eating dark chocolate helped people who have peripheral artery disease walk farther and longer.

Eating dark chocolate is linked to significantly lower blood pressure. Systolic blood pressure (top number) for people who ate dark chocolate went down by three points. Diastolic (bottom number) blood pressure went down by two points.

Researchers followed a group of more than 37,000 men for 10 years and counted instances of stroke. The numbers showed that those who ate about 63 grams (2 oz.) of chocolate per week had a lower risk of stroke, compared with those who ate no chocolate. Five additional studies also showed lower stroke risk, on average by about 20 percent for chocolate eaters.

> It takes only two to three ounces of dark chocolate per week to achieve these benefits.

Those who had the dark chocolate saw an average drop of 12 percent in their LDL cholesterol, known as bad cholesterol, which is linked to higher risks of heart disease.

A recent study found that eating dark chocolate helped people better cope with stress. *I could go on about the super benefits of dark chocolate covered bacon, but will save that for another day.*

Six Fruit Spreads

Jelly, jam, and preserves are all made from fruit mixed with sugar and pectin. The difference between them comes in the form that the fruit takes. Pectin is an indigestible carbohydrate, found in the cell walls of most fruit. When heated with sugar in water, it gels, giving jam, jelly, and preserves their thickness.

Jam is a thick mixture of pulp or crushed fruit, pectin, and sugar that is boiled gently and quickly until the fruit is soft and has an organic shape. It spreads easily and can form a blob. In addition to being a spread, jams are also good for fillings. Jam tastes much like the original fresh fruit.

Jelly is made from sugar, pectin, acid, and fruit juice. It is a clear spread that is firm enough to hold its shape. Jellies can also be made from ingredients other than fruit, such as herbs, tea, wine, liqueurs, flowers, and vegetables. Unlike a jam's fresh flavor of the original fruit, a jelly's flavor is that of the fruit after several hours of cooking.

Marmalade is a spread made from the peel and pulp of fruit. Marmalade is cooked for a long time, has no pectin, and is used as spreads and glazes. It is a balanced combination of clear jelly with pieces of fruit suspended in it. This fruit may or may not be citrus. Marmalade, like jelly, does not taste of fresh fruit, though the pieces of whole fruit maintain much of the original brightness of flavor.

Preserves are spreads that have chunks of fruit in a syrup or jam. It is a broad category that includes jam, jelly, and marmalade, as well as pickles, chutneys, and any other canned food. Basically, food which lasts longer than it would on its own is considered a preserve.

Fruit butter is a smooth and creamy spread that is created by slow-cooking fruit and sugar until it reaches the right consistency. These types of spreads are sometimes translucent and often opaque. Fruit butters are best used as a spread or filling. It is a variety of jelly and is whipped or cooked down until it becomes extremely thick.

Conserves are basically a jam, made with dried fruits and nuts and cooked. They have a very thick and chunky texture. Conserves work very well as a spread and as a condiment for meats and cheeses.

According to the US Food and Drug Administration, jam and preserves are considered the same thing. Generally a fruit spread is a preserve if the fruit chunks are somewhat large and it is called a jam if the chunks are relatively small and mashed.

Jams and jellies are sweeter and have about half the calories of butter or margarine and unlike butter and margarine, contain zero fat.

Nineteen Coffee Facts

Coffee is one of the most favorite morning beverages, but is also drunk at any hour of day or night.

1. There are two types of oils in coffee, good oils and bad oils. The good oils are good for your body and your health, the bad oils may give you ulcers and stomach problems. To avoid the bad oils in coffee use paper filters to minimize the effects.

2. Mocha Java Coffee has no chocolate in the Mocha or Java bean. Mocha is the name of the port in Yemen, where all African coffee beans are traded and transported. Java is the name of an island in Indonesia where the Java bean originates. Both coffees are dark bean and provide a bold coffee, when you mix the two together you get Mocha Java coffee.

3. Coffee starts out as a yellow berry, ripens into a red berry, and is then harvested by hand. Through water soaking process the red berry is de-shelled and leaves the green coffee bean. This bean then dries in the sun for 3-5 days before bagging.

4. In Africa, coffee beans are soaked in water mixed with spices and served as candy to chew.

5. Brazil is the largest coffee producer in the world and the US is the largest coffee consuming country in the world.

6. There are 65 countries in the world that grow coffee and they are all located along the equator.

7. Black coffee with no additives contains no calories.

8. There are two types of coffee plants, Arabica and Robusta.

9. Espresso Coffee has one third of the caffeine content of a cup of regular coffee.

10. James Mason invented the coffee percolator on December 26, 1865.

11. Instant coffee was invented in 1901 by a Japanese American chemist, Satori Kato. In 1906 English chemist, George Constant Washington claimed he invented instant coffee.

12. Melitta Bentz a housewife from Dresden, Germany, invented the first coffee filter in 1908.

13. It takes five years for a coffee bush/tree to reach full maturity, coffee trees can live up to 100 years and the average yield from one tree equals about one pound of roasted coffee.

14. A regular 6oz cup of coffee contains about 150 milligrams of caffeine.

15. Robusta coffee beans have twice as much caffeine as Arabica beans, but are of less quality.

16. Coffee was eaten long before it became a liquid refreshment. African tribes would mix the coffee berries with fat and create energy balls that they would eat once or twice a day, when they needed a boost of energy. Green coffee beans were ground up and mixed with fat, then made into small balls, which were eaten by travelers on long journeys. It was the first plant to be cultivated around the world.

17. The fruit, or cherry, is a reddish two-seeded berry. The two seeds are what we call coffee beans, but are actually seeds. The cherries and leaves also contain caffeine. In some countries, the berries are fermented into wine, but mostly they are used for fertilizer or cattle feed.

18. Coffee was the very first food to be freeze dried in 1938. Nestle invented the freeze dried coffee. It was a milestone that was unprecedented and set a new standard for how food could be packaged and sold.

19. Coffee is so popular and in such high demand that it is actually the second most traded commodity on earth, behind oil.

Bacon Trivia

Bacon and the N Words - Most discussions of eggs are followed by bacon and vice versa. Nitrates and nitrites may be unhealthy for your body, but what most nutritionists fail to tell you is that you can easily avoid nitrates and nitrites by simply not burning, charring, or over cooking your bacon, also avoid by baking in the oven.

By including some dairy and citrus with a bacon meal, the vitamins A, D and E work to effectively prevent conversion of nitrates and nitrites into nitrosamines in the stomach, rendering them harmless to the body. *Yea!*

Bacon Brain Building - Bacon is full of an important nutrient called choline, which helps increase intelligence and memory and has been shown in University studies to help fight off the debilitating effects of Alzheimer's Disease and other chronic mental impairments. *Bacon helps me to remember to eat more bacon.*

Bacon's Blood Balancing Bounty - Several university and medical center studies have shown that including bacon as a regular, moderate part of one's diet, naturally works to lower the body's blood pressure and blood sugar levels, helping to prevent and / or alleviate the effects of diabetes, as well as heart disease, and stroke.

> Center-cut bacon has only 25 calories per slice *and usually causes human faces to break into a smile.*

Bacon Fueled Motorcycle - Hormel created a motorcycle that is fueled by bacon grease and sent it on a journey from Minnesota to the San Diego Bacon Fest just in time for International Bacon Day, August 30, 2014. Likely some interesting exhaust fumes came from the bike.

Pork Powered Protein: The protein found in bacon is extremely valuable to maintaining our energy levels and a fully functioning, healthy body, with a minimum nasty, waist, thigh, and butt expanding, fat building carbohydrates.

Bacon's Blood Balancing Bounty - Several university and medical center studies have shown that including bacon as a regular, moderate part of one's diet naturally works to lower the body's blood pressure and blood sugar levels, helping to prevent and / or alleviate the effects of diabetes, as well as heart disease, stroke, and heart attack.

Bacon Elevator - Bacon is an effective mood elevator. Bacon makes us feel happy, satisfied, and blissful, which greatly reduces stress and effectively relieves the negative effects of frustration.

Flushing Fat With Flavor - People have heard horror stories for years that bacon is full of harmful fat, but the facts show bacon helps to fully satiate our appetite with high protein / low carb energy, raises metabolism, and builds leaner, stronger muscles.

Bacon actually has less total fat, saturated fat, and cholesterol than many popular cuts of beef and chicken. While some fish has less fat and cholesterol than bacon, bacon has more protein power and does not contain toxins, such as mercury.

French Fry Facts

The origin of French fries is Belgium. According to some historians, potatoes were being fried by 1680 in the Meuse Valley of Belgium. Locals often ate small fried fish, when the river was frozen they used potatoes as a substitute. They used to cut potatoes lengthwise and fry them in oil to use them as a fish substitute.

There is a museum in Belgium entirely devoted to the classic fast-food snack frites.

Belgians consume the most French fries per capita of any country in Europe. Belgians, who are the world's connoisseurs when it comes to French fries, occasionally will serve French fries with egg as a topping. The raw egg is cracked over the French fries immediately after the fries have been pulled from the fryer. This tends to mostly cook the egg, but leaves the yoke somewhat runny for dipping the fries in.

Thomas Jefferson gets the credit for introducing French fries to America when he served them at a White House dinner in 1802 after reportedly requesting, "Potatoes, fried in the French manner.

The average American eats thirty pounds of French fries per year.

The earliest known reference to fries in English literature is in A Tale of Two Cities. Charles Dickens refers to, "Husky chips of potato, fried with some reluctant drops of oil".

According to the Agricultural Research Service in Navarre, potato skins are packed with 60 phyto-chemicals, many of these are flavonoids which help lower bad cholesterol and keep arteries clear. Make fries with the skins on.

French fries are eaten all over the world and every culture has its own preferred condiment. Americans dunk them in ketchup, Brits eat their chips with salt and malt vinegar, mayonnaise is a popular accompaniment in Belgium and they look forward to steamed mussels and fries. In Vietnam they serve fries with soft butter and a sprinkling of sugar. "Clams and chips" is a very popular dish in Halifax, Nova Scotia, Canada. French fries served with hot mustard is very popular in Ireland.

French Fries in France are known as frites, patates frites, or pommes frites. These names are also used in many non-French areas.

About seven per cent of the potatoes grown in the US are sold by McDonald's. It sells more than one third of all the French fries sold in restaurants in the US each year.

Medicine and Healthcare

FACTS ABOUT OUR BODIES

Ten Amazing Body Facts

- An average red blood cell lives for 120 days.
- There are about 2.5 trillion red blood cells in your body at any moment.
- A red blood cell can circumnavigate your body in under 20 seconds.
- Nerve Impulses travel at over 400 km/hr (25 mi/hr).
- A sneeze generates a wind of 166 km/hr (100 mi/hr), and a cough moves out at 100 km/hr (60 mi/hr).
- Our heart beats about 100,00 times every day.
- Our blood travels about 60,000 miles each day.
- When we touch something, we send a message to our brain at 124 mph
- The life span of a taste bud is ten days.
- There are more living organisms on the skin of a single human being than there are human beings on the surface of the earth.

Seven Types of Twins - There are seven different types of twins: Identical, Fraternal, Mirror-Image, Polar Body (Half Identical), Mixed Chromosome, Superfecundation, and Superfetation. Some are obvious, such as identical and fraternal.

Mirror-Image twins occur only in *identical twins*. In approximately 23 percent of identical twins the egg splits later than usual, most often day seven or beyond. The original right half of the egg becomes one individual and the original left half becomes the other. These twins will often have "mirror images" of their features, such as hair whorls that run clockwise in one and counter clockwise in the other, a birthmark on the right shoulder of one and the left shoulder of the other, etc. The determination is made by observation only, and the twins must be identical. One twin will be right-handed, while the co-twin is left-handed. This may be a partial explanation for the fact that a little over one third of identical twins are left-handed, double the rate in the general population. In extreme cases, all of the internal organs are reversed in one of the twins, with the heart on the right, the liver on the left and the appendix on the left.

Two separate eggs are fertilized by two separate sperm, resulting in *fraternal* twins. These babies will be no more alike than siblings born at separate times. The babies can be either the same sex or different sexes, with the odds roughly equal for each.

Polar Body or Half Identical twins are unusual and rare. The polar body appears when the egg has been developing, even before fertilization. It is a small cell that does not function and will usually degenerate and die. It is thought that in some cases, when the egg is old, the splitting off of the polar body takes place in an abnormal way. It then becomes larger, receives more nourishment, and does not die as it usually does. Instead, it acts as a second egg. The polar body and the egg share identical genes from the mother, but they may then be fertilized by two separate sperm from the father. This will result in twins who share half their genes in common (from the mother) and the other half different (from the two sperm). They share some features of identical twins and some features of fraternal twins and thus are called half-identical twins.

Mixed Chromosomes or Chimerism is thought to occur if two separate sperm fertilize two separate eggs which then fuse, producing individuals with different sets of chromosomes. Some have been identified that have more than one distinct red blood cell type and individuals who are both XX and XY (the sex chromosomes - XX being female and XY being male.) This phenomenon might also be associated with fused placentas causing intermixing of the circulations. It is extremely rare and fewer than twenty-five cases have been identified.

Superfecundation Twins can have different fathers. It happens when the mother ovulates more than one egg and has more than one partner during her fertile period. One egg is fertilized with sperm from one partner, and the other egg from sperm of the second partner. These types of twins are always *fraternal* or dizygotic (two cell).

Superfetation occurs when a women ovulates more than one egg, but the eggs are released at different times, sometimes up to 24 days apart, and they are fertilized when they are released. The resulting twin pregnancy has different conception dates, so the babies may be quite different in size. Days or weeks may separate the births. It is quite an unusual event. This is called interval birth.

Eye Floaters - Eye floaters are little oddly shaped objects that appear in your vision, often when a person looks at bright light such as a blue sky. Their shapes vary greatly, but will often appear as spots, cobwebs, or randomly shaped stringy objects. These are not optical illusions, but rather something your eyes actually perceive. There are a few different things that can cause this, but in most cases these eye floaters are caused by pieces of the gel-like vitreous breaking off from the back portion of your eye and then floating about in your eyeball.

The vitreous humor, or often just "vitreous", is a clear gel that fills the gap between your retina and lens, helping maintain the round shape of your eye in the process. This gel is about 99% water and 1% mostly consisting mostly of a network of hyaluronic acid and collagen. Hyaluronic acid ends up retaining water molecules. Over time though, this network breaks down which results in the hyaluronic acid releasing its trapped water molecules. When this happens, it forms a watery core in your vitreous body.

As you age, pieces of the still gel-like collagen/hyaluronic acid network will break off and float around in this watery center. When light passes through this area, it creates a shadow on your retina. This shadow is actually what you are seeing when you see the eye floaters.

Children and teenagers almost never experience these types of eye floaters as there must first be some deterioration of the gel-like substance in their eye for these floaters to appear. However, they do still sometimes experience a certain type of eye floater that often appears more like a crystallized web across their vision. These floaters aren't found in the vitreous humor like the other floaters. Instead, they are found in the Premacular Bursa area, right on top of the retina. These floaters are microscopic in size and only appear as big as they do because of their proximity to the retina.

Bone Fusion - Babies are born with 300 or more bones and adults have 206, because the bones have fused together. The bones that fuse (in general order of fusion) are those of the: Skull, Elbow, Hip, Ankle, Knee, Wrist, and Shoulder. Some of a baby's bones are made entirely of cartilage. Other bones in a baby are partly made of cartilage. This cartilage is soft and flexible. During childhood growing, the cartilage grows and is slowly replaced by bone, with help from calcium. It may take until between ages of 18 to 25 for all bones to completely fuse.

> Of the 206 bones in a body, 106 are located in the hands and feet.

Brain Cell Myths Debunked - Brain cells can't regenerate is an old myth. Also drinking kills brain cells is another old myth.

The reason for the regeneration myth is that it was believed and taught by the science community for a long time. In 1998, scientists at the Sweden and the Salk Institute in La Jolla, California discovered that brain cells in mature humans can regenerate.

It had previously been long believed that complex brains would be severely disrupted by new cell growth, but the study found that the memory and learning center of the brain can create new cells.

Even in alcoholics, alcohol use does not actually result in the death of brain cells. It may temporarily damage the ends of neurons, called dendrites. This results in problems conveying messages between the neurons. The cell is not damaged, but the way that it communicates with others is temporarily altered.

Scientific medical research has actually demonstrated that the moderate consumption of alcohol is associated with better thinking and reasoning skills and memory than is abstaining from alcohol. Moderate drinking helps the brain function better into old age.

High Temperature - When it comes to body temperature, anything up to 102°F is mild and can be treated by drinking plenty of fluids. To quickly bring down a temperature above that, put an ice pack under your arm or near your groin. Icing either spot will cool your body's core. Another remedy is to take a cool, but not cold bath.

For children, take a pair of cotton socks that are long enough to cover the child's ankles. Thoroughly wet the socks in cold tap water. Wring out excess water. Put the socks on the child's feet and repeat process when the socks dry out.

Wenis - Wenis has achieved the status of a dictionary word and can be found in the online Merriam Webster dictionary. Even Wikipedia is reserving the word for inclusion. It refers to the skin on the outside of the elbow. The excess skin allows your elbow to move and flex. Medically speaking, it is called the olecranal skin. The word wenis has long been used as slang, because it sounds like the male appendage. Sample usage, "I fell and scraped my wenis."

Eye Goop - Other names include; eye crusties, eye gunk, sleepy dust, sleepy boogers, eye discharge, eye goop, eye crud, eye jelly, eye crust, eye bogeys, eye boogers, eye-sand, sleepy dirt, eye sand.

It is a type of 'rheum', which is the name for discharge from your nose, mouth, or eyes during sleep. More specifically, eye rheum is known as gound. Gound is made up of a mixture of dust, blood cells, skin cells, etc., mixed with mucus secreted by the conjunctiva, as well as an oily substance from the meibomian glands (named after German, Heinrich Meibom).

The meibomian glands are a type of sebaceous gland that line the rim of the eyelids with about fifty on the top and twenty five on the bottom of each eye. They secrete an oily substance called meibum that performs a variety of functions including: helps seal your eyes in an air tight fashion when they are closed; prevents tears from spilling onto your cheeks; and helps keep tears that coat your eyes from evaporating. It is this oily substance that is one of the primary components in gound, mixed with mucin from the conjunctiva and various foreign particles in your eye.

> The tragus is located in the middle of the outside of the ear.

Normally, when you are awake, the gound is naturally washed away via tears and the blinking motion. As you sleep, the meibomian secretions and other components of the gound tend to gather in the corners of your eyes, as well as along your eye lines and dries out. *Sleepy eyes suddenly takes on a whole new meaning.*

Bad Breath Eliminators - If you do not have any Listerine handy, here are a few other options. Sugar may cure hiccups, but it also can cause plaque, which is one cause of bad breath. Bad breath usually results from poor oral hygiene and gastrointestinal health. Breath odors originate inside the mouth and also from the digestive tract. The cause in both is mostly bacteria.

Coriander, spearmint, tarragon, eucalyptus, rosemary, and cardamom are all good for fighting bad breath, either by chewing, or steeping in hot water, as a tea.

Research also shows that live microorganisms in sugar free yogurt may reduce levels of bad breath germs. A serving of yogurt each day reduces the level of odor-causing hydrogen sulfide in the mouth. It also reduces bacteria in the mouth as well as reduces plaque and gum disease.

Apples, carrots, celery, and any fiber-rich fruits or vegetables also help fight halitosis (bad breath). Plaque build-up causes odors and eating foods that increase saliva production keep the mouth moist and rinsed. Eating berries, citrus fruits, melons, and other vitamin C foods create an inhospitable environment for bacteria growth and prevent gum disease and gingivitis.

Sunburn and SPF - SPF is an acronym for Sun Protection Factor. SPF is actually a measure of protection from amount of UVB exposure and it is not meant to help you determine duration of exposure. Sunbathers often assume that they get twice as much protection from SPF 100 sunscreen as from SPF 50. In reality, the extra protection is negligible. Properly applied SPF 15 blocks 93% of UV-B rays; SPF 50 sunscreen blocks 98 percent of sunburn rays. Dermatologists recommend using a SPF15 or SPF30 sunscreen. Higher SPFs do not actually give much more protection.

Sunblock and sunscreen block the rays from the sun being absorbed by our skin. Ninety five percent of the UV (Ultra violet) energy hitting the earth's surface is UV-A. The other 5% is UV-B. Most of UV-B radiation is absorbed by our atmosphere. UV-A penetrates the skin more deeply than UV-B. However, UV-B causes more problems generally associated with exposure to the sun's rays, like skin cancer, aging, and DNA damage. UV-B waves are primarily responsible for sunburned skin. Scientists know less about the dangers of UV-A radiation, but the general consensus is that it is less obvious than UV-B damage, but possibly more serious.

Sunscreens generally only block UV-B rays, and not UV-A. To get broad spectrum protection, sunscreen must contain both the organic compounds associated with UV-B absorption and an inorganic associated with UV-A reflection.

Sunburn reactions usually begin about 4 hours after exposure and peak between 8-24 hours, so what we feel while being exposed is just the beginning.

Using Vocal Cords - Your vocal cords are an instrument that you use every day. The human vocal range extends from the depth of whispering to shouting. In between are talking, laughing, crying, humming, singing, and more. The entire vocal range is both attenuated and enhanced by emotions. For instance, it is not necessary to see a person speaking with fear, or happiness to notice the differences in tone and inflection.

One often underused quality of voice is silence. Most of us are familiar with the 'the silence was deafening'. *If you cannot improve the silence, do not waste your time exercising your vocal cords.*

Bitter, Sweet, and Salty - Salty and sweet are distinct tastes which our taste buds are usually able to detect. However, if you add salt to some foods, they do not taste salty, but become sweeter tasting. This is because salt is not just a taste, it is also a taste enhancer.

Bitter and sweet cancel each other out to some degree. Think of adding sugar to naturally bitter coffee and you get the idea. It cancels/masks the bitterness. Some people add a bit of salt to the grounds before making coffee, for the same reason.

Pineapples are sweet, but also have some bitterness to them. If you neutralize the bitterness, it should taste sweeter. Adding salt can do this. When salt mixes with the pineapple, the salt splits up into sodium and chloride ions. The chloride is tasteless and our tongues ignore it. The sodium bonds with the acids in the pineapple and forms a similarly tasteless salt, but the bitterness effectively disappears. What remains is the sweetness of the pineapple. Add a little bit of salt to your fresh pineapple and enjoy the enhanced sweetness. It also works with watermelon, oranges, grapefruit, dark chocolate, and other foods that are both bitter and sweet. Perhaps this is one reason why it is said that bacon is the food that makes other foods taste better. My father always salted apples before eating and usually paired with extra sharp cheddar cheese.

Adding salt works less well with canned or other processed fruits as many are already artificially sweetened.

Calories, Sleep, and Laughter - Many variables that go into the calorie-burning equation, such as age, sex, weight, metabolism, diet, and physical and nonphysical daily habits. The two most important factors in determining how many calories you burn while sleeping are weight and number of hours slept. On average, a person burns between 0.4 and 0.5 calories per pound, per hour. For example, a 100 lb. person burns 40-50 calories per hour. In eight hours of sleep, this person will burn approximately 360 calories.

> Laughing 100 times is equivalent to 15 minutes of exercise on a stationary bicycle.

A pound of muscle burns fifty calories a day on average and a pound of fat burns nine calories. A leaner, more muscular person is going to burn up to five times more calories per pound.

If you weigh 160 pounds, you burn 69 calories per hour while sleeping, the FitWatch website calculates up to 552 calories burned during eight hours of sleep. A 120-pound person burns about 51 calories per hour sleeping, or 408 for eight hours; a 200-pound person burns 86 calories per hour, or 868 for eight hours of sleep.

Fifteen minutes of laughter a day will burn ten to forty calories, depending on a person's weight and the intensity of the laughter. A study by Loma Linda University found that laughing raises the levels of immunoglobulins, which ward of disease, by fourteen percent. Laughter also has other benefits, including increased pain tolerance, relief of emotional stress and a workout for the muscles of the diaphragm, abdomen, back, and shoulders.

Circadian Rhythms - These are physical, mental, and behavioral changes that follow an approximately 24-hour cycle, responding primarily to light and darkness in an organism's environment. The study of circadian rhythms is called chronobiology.

The master clock that controls circadian rhythms consists of a group of nerve cells in the brain called the suprachiasmatic nucleus, or SCN. The SCN contains about 20,000 nerve cells and is located in the hypothalamus, an area of the brain just above where the optic nerves from the eyes cross. SCN controls the production of melatonin, a hormone that makes us sleepy. When there is less light, like at night, the SCN tells the brain to make more melatonin so we get drowsy.

Circadian rhythms can influence sleep-wake cycles, hormone release, body temperature, and other important bodily functions. They have been linked to various sleep disorders, including insomnia. Abnormal circadian rhythms have also been associated with obesity, diabetes, depression, bipolar disorder, and seasonal affective disorder.

Clock genes contain instructions for making clock proteins, whose levels rise and fall in a regular cyclic pattern. This pattern in turn regulates the activity of the genes.

Many of the clock genes and proteins are similar across species, allowing researchers to make important findings about human circadian processes by studying the clock components of other organisms. They have identified genes that direct circadian rhythms in people, fruit flies, mice, fungi, bread mold, plants, and several other model organisms used for studying genetics.

Jet lag occurs when travelers suffer from disrupted circadian rhythms. When you pass through different time zones, your body's clock will be different from your wristwatch. For example, if you fly in an airplane from California to New York, you 'lose' 3 hours of time. So when you wake up at 7:00 a.m., your body still thinks it is 4:00 a.m., making you feel disoriented. Your body's clock will eventually reset itself, but this often takes a few days.

Straight Teeth Talk - Though fillings do crack and decay over time, you rarely need all of them replaced at once. Some dentists claim that old silver fillings need to be removed for safety reasons, because they leech mercury, but that idea is a myth.

There is enough fluoride in our drinking water and in over-the-counter toothpastes to prevent cavities in most people, so additional fluoride from a dentist is additional cost, with little benefit.

Eye Colors, Brown - Each of the various eye colors show something about us.

Brown is the most common eye color in the world, because it is caused by a dominant gene. Brown eyes contain large amounts of melanin, a pigment that also causes skin to darken in the sun. If you are lucky enough to have brown eyes, you are much less likely to develop melanoma skin cancer than those with less melanin and those with fairer coloring.

There is a common myth that people with brown eyes are very confident, but it is not always true, as eye color does not determine confidence.

Very dark eyes are sometimes mistaken for being black, but truly black eyes only exist in fiction. Those people who do have incredibly dark brown, almost black, eyes share many of the same traits as those with a lighter shade of brown.

It is very uncommon to find people with brown eyes in some parts of the world, especially Iceland and parts of Scandinavia. Conversely, brown eyes are everywhere in Africa and Asia.

Technically in the brown eye family, amber eyes are of a solid color and have a strong yellowish/golden and russet/coppery tint from the yellow colored pigment lipochrome in the iris (which is also found in green eyes). Amber eyes should not be confused with hazel eyes; although hazel eyes may contain specks of amber or gold, they usually tend to comprise many other colors, including green, brown, and orange. Amber eyes are very rare worldwide, and are most common in Asia and South American countries. Amber eye color can range from golden yellow to a more copper tone.

Brown Eye Stroma Procedure - There is a laser treatment, pioneered by California-based Stroma Medical and it is currently available in several countries. It is undergoing human testing in Costa Rica that turns brown eyes blue. The Strōma laser disrupts the brown layer of pigment, causing the body to initiate a natural and gradual tissue-removal process. Once the tissue is removed, the patient's natural blue eye is revealed. The procedure is totally non invasive and takes about 20 seconds to perform, but two to four weeks to see final results.

Eye Colors, Grey - The exact causes of grey eyes are a bit uncertain, but there is a possibility that it is the eyes having more collagen and less melanin than blue eyes. As a result, when light enters the eye it is scattered slightly different, causing them to look grey, rather than blue.

Those with grey eyes are generally believed to have strong characters, with a dominant, rational, analytical mindset, although character is not a function of eye color.

Grey eyes are most commonly found in Northern and Eastern areas of Europe. They can also be found at various locations around the world, including North West Africa, Asia, and the Middle East.

Incidentally, Gray and grey are different spellings of the same word, and both are used throughout the English-speaking world. Gray is more common in American English, while grey is more common in all other varieties of English.

Eye Colors, Hazel - Hazel eyes appear to be a mixture of brown and green. They are very uncommon so it is thought that they are caused by a recessive gene, but in fact, very little is known about hazel eyes and what causes them. This is a much less common eye color than brown, but it is more common than green.

Myths state that hazel eyes change color according to mood and the person's surroundings. This is actually true - the subtle blend of green and brown coloring means that different lighting brings out different effects from the hazel eye color, sometimes looking more green, while other times having a browner tone.

Most people with hazel eyes descend from European ancestors, so many can be found in the USA and Europe. Hazel eyes are very rare in Africa and Asia, where brown eyes are the most common. *My eyes are hazel.*

Eye Colors, Green - Just two percent of people in the world have green eyes, making it the least common eye color. Green eyes originate from Siberia and now can mostly be found in Europe. Interestingly, in Iceland the number of females with green eyes is greater than the number of males with green eyes. Ireland is also a hotspot for green eyes as they are believed to have Celtic ancestry, making green eyes and red hair a typical combination. Elsewhere around the world green eyes are very uncommon, but individuals can be found in all corners of the globe, including the USA, Europe, Asia, South America, and Northern Africa.

Sometimes green eyes can bear a striking resemblance to cat's eyes, resulting in the myth that people with green eyes were evil. History is full of stories of women being condemned as witches, simply because of their green eyes. *My cousin tells me she and her brother were born with brown eyes, but they are now most often hazel, and sometimes green.*

Eye Colors, Blue - Naturally blue eyes are caused by having low melanin levels in the iris - the same stuff that gives skin its pigment and color. In fact, we have all had blue eyes at one point in our lives, because all babies are born with blue eyes. For most people, their eyes change color as they grow older and develop melanin, but for a select few who do not develop as much melanin, their eyes stay blue forever. Eyes appear blue for the same reason as the sky is blue. It is a process called Rayleigh Scattering.

In Iceland, 80% of the population has blue eyes. The statistics are similar in the rest of Northern Europe and Scandinavia, where blue eyes are very common. Blue eyes can also be found in some areas of Western Asia, as well as in Israel. Blue eyes are extremely rare in Africa. People with blue eyes are becoming less common in the US.

For a long time it was believed that blue eyes were caused by a recessive gene, but lately this has been found to be untrue. People with blue eyes tend to have a higher tolerance to alcohol than those without.

Silver eye color is quite rare, although many consider silver eyes to be a variation of blue eye color. Like blue eyes, silver eyes are the result of a very low amount of pigmentation in the eye, which reflects a gray-silver appearance. Silver eye color is most common in eastern European countries, and is one of the more rare eye colors worldwide.

Eyelash Facts - A study published in the Journal of the Royal Society Interface reports that eyelashes divert airflow to prevent drying of the eyes and protect against airborne particulates.

Twenty two species of mammals possess eyelashes of a length one-third the eye width. Wind tunnel experiments confirm that this optimal eyelash length reduces both deposition of airborne particles and evaporation of the tear film by a factor of two. This happens because of the incoming flow's interactions with both the eye and eyelashes.

Another study found that growth of eyelashes occurs in response to exposure to allergens. Children with allergies have ten percent longer and denser lashes than those without allergies. Allergens trigger mast cells within the inside of the eyelid to release prostaglandins that promote hair growth, which presumably protects the eye. *If models only knew their long lashes make them look like they have allergies.*

Contact Lenses - Eyeglasses have been around since 13th century Italy, and the design has not changed much over the years, except for different types of frames, which change with fashion.

During 1887, a German named Adolf Fick decided to do away with frames altogether and simply stick the lens directly on his eye.

The first contact lenses were 21mm (0.8 inches) wide and made from blown glass, with a sugar solution between the lens and the eye to cut down on friction. They were bulky and uncomfortable, but blown glass contacts lasted for 50 years until they were replaced with plastic ones in 1936.

Even though Adolf Fick was the first person to make a practical contact lens, he was not the first to try. Leonardo da Vinci is said to have invented a type of contact lens in 1508 made out of a bowl of water. Rene Descartes supposedly built a water-filled tube that was designed to go into the eye, but the idea never took off because it stuck out so far a person could not blink.

Fur and Hair - There is no difference between fur and hair; it is all just hair. Most refer to animal hair as fur, while referring to our own hair as just hair. However, hair and fur are chemically indistinguishable, both made up of keratin.

Human hair does not grow forever nor does animal hair/fur, although the length of the growing cycle can be longer or shorter for both. Various mammals have different growth cycles for their hair than humans do. Cat hair seems to stop growing at a relatively short length, similar to the growth rate and length of the hair on a human's arms and legs.

The maximum length of hair on various parts of a body is entirely determined by genetics and varies widely from person to person and animal to animal.

A cat's whiskers are just hair, though these hairs are attached to special nervous system connections allowing them to work as sensory receptors.

A Porcupine's quills are extremely enlarged hairs.

Incidentally, shaving does not make your hair grow back thicker, stronger, or faster. It has been proven by numerous studies that shaving has absolutely no effect on hair growth rate or shape.

Body Odor Facts - Body odor is a uniquely personalized thing. Just what kind of body odor each individual person has is determined by a combination of a certain area of their genetic makeup called the major histocompatibility complex and, partially by what they eat. The basic composition of a person's body odor remains the same, however, and it has been suggested that one of the reasons for it is to help us choose a genetically appropriate mate. Change in body odor has also been linked to the development of certain cancers and viral diseases.

The body odor fingerprint is not the only thing scientists have discovered about body odor. They found that the older people get the worse they stink. A substance called 2-Nonenal has been identified as the reason some people have a faintly greasy odor about them. The substance has only been found in people over the age of 40 and the older people get, the more of the substance the body produces. Sweat itself is pretty much odorless, but the bacteria that reacts with sweat is what produces the odor.

DNA - DNA is DeoxyriboNucleic Acid. The blueprint of every living thing on the planet is encoded in DNA. It can hold a lot of information. We could theoretically encode all the world's data (emails, movies, books, pictures, etc.) on just a few grams of DNA.

According to New Scientist, a gram of DNA could theoretically store 455 exabytes of data. The world has about 1.8 zettabytes of data, according to a 2011 estimate.

All the world's information would fit on a four-gram DNA hard drive the size of a teaspoon.

Also, given the right conditions, DNA can survive for thousands of years. Long past the time traditional hard drives have degraded.

Scientists at the Swiss Federal Institute of Technology in Zurich encapsulated DNA in tiny, dry glass spheres. The researchers say that DNA kept at a temperature of 10 °C would remain uncorrupted and readable for 2,000 years. At even lower temperatures the data could last two million years.

However, preserving data in DNA is currently very expensive. Swiss researchers spent $1,500 to encode 83-kilobytes, which is smaller than the size a picture taken on a smartphone uses. There are a nearly two quintillion kilobytes in the world's 1.8 zettabytes.

Seventeen Fascinating Body Facts

1. From the age of thirty, humans gradually begin to shrink in size.

2. Most people lose fifty per cent of their taste buds by the time they reach age sixty.

3. Your body contains enough iron to make a spike strong enough to hold your weight.

4. The amount of carbon in the human body is enough to fill about 9,000 'lead' pencils.

5. One square inch of human skin contains 625 sweat glands.

6. The surface area of a human lung is equal to that of a tennis court.

7. Give a tennis ball a hard squeeze and you use about the same amount of force your heart uses to pump blood around your body.

8. When you blush, your stomach lining also reddens.

9. The human body has less muscles in it than a caterpillar.

10. Your eyes blink enough times in a lifetime to see blackness for over a year.

11. More germs are transferred shaking hands than kissing.

12. The aorta, the largest artery in the body, is almost the diameter of a garden hose.

13. Capillaries are so small that it takes ten of them to equal the thickness of a human hair.

14. Your body has about 6 quarts (5.6 Liters) of blood. It circulates through the body three times every minute.

15. The heart pumps about 1 million barrels of blood during an average lifetime.

16. The human body can function without a brain (although not long).

17. Humans are the only primates that do not have pigment in the palms of their hands
A man's testicles manufacture 10 million new sperm cells each day, enough to repopulate the entire planet in 6 months.

Eight Eyebrow Facts

Eyebrows are tufts of hair that follow the shape of the ridge of the brow in mammals. They are very small and personal, but (mostly women) annually spend billions to pluck, tweeze, paint, scarify, shape, tattoo, pierce, puff, and generally do many unnatural things to this unique part of the human body. They are profoundly expressive of mood.

- The function of our brows is to keep moisture out of our eyes when it is raining or when we sweat. That arched shape helps divert liquid to the side of our faces.

- According to the Bosley hair transplant company, the average person has about 250 hairs per eyebrow.

- The average lifespan of an eyebrow is four months.

- A study done by MIT found that people had more trouble correctly identifying the faces of people they knew when they were presented with images of them missing their eyebrows and concluded that brows may be more important for facial recognition than eyes.

- Brows help us signal emotions, as the pitch of your voice rises, so do your eyebrows and vice versa.

- When you make an expression without thinking, eyebrows move in a way that is symmetrical to each other. Conversely, when you make what's called an 'intended' expression, like suspicion and curiosity, your brows will furrow asymmetrically.

- Man is the only species that has eyebrows against bare skin.

- Every culture and time period has had a different way of shaping their brows: In Florence during the Renaissance, people shaved their eyebrows off completely, while the colonial elite in 18th-century America preferred to beef their brows up using grey mouse skin.

20/20 Vision

The 20/20 scale is different in different parts of the world. After examining a large number of people, American ophthalmologists decided on the 20/20 scale, saying that "20/20" is the normal visual acuity of the average person. That means standing 20 feet away from something, you can see what the average person can see standing 20 feet away from the same thing. In metric countries doctors measure how well a person can see at 6 meters away (19.69 feet).

The Snellen eye chart is the chart topped with the big E and consists of 11 rows of capital letters that get progressively smaller toward the bottom of the chart. A person is placed 20 feet away from the chart. Since most doctors' offices are too small, mirrors are often used to simulate 20 feet. The doctor asks the person to read out the smallest line of letters that can be seen at that distance. Most people can read the fourth line up from the bottom without trouble, so if a person can do this, the vision is considered 20/20.

Using the Snellen chart, if a person can only see the big E up top and none of the other lines of text, he is considered to have 20/200 vision, meaning he sees at 20 feet what an average person can see at 200 feet away. 20/200 visual acuity and worse is considered legally blind in the United States, unless it can be corrected to better with glasses or contacts.

If a person can read the tiny bottom line of text on the chart at 20 feet away, it is considered 20/5 visual acuity. Most humans do not have the ability to have much better than 20/10 vision.

The 20/20 or 6/6 visual acuity is not a measure of a prescription as it does not take into account the nature of the problem, only the result of it.

Ten Teeth Facts

1. Teeth in a growing fetus begin to develop at six weeks after conception.
2. About one in every 2,000 babies is born with natal teeth.

3. Not everyone loses their baby teeth. By age 3, the average child has a full set of 20 temporary teeth. Children typically start losing teeth around 5 or 6 and finish in their early teens. If a person does not have a replacement permanent tooth, that baby tooth will stay put.

4. Thirty five percent of people are born without wisdom teeth.

5. About 2,500 years ago, the Maya already had a very advanced understanding of teeth. They would have their dentists use a primitive drill to decorate their teeth. Sometimes they would have parts of the tooth cut out or shaped to make it look more interesting. Their most extreme modification was the bejeweling of teeth.

6. Ancient Egypt people were using primitive tools made from twigs to brush their teeth. Many countries still use twigs from trees with antibacterial properties, such as cinnamon and neem, and they have been found to be as effective as modern toothbrushes.

According to a Time Magazine Survey, 59% of Americans would rather sit in a dentist's chair than sit next to someone on a cell phone.

7. Acidic foods, like sour candy, soft drinks, and fruit juices soften teeth. The result is enamel erosion and diminished tooth size.

8. Paul Revere, in addition to earning a living as a silversmith and copper plate engraver, also worked as a dentist. Revere is the first person known to use dental forensics to identify the body of a colonial colonel killed at the Battle of Bunker Hill by his dental bridge.

9. Some cheeses, including aged cheddar, Swiss, and Monterey Jack have been found to protect teeth from decay. *Grilled cheese and bacon immediately springs to mind.*

10. Every person has a set of teeth as unique as his or her fingerprints, and dental fingerprints of identical twins are different.

MEDICAL FACTS

Cold or Flu - During winter, many will get one or the other, or both. However, there is a difference that is quite striking. Both can share a number of the same symptoms, including a runny or stuffy nose, sore throat, and cough. Because both the common cold and flu are caused by viruses, neither responds to antibiotics, which only work on bacterial infections. Antiviral medications can be prescribed by a physician to treat the flu and should be administered within 48 hours of when people begin to feel ill.

Colds tend to be relatively mild and typically last only a few days. Colds also have a more gradual onset with mild aches, and pains. Common colds are caused by many different viruses and high fever is rare. Colds are much more common than cases of flu.

The flu, short for influenza, usually comes on suddenly and is accompanied by fever, severe aches, chills, and fatigue. Effects of the flu can last for weeks.

Treatment for both includes plenty of rest, drinking fluids, taking antihistamines, pain relievers, and decongestants. *Don't forget to keep a good supply of chicken soup, just in case.*

Nuts are Healthy - Had been thinking about this and it seems to fit with National Peanut Butter Day. According to data analysis conducted by researchers at the Dana-Farber Cancer Institute, Brigham and Women's Hospital, and the Harvard School of Public Health and published in the New England Journal of Medicine, those who ate nuts nearly every day were 20 percent less likely to die in the course of two 30-year cohort studies.

Nut eaters were almost 30 percent less likely to die of heart disease and more than 10 percent less likely to die of cancer than those who never ate them, even after adjusting for other lifestyle factors. The nut eaters were also slimmer and had lower rates of type 2 diabetes.

The study found that nuts, such as almonds, cashews, Brazil nuts, and peanuts delivered the health and longevity benefits in direct proportion to consumption.

Researchers tracked the health of 119,000 men and women for 30 years and included detailed dietary questionnaires every four years. "What we find is regular nut consumers are actually lighter; there is less obesity in that group," said Charles Fuchs, director of the

Gastrointestinal Cancer Treatment Center at Dana-Farber and senior author of the paper.

Previous studies have also pointed to a correlation between eating nuts and lower risks of heart disease, type 2 diabetes, colon cancer, and diverticulitis. Higher nut consumption also has been linked to reductions in cholesterol levels, inflammation, and insulin resistance. *It is nuts not to eat nuts.*

How Many Kisses - A popular study showed that , because you do not know what someone has been touching.

What we call the 'Eskimo kiss', or rubbing noses is called a kunik by the Inuit. It is an expression of affection, usually from an adult to a child. The Inuit also kiss on the lips as we do. The myth of rubbing noses grew out of a Hollywood silent documentary.

Kissing as a greeting is healthier than a handshake

French disagree on the number of greeting kisses, but mostly for central France it is two kisses, and for the North, four. There are exceptions - in Finistère, one kiss is normal - and even disparities within the same area: half the population of Calais prefer deux bises, while the other half will greet you with quatre. The number of kisses can depend on whether someone is a friend or family member, and varies between generations. To the upper-class French any more than two kisses is a faux pas.

Of course, it is not just in France that people greet each other with a kiss; in the Netherlands three is normal, and in Belgium it is one kiss for your peers, but if someone is ten years older than you, then three is respectful. In Spain, two is normal, but you must kiss the right cheek first.

The French don't necessarily French kiss more than anyone else; the term probably comes from our belief that French sexuality is more sophisticated. In France, it is known as baiser anglais ('English kissing'), baiser florentin (Florentine kiss) or rouler une pelle (to roll a spade). In Quebec, it is frencher.

Kissing in public is illegal in India and a similar law has been proposed in Russia and Indonesia.

How Much Water - North American companies use 1.39 liters of water to make one liter of bottled water. That is less than the global averages of a liter of soda, which requires 2.02 liters of water. A liter of beer needs 4 liters of water, wine needs 4.74 liters. Hard alcohol requires 34.55 liters of water for every liter.

Medical Errors - The thing we see cited among the top causes of death is medical errors, also known in the literature as 'preventable adverse events'. That means when medical personnel do the wrong thing, or fail to do the right thing, or do the right thing, but do it wrong. This can often take the form of misdiagnosis, or miscommunication between various healthcare providers, or between providers and patient. *Medical errors are the third leading cause of death in America.*

Placebo and Color Affect - Researchers found the color of a package and a pill makes a difference in how it works. In one study, every patient was given the exact same sedative, but some patients received it in a blue pill and others in an orange pill. The blue pill takers reported falling asleep 30 minutes faster, and sleeping 30 minutes longer, than the orange pill takers.

You likely know that you can give a person with a headache a Tic Tac, say it is medicine, and it may eliminate a headache just like an aspirin would, for reasons science does not completely understand. This phenomenon is also affected by color. In other words, how you perceive effectiveness affects effectiveness and color matters.

Subjects, in another study were told they would get a sedative or a stimulant, when they were actually getting placebos. Sixty six percent of the subjects who took blue pills reported feeling less alert, compared to only twenty six percent of those who took pink pills. It is because we have been conditioned to think that blue is tranquil.

In yet another study, when researchers put various fake medicine packages in front of subjects, the subjects picked certain colors of boxes over others. Warm colors like brown and red were perceived as more potent, especially if the shades were darker. This is why heart medicines are often red and brown, while skin medicines are yellow, and sleeping pills are often blue. Painkillers are most often white. All carefully chosen to match our perceptions.

> How you perceive effectiveness affects effectiveness and color matters.

The majority of fast food chains have red and yellow or orange in their logo, because these are stimulating colors. Lowfat containers, more often than not have blue on the package.

Color associations are also cultural. In America blue is a calming and peaceful color, but in Italy it is associated with the national soccer team. Researchers found that, rather than making him drowsy, a blue pill might invigorate an Italian.

Sugar Stops Hiccups - This remedy is no placebo. Hiccups occur when a spasm contracts the diaphragm, a large sheet of muscle that separates the chest cavity from the abdominal cavity. This spasm causes an intake of breath that is suddenly stopped by the closure of the vocal cords. This closure causes the 'hiccup' sound.

Hiccups are irritating, but it is possible to stop them within sixty seconds or so by swallowing a teaspoon filled with dry sugar or honey. Specialists believe the abrupt sweetness on the tongue overloads the nerve endings in the mouth and blocks the hiccup spasm.

How to Stay Young - It need not take a lot of effort. John Morley, M.D., director of the division of geriatric medicine at Saint Louis University outlines a ten-step program to improve quality of life as we age.

He suggests little changes that involve good eating, such as including dark chocolate in your diet, drinking wine, socializing, adding simple exercises, fidgeting in your office chair to burn calories, spending time walking from your car to the store rather than driving to find a close parking space, working in your garden, taking the stairs instead of the elevator or going dancing once a week. *I already socialize, drink wine, and eat chocolate, but need to practice fidgeting a bit more.*

Origin of Gin and Tonic - British soldiers fighting in the Indies had a serious problem with Malaria. The British also had a tonic water that contained quinine, which was effective at fighting malaria. The tonic water tasted terrible, so the British soldiers mixed gin with it to make it palatable. Upon returning home after the war, they continued to drink the mix and it became quite popular.

Incidentally, Malaria comes from the Italian, meaning 'bad air' as it was originally thought to be caused by dirty air.

Tonic water still contains some quinine, but much less than the original, and now usually has artificial sweeteners to moderate the bitter taste. Interesting to note the sensitivity of quinine to UV makes it appear fluorescent in direct sunlight and glows blue under black lights.

Virus vs. Bacteria - Viruses and bacteria are very different and they can both be either beneficial or harmful. A virus is both living and non-living, and is incapable of reproducing on its own, while bacteria are complete, living organisms that can self-replicate. Bacteria are usually much larger, come in a wider variety of shapes, and serve in more beneficial roles than a virus.

Infections and illnesses can be viral or bacterial. We often hear the terms, and we might even have a vague idea of what they mean, but a complete understanding of the difference between the two can help you treat the illnesses they cause.

Viruses are tiny, microscopic things that exist in two different states. When they are floating in the air or lying on a table waiting for someone to come by and inhale them, they are non-living and inert. Once they are absorbed into a living host, they activate. A virus cannot replicate on its own, and requires a host cell to attach itself to in order to multiply. Some microbiologists classify viruses as microorganisms, while others do not, because they are "nonliving" and describe viruses as microscopic infective agents.

After contacting a host cell, a virus will insert genetic material into the host and take over that host's functions. The infected cell continues to reproduce, but it reproduces more viral protein and genetic material instead of its usual products. It is this process that earns viruses the classification of 'parasite'.

However, a virus can also be useful, because a virus will naturally attach itself to a healthy living cell, a virus can be used as a delivery system when genetic material needs to be transferred to a human body. Injecting a virus with genetic material then releasing it into the body can result in the delivery and replication of cells. This type of gene therapy is still experimental, but showing good progress. Some types of viruses can also target and destroy many types of bacteria, like E. coli.

Bacteria are tiny, living organisms that are not classified as either plant or animal. As such, they do not rely on hosts in order to reproduce, and can exist, grow, and multiply outside of a living body. Few know that many bacteria not only coexist with us all the time, but help us do an array of useful things, like make vitamins, break down garbage, and maintain our atmosphere.

Bacteria consist of a single cell and have been found living in temperatures above the boiling point and in freezing cold. They consume everything from sugar and starch to sunlight, sulfur, and iron. There is a species of bacteria that can withstand blasts of radiation 1,000 times greater than would kill a human being. A gram of soil typically contains about 40 million bacterial cells. A milliliter of fresh water usually holds about one million bacterial cells.

A single bacterium contains more than a virus and can reproduce on its own. That means a cell wall, genetic material, and an appendage to propel itself. It is different from plant and animal cells, however, as there is no nucleus to contain the genetic material.

When magnified, a virus appears round, but bacteria can be a number of different shapes, including ball-shaped, rod-shaped, and spiral. Within each general group of shape types, there is a wide variety that separates bacteria even further.

After age 30, our chances of dying double every ten years.

Because of their simplicity, a virus can be 10,000 times smaller than a bacterium. Examples of both can be found just about anywhere on Earth, in any environment.

Determining whether an illness is caused by bacteria or a virus determines how it is treated. Bacteria are vulnerable to antibiotics, while anti-viral agents are required to kill a virus, and vaccinations can help prevent them from infecting a body.

Gluten Fad and Facts - As with most fads, gluten has way too many headlines and gluten free diets are popular, without much knowledge of what it is or why we should or should not eat gluten. In fact, the majority of Americans do not know which foods contain gluten.

Gluten is a protein composite found in foods processed from wheat and related grain species, including barley and rye. Gluten gives elasticity to dough, helping it rise and keep its shape and often gives the final product a chewy texture. Worldwide, gluten is a source of protein, both in foods prepared directly from sources containing it, and as an additive to foods otherwise low in protein.

Gluten, especially wheat gluten, is often the basis for imitation meats resembling beef, chicken, duck, fish, and pork. When cooked in broth, gluten absorbs some of the surrounding liquid and becomes firm to the bite. Gluten is often present in beer, soy sauce, some chocolates, and deli meats. It can be used as a stabilizing agent in more unexpected food products, such as ice cream and ketchup.

Experts estimate that about .75% to 1% of Americans have celiac disease. The condition, caused by an abnormal immune response to gluten, can damage the lining of the small intestine. For people with celiac disease, a gluten-free diet is essential, but for others, "unless people are very careful, a gluten-free diet can lack vitamins, minerals, and fiber," according to the Celiac Disease Center at Columbia University.

Many whole grains that contain gluten are rich in an array of vitamins and minerals, such as B vitamins and iron, as well as fiber. Studies show that whole grain foods, as part of a healthy diet, may help lower risk of heart disease, type-2 diabetes, and some forms of cancer. Dietary Guidelines for Americans recommends that half of all carbohydrates in the diet come from whole grain products.

Gluten sensitivity is classified as intolerance, not an allergy.

Gluten does not make you fat and cutting gluten will not help you lose weight. Gluten-free does not mean fat-free or calorie-free. "Gluten does not make you fat," according to the Cleveland Clinic. "Calories make you fat regardless of where those calories are coming from, whether they are coming from brown rice, which is gluten-free or a wheat bagel." If you eat more calories in a day than you use, the extra calories will be stored as fat.

Some gluten-free foods contain extra sugar and/or calories to make them more palatable and make up for the loss of the gluten.

You can eat a clean diet that includes gluten or a clean diet that does not.

> French fries are gluten-free and vegetarian.

There is nothing unhealthy about gluten. Gluten alone doesn't have many health benefits, but foods that contain gluten, like whole grains, tend to be higher in fiber and contain vitamin B, zinc, and iron. As a result, cutting gluten could actually result in nutritional deficiencies.

Gluten does not cause cancer. The exception is an increased risk of intestinal cancer for only those who have celiac disease, or true gluten intolerance. The Mayo Clinic lists cancer as a complication of celiac disease (not gluten). People with celiac disease who do not maintain a gluten-free diet have a greater risk of developing several forms of cancer, including intestinal lymphoma and small bowel cancer.

Numerous observational studies show that the more whole grains a person eats, including the gluten-containing grains (wheat, rye, barley), the lower risk of most cancers. This is true for some of the most common types of cancer, such as breast, prostate, and colon cancers, as well as for less common cancers, such as cancer of the pancreas. Whole grains contain fiber, which can stabilize blood sugar and hormone level.

Morbidity vs. Mortality - Was listening to radio the other day and the announcer was talking about morbidity and mortality, but was incorrectly mixing them together.

Morbidity refers to the disease state of an individual or the incidence of illness in a population. Morbidity scores or predicted morbidity are assigned to ill patients with the help of systems. Morbidity scores help decide the kind of treatment or medicine that should be given to the patient. Predicted morbidity describes the morbidity of patients, and is also useful when comparing two sets of patients or different time points in hospitals. The general definition of morbidity is the state of being unhealthy or diseased.

Mortality refers to the state of being mortal, or the number of deaths in a population. If you refer to the infant mortality rate, you would be referring to the mathematical equation of dividing the number of infant deaths by the number of live births.

Definition Morbidity refers to the state of being diseased or unhealthy within a population.

Mortality is the term used for the number of people who died within a population and incidence of death or the number of deaths in a population.

Caffeine - After as little as 10 minutes, the caffeine concentration in your blood reaches half the maximum concentration, which is enough to have an effect. The caffeine reaches maximum levels, making you most alert after 45 minutes. Depending on how fast or slow your body is able to break down the drug, you could feel the effects of caffeine for 3 to 5 hours.

Coffee contains hundreds of different compounds. These include many antioxidants that protect our bodies from damaging chemicals called free radicals. These molecules cause aging and are associated with illnesses such as cancer and heart disease. NIH studies show that coffee drinkers have a reduced risk of Alzheimer's, Parkinson's, type 2 diabetes and many other diseases.

Calcium Facts - Calcium is essential for human, plant, and animal nutrition. Animals skeletons get their rigidity primarily from calcium phosphate. The eggs of birds and shells of mollusks are comprised of calcium carbonate. Calcium is used as a reducing agent when preparing metals from their compounds; as a reagent in purification of inert gases; to fix atmospheric nitrogen; as a scavenger and decarbonizer in metallurgy; and for making alloys. Calcium compounds are used in making lime, bricks, cement, cheese, glass, paint, paper, sugar, glazes, as well as many others, including fireworks.

Calcium is not found free in nature, but it can be purified into a soft silvery-white alkaline earth metal. Though calcium has been known for thousands of years, it was not purified as an element until 1808 by Sir Humphrey Davy from England.

The element name 'calcium' comes from the Latin word 'calcis' meaning 'lime'. It is the fifth most abundant element in the Earth's crust at a level of about 3% in the oceans and soil.

Vitamin D is essential for calcium absorption by the human body. It is converted to a hormone which causes intestinal proteins responsible for calcium absorption to be produced.

Calcium is the main component of teeth and bones. Approximately one third of the mass of the human body is calcium after all water is removed.

The top three countries that produce calcium are China, United States, and India.

Sports Drinks - A study found that sports drinks work because they activate the pleasure center of your brain. You do not even have to drink them, just swishing some around in your mouth and spitting out has the same effect.

The carbohydrates in the drink stimulate receptors in your mouth that then send your brain messages that things are all great. Your brain then becomes more active in the pleasure center, allowing you to enjoy feeling the burn longer than someone without a sugary drink.

The oldest person in the world was born with a completely different set of humans than now are alive.

Sleep Juice - New research finds drinking tart cherry juice twice a day can help you sleep almost 90 more minutes a night. Cherry juice is a natural source of the sleep-wake cycle hormone melatonin and amino acid tryptophan.

The ruby red pigments in tart cherry juice, contain an enzyme that reduces inflammation and decreases the breakdown of tryptophan.

Researchers had seven older adults with insomnia drink eight ounces of Montmorency tart cherry juice twice a day for two weeks, followed by two weeks of no juice, and then two more weeks of drinking a placebo beverage. Compared to the placebo, drinking the cherry juice resulted in an average of 84 more minutes of sleep time each night.

Another thing you might try is kiwi. Eating two kiwi fruits an hour before bed was shown to increase sleep time by 13% and decrease mid-sleep waking periods by 29% after just four weeks. *Zzzzzz*

Embalming Facts - This was something of a surprise to me. No state requires routine embalming and some do not require it at all. It is also not required for cremation if it is performed immediately. Some states require embalming for remains that are to be shipped out of state. Embalming provides no public health benefit, according to the US Centers for Disease Control and Canadian health authorities. Hawaii and Ontario forbid embalming if the person died of certain contagious diseases.

Modern embalming consists primarily of washing with a germicide-insecticide-olfactant. Removing all blood and gases from the body and the insertion of a disinfecting fluid. Funeral home effluent is not regulated, and waste is flushed into the common sewer system or septic tank. Embalming does not preserve the body for any great length of time. It also serves no useful purpose in preventing the transmission of communicable disease. Refrigeration is just as effective as embalming for short periods of time, such as for viewing.

Next time you feel some pain, such as a shot from the doctor, or paper cut, or a prick from a plant thorn, force a rough cough or a few coughs. Coughing has been shown to moderate the feeling of pain.

The US Federal Trade Commission says, "Except in certain special cases, embalming is not required by law. Embalming may be necessary, however, if you select certain funeral arrangements, such as a funeral with viewing. If you do not want embalming, you usually have the right to choose an arrangement that does not require you to pay for it, such as direct cremation or immediate burial." Refrigeration is an alternative to maintain a body while awaiting a funeral service or when there is a delay in making arrangements.

Charges for embalming, dressing, and cosmetology can be covered under one charge and can vary from $500 to $1500, or more. Sheltering and refrigeration of a body for up to 3 days can vary from no charge to a few hundred dollars.

High Tech / Low Tech - An inexpensive diagnostic test made from paper has been developed that can assess liver health in 15 minutes and costs pennies. The test uses a single drop of blood from a finger prick to measure the presence of liver enzymes, and does not require a laboratory, instruments, or syringes.

If liver enzymes are present in the blood, wells within the paper will show a color change, which are be color matched to a scale to determine approximate degree of concentration. A color change indicates the concentration range of enzymes present. Though this can be checked by eye, greater accuracy could be achieved by scanning the paper with a smartphone.

Liver damage can be a consequence of taking antiretroviral drugs, which are prescribed to HIV patients. Because of the high HIV infection rates in poor countries, liver problems are on the rise, so the ability to cheaply monitor blood is important to prevent potentially fatal side effects of the drugs meant to save people's lives.

> Of all the people in history that have reached age 65, half are still living.

The paper uses patterns, channels, and assay zones (or wells) of water-repellent materials on a piece of paper about the size of a postage stamp. Biological and chemical assay reagents are then deposited in the wells. When blood, urine, saliva, sweat or other biological samples are applied to it, the paper wicks the sample through the channels to the assay zones, without external pumps or power. After use, it can be disposed of by burning.

These patterned paper-based devices can be embedded with electrical circuitry to enable resistive heating, electrochemical assays, or initial processing of assay results. Multiple sheets of patterned paper can be stacked to generate three-dimensional devices capable of automatically performing a variety of complex fluid operations such as splitting, filtration, mixing, and separations.

The postage stamp-sized paper diagnostics system was developed in the laboratory of Harvard Professor George Whitesides. With funding from the Bill and Melinda Gates Foundation, Professor Whitesides started the non-profit organization, Diagnostics For All, and looked to improve the health of the poorest areas of the world. The team is also working on malaria and dengue fever tests.

An ink jet printer using wax ink prints a pattern on two sheets of paper. One sheet contains reagents that react with liver enzymes, the other dyes that change color if a reaction occurs. The two sheets are fused together by heating, so that channels or wells that can be used as miniaturized test tubes for reactions are produced. A plasma filter is added and the three are laminated together, and cut into postage stamp size squares. *The rest of the world could also benefit from this low cost efficient healthcare.*

Loneliness vs. Being Alone - Being lonely increases the risk of everything from heart attacks to dementia, depression and death. People who are satisfied with their social lives sleep better, age more slowly, and respond better to vaccines. Those who have rich social lives and warm relationships do not get as sick and they live longer. A person can be lonely in a crowd or be alone and not be lonely.

Research shows, our bodies have evolved so that in situations of perceived social isolation, they trigger branches of the immune system involved in wound healing and bacterial infection. Differences relate most strongly to how lonely people think they are. Ending loneliness is not about spending more time with people, but about our attitude to others. Changing this attitude reduces loneliness more effectively than giving people more opportunities for interaction.

Meditation is typically done while a person is alone and there is evidence that meditation boosts the immune response in vaccine recipients and people with cancer, protects against a relapse in major depression, soothes skin conditions, and even slows the progression of HIV. As with social interaction, meditation works largely by influencing stress response pathways. People who meditate have lower cortisol levels.

Loneliness is more of an attitude than a state of physical being.

In a study of fifty people with advanced lung cancer, those judged by their doctors to have high spiritual faith responded better to chemotherapy and survived longer. More than forty percent were still alive after three years, compared with less than ten percent of those judged to have little faith.

Some think that what matters is having a sense of purpose in life. Having an idea of why you are here and what is important increases your sense of control over events. Spending more time doing what you love, whether it is gardening or volunteer work has a similar effect on health. *Bottom line, loneliness is more of an attitude than a state of physical being. You have the power to be happy, alone or with others.*

Attitude Changers - Here are some ideas to perk up your attitude.

Asking people to list three things they are grateful for in life or three events that have gone well during the past week can significantly increase their level of happiness for about a month.

People become much happier after the smallest acts of kindness.

Adding plants to an office results in a fifteen percent boost in the number of creative ideas and helps produce more original solutions to problems.

Lightly touching someone on their upper arm makes them far more likely to agree to a request. In one study, the touch produced a twenty percent increase in the number of people who accepted an invitation to dance in a nightclub and a ten percent increase in those who would give their telephone number to a stranger on the street.

Praising a child's effort rather than their ability encourages them to try.

Visualizing taking steps required to achieve a goal is more effective than dreaming about the goal.

Alzheimer's vs. Dementia - Both Alzheimer's and dementia are associated with a loss of memory, but there is a difference. Alzheimer's refers to a physical change in the makeup of the brain, which causes dementia as one of its major symptoms. Dementia can be a symptom of other diseases as well.

Dementia is one of the major symptoms of and the final stage in the progression of Alzheimer's (an age-related disease that is characterized by symptoms other than just memory loss, as well as by a physical change in brain tissue). When a person suffers from the symptom of dementia, it means that they are afflicted by memory loss and an overall decline in their ability to process information. In order to be diagnosed with dementia, a person must demonstrate impaired abilities in two of the following areas: memory, ability to focus, reasoning and judgment, visual perception, and communication.

Dementia is diagnosed when the symptoms get so bad they interfere with a person's ability to function on a daily basis. Forgetfulness and memory loss is a normal part of aging, but dementia is defined as severe instances of those.

Common causes for dementia can include vitamin deficiencies or problems in other parts of the body, such as the thyroid. Some medications can cause dementia as one of their side effects, and excessive use of alcohol can also lead to dementia. It generally starts out mild and progresses slowly over years. In some cases it can be treated and reversed.

Alzheimer's can be one of the causes of dementia. It describes a physical condition in which there is a change in the tissue of the brain, including the formation of structures called amyloid plaques and neurofibrillary tangles. They are blockages in the brain that prevent the transmission of signals. The loss of signals between the brain's neurons results in dementia, among other symptoms.

In addition to dementia, those who suffer from Alzheimer's often show other signs of cognitive difficulty. This can include a loss of depth and spatial perception, abnormal sleep patterns, and an inability to visualize and understand abstract concepts, such as numbers. There is often a change in personality, as well, and a person can become angry, restless, or paranoid. Those afflicted with the disease often have trouble following directions or fulfilling requests, and may also lack the motivation to do so. This lack of motivation can extend to all areas of life, from getting up in the morning to interacting with other people.

Alzheimer's also worsens over time, and three distinct stages have been identified. The first is a stage where there are no symptoms, but the disease it starting to develop in the brain. In the second, symptoms begin to manifest themselves and the person suffers from mild, but not complete cognitive impairment. In the third stage, symptoms progress to full-blown dementia.

Currently, there are no cures or preventative methods for Alzheimer's, and those who are diagnosed with it will eventually need around-the-clock, complete care. What triggers the development of Alzheimer's is unknown, although many doctors point to an all-around healthy lifestyle as the best way to keep brain function at healthy levels, regardless of age. *Bottom line, Alzheimer's and other diseases can cause dementia, while dementia can be a symptom of Alzheimer's.*

Cat Scan Origin - The Beatles were indirectly responsible for funding the development of the CT scanner. Their record label, EMI, also operated a computer research facility that once employed Godfrey Hounsfield, who had been developing X-ray computerized tomography (CT) in the late '60s. Researchers and radiologists claim that EMI invested the profits they earned from the Beatles' music into Hounsfield's technology, allowing for the invention of a commercial CT scanner (then known as an EMI scanner) by the early 1970s.

Phytonutrients - A buzzword we hear in many commercials these days is phytonutrients. They are also called phytochemicals, chemicals produced by plants.

Plants use phytonutrients to stay healthy, protect from insect attacks, and protect against radiation from UV rays. There are more than 25,000 types of phytonutrients.

Phytonutrients affect human health, but are not considered nutrients that are essential for life, like carbohydrates, protein, fats, vitamins, and minerals. They can provide significant benefits for humans who eat plant foods. Phytonutrient-rich foods include colorful fruits and vegetables, legumes, nuts, tea, whole grains and many spices.

Among the benefits of phytonutrients are antioxidant and anti-inflammatory activities, enhanced immunity and intercellular communication, repair DNA damage from exposure to toxins, detoxify carcinogens and alter estrogen metabolism.

Many phytonutrients give plants their pigments, so a good way to tell if a fruit or vegetable is rich in phytonutrients can be by its color. Look for a deep-hue like berries, dark greens, melons, and spices. These foods are usually rich in flavor and aroma. However, some phytonutrient-rich foods have little color, like onions and garlic.

Resveratrol has generated much buzz, because large concentrations of it are found in red wine. The best-known source of resveratrol is grapes, with a high concentration in grape skin. It is also found in peanuts, grape juice, cocoa, blueberries, and cranberries. Resveratrol has been shown to reduce the risk of heart disease through antioxidant and anti-inflammatory activities.

Overweight Redefined - During 1998, twenty nine million Americans suddenly became overweight without gaining an ounce. The US government announced new guidelines lowering the threshold of what classifies a person as overweight.

Previously, if your body mass index (BMI) was less than 28 for men or 27 for women, you were considered 'normal'. Since then only BMIs of 25 or below are considered healthy. That was a reduction of about 20 pounds for the average male. *BMI is a ratio of weight to height, and is considered an indicator of how much body fat a person has.*

Compulsion, Obsession, Anal, and OCD - The holidays are the time many people meticulously clean the house and fastidiously prepare large tasty meals. Both of these activities can seem obsessive or compulsive, but neither is considered medically significant. However, for some these obsessions and compulsions last all year.

Anal-retentive (anal) is used to describe a person who pays such attention to detail that the obsession becomes an annoyance to others, and potentially to the detriment of the anal-retentive person. Traits include orderliness, stubbornness, a compulsion for control, as well as a generalized interest in collecting, possessing, and retaining objects. Those who are anal can take pleasure in organizing and re-organizing, in keeping things neat and in their proper place.

Obsessive–compulsive disorder (OCD) people can have obsessions, compulsions, or both. OCD is a mental illness. Usually the person has a feeling that they are staving off unspecified doom, such as "Something terrible will happen if I do not wash my hands exactly seven times and tap my toes in rhythm." The acts of those who have OCD may appear paranoid and potentially psychotic. However, people with OCD generally recognize their obsessions and compulsions as irrational and may become further distressed by this realization. Those who have OCD suffer extreme distress from a disruption in their routine.

Obsessions are intrusive thoughts that produce fear, worry, uneasiness, or apprehension. If the obsession is with a certain activity, performing it, or thinking about performing it later does not relieve the stress, pressure, or obsession. We all have things that distract us from our daily routines, but those with true obsessions try to make them go away with no success.

Compulsions are repetitive behaviors that a person must perform, such as checking to make sure the front door is locked, organizing items in groups of arbitrary size, or keeping things in a specific order or position. Compulsions are aimed at reducing the associated anxiety. Most often these rituals become not just a part of daily life, but the person feels that they must repeat them every day in order to keep something horrible from happening.

Bottom line - If you must get things done perfectly and meticulous, you might be anal, but if you must get things done perfectly and meticulous or you will be continuously and seriously agitated and upset, you could have OCD.

XPRIZE Blood Test Prize - On November 10, 2014, the XPRIZE Foundation announced the winner of the Nokia Sensing XCHALLENGE, the global competition aimed at accelerating the availability of hardware sensors and software sensing technology as a means to smarter digital health solutions.

The winning device, called the Reusable Handheld Electrolyte and Lab Technology for Humans (rHEALTH) system, can potentially run hundreds or even thousands of lab tests using a single drop of blood, and those tests, in turn, can be used to diagnose a range of diseases.

Along with a number of distinguished awards, the $525,000 grand prize was presented to Eugene Chan, founder and CEO of the device's maker, DNA Medicine Institute (DMI), at Singularity University's Exponential Medicine conference.

The rHEALTH system reacts to a sample of blood, about 1,500 times less than is usually required, with a series of nanostrips. These strips are a bit like pH test strips, but they are on the scale of blood cells. The system reacts to the blood sample with tens of thousands of nanostrips, each running a different test, then shines a laser on them in rapid succession. The whole process yields results in about two minutes and currently runs about 22 lab tests, ranging from vitamin D to HIV.

Size Matters - An easy way to keep things in perspective.

Flea	1 million nanometers
Human hair	80,000 nanometers
Red blood cell	7,000 nanometers
Virus	100 nanometers
Intel processor	14 nanometers
Strand of DNA	2.5 nanometers

Cholesterol and Salt Update - Hooray, bring on the bacon and eggs! Two recent reports are shaking up the food industry. Salt has recently been vindicated by scientists. "Cardiovascular disease, heart failure, or death in older Americans are not linked to salt intake", according to research published in JAMA Internal Medicine on January 19, 2015. This follows the previous year's Institute of Medicine report, which also raised questions about sodium recommendations. The IOM committee found that there was no clear evidence to support limiting sodium to 1,500 milligrams or less per day.

The New England Journal of Medicine published a study which reported that people who consume less 1,500 milligrams of sodium are more likely to die than people who eat between 3,000 to 6,000 milligrams of sodium per day.

Now the new report says, cholesterol is no longer a "nutrient of concern," according to the US leading nutritional panel in February 2015.

In its 2015 version of the guidelines from the US Department of Agriculture, it will no longer place an upper limit on cholesterol, "because available evidence shows no appreciable relationship between consumption of dietary cholesterol and serum cholesterol."

The draft report said, "Cholesterol is not a nutrient of concern for over consumption." The recommended changes were compiled by 14 nationally recognized nutrition, medicine, and public health experts. *It makes Dr. Adkins appear absolutely prescient.*

Health experts agreed it is no longer necessary to consider a food's cholesterol content when making dietary decisions. The committee's new report also advised eliminating 'lean meat' as well as 'cutting back on red and processed meats' from the list of recommended healthy foods. The panel also said it OK to have three to five cups of coffee per day.

The science connecting high-cholesterol foods to the accumulation of bad cholesterol in the blood is lacking - not conclusive enough to warrant federal intake recommendations. Even the predictive value of bad cholesterol levels in looking at heart attack risk has shown to be weak by recent studies.

The new enemy is increased carbohydrates, according the current analysis of government data. It says that, "Over the past 50 years, we cut fat intake by 25 percent and increased carbohydrates by more than 30 percent." That is what has led to the increase in obesity.

Other countries that offer dietary guidelines have long abandoned specific caps on cholesterol. According to David Klurfeld, a nutritional scientist at the USDA, "The US is the last country in the world to set a specific limit on dietary cholesterol." Finally science begins to trump headlines. *Many of my friends know I have been a Cassandra of cholesterol for years. I wonder how long it will take for 'artery clogging' to be banished from the lexicon.*

Beer Benefits and Sexual Performance - Moderate beer drinking decreases risk of heart disease by 31 percent (the same as wine). A study published in the Clinical Journal of the American Society of Nephrology also found that moderate consumption of beer reduces the risk of developing kidney stones by 41 percent, and is one of the few plant sources of vitamin B12.

The phytoestrogens in beer can help delay premature ejaculation.

Dark brews can help get you in the mood better, because they increase both red blood cells and overall circulation. Dark contains more iron than pale beers.

Beer increases stamina and is good for heart health.

Guinness is great for stomach issues, low in calories and alcohol content, and is rich in vitamins, minerals, and probiotics. It contains only 128 calories and 11 grams of carbohydrates per serving.

50 Shades of Green beer is like green juice and Viagra combined. It is specifically engineered to enhance performance. It contains ginseng, ginkgo biloba, and damiana to achieve increased sexual desire, blood flow, and nerve stimulation. *Gives a whole new meaning to 'Bottoms up!'*

Cancer and Chemotherapy Facts - Not usually a positive topic, but it is nice to get a few facts and dispel some myths.

There are over 200 different types of cancers and 200 different types of cells in the human body with all of these having the potential to become cancerous. All types of cancer are a result of unregulated cell growth. The result is excessive tissue, known as tumors. These tumors can be localized, or they can spread to surrounding areas through your lymphatic system or your blood stream.

Normal healthy cells divide and die as they should. The average number of times normal healthy cells divide is known as the Hayflick Limit. It was named after Dr. Leonard Hayflick, who in 1965 noticed that cells divide a specific number of times before the division stops. The average was between 40-60. If you took every cell in your body, at the time you were born, and accounted for all the cells they would produce and so on, multiplied that number by the average time it takes for those cells to die, you get what is known as the ultimate Hayflick limit, or the maximum number of years you can theoretically live, 120 years.

Chemotherapy, by definition is "a chemical that binds to and specifically kills microbes or tumor cells." It is a drug treatment that uses powerful chemicals to kill fast-growing cells in your body. It is usually systemic treatment, meaning that the drugs flow through the bloodstream to nearly every part of the body. Chemotherapy is generally given in cycles: a treatment period is followed by a recovery period, then another treatment period, etc.

It is most often used to treat cancer, since cancer cells grow and multiply much more quickly than most cells in the body. Many different chemotherapy drugs are available and can be used alone or in combination. Chemotherapy treatments carry risks of side effects, some mild and treatable and others which can cause serious complications.

Most chemotherapy cannot differentiate between abnormal cancer cells and normal healthy cells. Because of this, cells that multiply rapidly can also be affected by chemotherapy. Not all chemo drugs will make you lose your hair. Some people have mild thinning that only they notice and some show no loss. Hair loss includes eyelashes, eyebrows, under arms, legs, and even pubic hair. Whether you lose hair depends upon the medication, dosage, combinations, and individual sensitivity. Hair loss happens because the chemotherapy affects all cells in the body, not just the cancer cells. The lining of the mouth, digestive tract (that is why many have nausea and vomiting as side effects), stomach, bone marrow, and the hair follicles are especially sensitive because those cells multiply rapidly just like the cancer cells.

Chemotherapy can also decrease in production of white blood cells (causing immune-suppression), and inflammation of the digestive tract. Other areas that can be affected include, kidneys, liver, heart, and lungs. *Many healthy cells repair themselves during or shortly after therapy.*

Genetics vs. Genomics - The words genetic and genomic are often used interchangeably. However, they have different and specific meanings.

It is the study of how inherited traits are passed from one generation to the next through the genes, and how new traits appear by way of genetic mutations or changes. These traits may be characteristics like eye or hair color.

Genomics is a more recent term that describes the study of all of a person's genes (the genome). Genomics is defined as the study of genes and their functions, and related techniques.

The main difference between genomics and genetics is that genetics looks at the functioning and composition of a single gene and genomics addresses all genes and their inter-relationships in order to identify their combined influence on the growth and development of an organism, such as a person.

Genetic information is stored in the molecule DNA. Gene refers to a specific sequence of DNA on a single chromosome that encodes a particular product. Humans have many thousands of genes, spaced across the entire set of DNA.

The word genome encompasses the entire set of genetic information across all 23 chromosome pairs, including all genes, as well as gene-modifying sequences, and everything in-between.

In the context of clinical and research settings, "genetic" testing refers to the examination of specific bits of DNA that have a known function.

Genomic testing looks for variations within large segments across the entirety of genetic material, both within and outside known functional genes. It looks at groups of genes and how active they are, such as how a cancer is likely to grow and respond to treatment.

> Genetics is the study of heredity.
>
> Genomics is the study of genes and their functions.

All the genes make up the genome. Both are important because understanding more about diseases caused by a single gene using genetics and complex diseases caused by multiple genes and environmental factors using genomics can lead to earlier diagnoses, interventions, and targeted treatments.

Condom Facts - For most of their history, condoms have been used both as a method of birth control, and as a protective measure against sexually transmitted diseases. Condoms have been made from a variety of materials. Prior to the 19th century, chemically treated linen and animal intestine or bladder were used.

The oldest condoms excavated were found in a cesspit located in the grounds of Dudley Castle and were made from animal membrane, the condoms dated back to as early as 1640s. Condoms during the Renaissance were made out of intestines and bladder. Cleaned and prepared intestine for use in glove making had been sold commercially since at least the 13th century.

The story of the Earl of Condom, a knighted personal physician to England's King Charles II in the mid-1600's, who was requested to produce a method to protect the King from syphilis is completely false.

Mind Control - Our minds are so powerful, that we can actually heal ourselves through the power of thought. The difficulty is that sometimes we need to be tricked into it. We need a reason to believe we have the power. The placebo effect gives us a reason and has been well documented.

In a recent study, researchers found a patient's perception or expectation of a drug based on how much it costs, significantly affects the drug's efficacy. The medical team gave a group of volunteers with Parkinson's disease two shots of a placebo drug for the disease and participants were not told it was a simple saline solution. Doctors told the patients they were receiving two drugs, one shot and then the second after the first wore off. Prior to administering the shots, doctors told the participants each drug had proven equally effective, but one cost $100 per dose and the other cost $1,500 per dose. Both doses were the exact same saline solution.

Results showed the 'expensive' placebo minimized hand shaking and improved motor skills among the Parkinson's disease patients more effectively than did the 'cheap' placebo. Researchers also found the difference in efficacy was most pronounced among patients who admitted to expecting an improved result from the expensive version of the drug. The study was recently published in the journal Neurology. *I think I can. I think I can...*

Placebo Affect - Ted Kaptchuk's first randomized clinical drug trial, All the patients had joined the study hoping to alleviate severe arm pain: carpal tunnel, tendinitis, chronic pain in the elbow, shoulder, and wrist.

In one part of the study, half the subjects received pain-reducing pills; the others were offered acupuncture treatments. The pills his team had given patients were actually made of cornstarch; the acupuncture needles were retractable shams that never pierced the skin. The study was designed to compare two fakes.

In both cases, people began to call in, saying they could not get out of bed. The pills were making them sluggish, the needles caused swelling and redness; some patients' pain ballooned to nightmarish levels. Almost a third of his 270 subjects complained of bad side effects. The side effects were exactly what patients had been warned their treatment might produce. Most of the other patients reported real relief, and those who received acupuncture felt even better than those on the anti-pain pill.

In-Vitro vs. In-Vivo - We hear these terms in the medical context, but they can be confusing. In vivo, (within the living) means within the body and in vitro, (within the glass) means outside of the body, such a test tube.

Daylight Saving and Heart Attacks - A team of Swedish researchers conducted a study in 2008 that showed the rate of heart attacks during the first three weekdays following springtime daylight saving time increased by about 5 percent from the average rate during other times of the year. The effect did not arise at the end of daylight saving time in the fall.

The researchers attributed the small surge in heart attacks in the springtime to changes in people's sleep patterns. Lack of sleep can release stress hormones that increase inflammation, which can cause more severe complications in people already at risk of having a heart attack.

The 2009 Journal of Applied Psychology study found that mine workers arrived at work with 40 minutes less sleep and experienced 5.7 percent more workplace injuries in the week directly following the springtime daylight saving transition than during any other days of the year. The researchers attribute the injuries to lack of sleep.

A 2012 Journal of Applied Psychology study found that the incidence of cyberloafing significantly increased in more than 200 metropolitan US regions during the first Monday after daylight saving time in the spring, compared with the Mondays directly before and one week after the transition. The team attributed the shift to a lack of sleep, thus lack of workday motivation and focus.

Doctor Codes - "Doctor" codes are often used in hospital settings for announcements over a general loudspeaker or paging system to avoid panic or endanger a patient's privacy. Most often, "Doctor" codes take the form of "Paging Dr. _____", where the doctor's name is a codeword for a dangerous situation or a patient in crisis. These are used in the same way as code blue, code red, etc., are used.

Doctor Brown: To alert security staff of a threat to personnel. If a nurse or doctor is in danger from a violent patient or non-staff member, they can page Doctor Brown to their location and the security staff will rush to their aid.

Dr. Allcome: Serious emergency. "Doctor Allcome to Ward 5." indicates all medical staff not presently occupied are needed.

Dr. Firestone: Fire in the hospital. If a fire's location can be isolated, the location of the fire is included in the page, e.g. "Paging Dr.

Firestone to 3 West" indicates "Fire in or near west wing on third floor" (William Beaumont Hospitals, MI).

Dr. Pyro: Fire in the hospital. "Paging Dr. Pyro" indicates a fire and its origin or current location, e.g. "Paging Dr. Pyro on 3" means "Fire on third floor" (Kaiser Permanente, system-wide).

Dr. Strong: Patient needs physical assistance or physical restraint. "Paging Dr. Strong ..." indicates that any physically capable personnel (orderlies, police, security officers, etc.) in the proximity should report and be prepared either to move a patient who fell down and cannot get back up or to capture and restrain an uncooperative patient.

Essential Oils

An essential oil is a concentrated liquid containing volatile aroma compounds from plants. Essential oils are also known as volatile oils, or ethereal oils. An oil is 'essential' in the sense that it carries a distinctive scent, or essence, of the plant. Essential oils do not form a distinctive category for any medical, pharmacological, or culinary purpose. They are not essential for health.

Sage is best for blood-pressure reduction. In a 2013 study, women who smelled clary sage experienced reduced blood pressure and breathing rates. They were also able to relax during a stressful medical exam. Sage also increases memory and attention

Peppermint is best for stress relief. Research shows that breathing in eau de peppermint can decrease the body's levels of cortisol, a stress hormone. It also reduces fatigue.

Orange is best for decreasing anxiety. A study found that people who sniffed it before a stressful test were able to stay calm under pressure without anxiety spikes.

Rosemary is best for enhancing brainpower. Breathing it in can improve speed and accuracy during demanding mental tasks, per a 2012 study. Other research found its scent left people feeling refreshed and mentally stimulated. It also has been known to reduce fatigue.

Cinnamon is best for improving focus. It may stoke the area of the brain that governs alertness. Research found that drivers were more focused after breathing in cinnamon-oil scents.

Lavender increases relaxation and relieves some symptoms of PMS. A 2013 study found that it also eases pre-period symptoms such as mental confusion and depression. It also reduces some migraine pain.

Olive Oil may help you lose weight, according to a recent study in the American Journal of Nutrition. It says the scent of olive oil might help you feel more full.

A diffuser is the most effective way to unleash essential oils into the air, but you can add one or two drops of oil into a bowl of steaming hot water. Another option is to place one drop of oil on a cotton ball, put it under your nose, and inhale normally for one to two minutes.

Essential oils should never be used for more than one hour at a time. Look for 100 percent pure and organic oils free of fillers, pesticides, and synthetic chemicals.

Fourteen Uses for Aloe Vera

A friend recently dropped off some Aloe Vera for the garden. I knew it had some great medicinal properties, but found more information on the web. Also found it survives the winter in Texas. It is antibacterial and contains vitamins and minerals. Here are a few topical and other uses.

1. Slice aloe leaves lengthwise and use the inner sides as a biodegradable body scrub in the shower.
2. Rub on to treat burns from grease splatters or hot utensils.
3. Rub on to reduce sunburn sting.
4. Rub on to eliminate sting or itch from insect bites and allergic skin reactions.
5. Rub on to fight Athlete's Foot.
6. Rub on as moisturizer for dry skin, remove makeup, or for shaving.
7. Soothe Psoriasis, Rosacea, Eczema, blisters, bruises, and rashes.
8. Prevent scarring and stretch marks.
9. Reduce facial wrinkles.
10. After washing, apply to eliminate acne.
11. Decrease skin pigmentation and dark spots.
12. Drink to relieve indigestion, but too much can cause diarrhea.
13. Take aloe orally to relieve heartburn, arthritis, and rheumatism pain.

14. Boil leaves in a pan of water and breathe in the vapor to reduce affects of asthma.

Six More Home Remedies

Feeding a cold, even when you are overfeeding it vitamin C supplements, is not supported by science. However there are many other home remedies that have been proven to work.

1. In three separate studies since 2001, scientists have directly measured a reduction in acid reflux in subjects who chewed sugar-free gum after a meal that was designed to give them heartburn, versus those who did not. The saliva you secrete when chewing gum has a calming effect on acid reflux.

2. Oats have anti-inflammatory compounds that are effective when applied directly to the skin and can be applied as oatmeal or adding ground oats to a bath. Good for treating poison ivy, irritated skin, or itching due to eczema.

3. One way to reduce sunburn pain is cucumber. Use a food processor to turn it into paste, apply it to sunburned skin and leave it on until it dries.

4. In a small study published in the American Journal of Physiology, researchers induced nausea by spinning subjects in a large drum after a heavy meal. Ginger helped ease the nausea of the subjects. Try drinking ginger ale, eating a ginger candy, or dissolving a teaspoon of ginger powder in a cup of water or tea.

5. According to research in the Journal of Family Practice, nasal irrigation with a saltwater solution relieved the symptoms of sinus congestion and improved sinus-related quality of life. Add half a teaspoon of salt for every eight ounces of warm water. Use a neti pot or a squeeze bottle to pour the solution into your nostrils while leaning over a sink to catch the drainage.

6. Apple cider vinegar is an antibiotic and can be used to treat fungus. Soak toes or fingers in apple cider vinegar for twenty minutes twice a day until symptoms go away. It is also good to combat acne as it kills bacteria on skin and shrinks blood vessels around the acne. Soak a cotton ball with apple cider vinegar, and apply it to affected skin after washing.

HAPPY FACTS

Laughter Studies- We all know laughing is good for you, and now, here are some studies that prove it. A 2013 review of studies found that among elderly patients, laughter significantly alleviated the symptoms of depression. Another recently published study found that firefighters who used humor as a coping strategy were somewhat protected from PTSD. Laughing also seems to ease more-quotidian anxieties. One group of researchers found that watching an episode of Friends was as effective at improving a person's mood as listening to music or exercising, and more effective than resting.

Laughter even seems to have a buffering effect against physical pain. A 2012 study found that subjects who were shown a funny video displayed higher pain thresholds than those who saw a serious documentary. In another study, postsurgical patients requested less pain medication after watching a funny movie.

Other literature identifies even more specific health benefits: laughing reduced arterial-wall stiffness, which is associated with cardiovascular disease. Women undergoing in-vitro fertilization were sixteen percent more likely to get pregnant when entertained by a clown.

A clown also improved lung function in patients with chronic obstructive pulmonary disease. A study of Norwegians found that having a sense of humor correlated with a high probability of surviving into retirement. *Not new news, but always good to get positive reinforcement.*

Laughing Buddha - The Laughing Buddha also Happy Hotei is the nickname for Budai or Pu-Tai, which means "Cloth Sack". Budai was a real zen monk who lived in China during the 10th century, and he has always been portrayed as a smiling or laughing fat man. Though he is called the Laughing Buddha, do not confuse him with Gautama Buddha, the sage on whose teachings Buddhism was founded.

Budai or Hotei (in Japanese) is one of the seven lucky gods in Japan, and you can find statues of him in many shrines and temples just like in China and other East Asian countries.

Global Belly Laugh Day - Today is Global Belly Laugh Day. Laughter causes the tissue lining our blood vessels to expand and increase blood flow. This makes us feel more positive, boosts our immune systems, increases pain tolerance and makes us feel good. It is appropriate to be celebrated this time of year as Victor Hugo said, " Laughter is the sun that drives winter from the human face."

Send out an email, put up posters, and tell everyone you meet to laugh out loud. Share your laughs with others. Look through old photos of you, family, and friends wearing crazy outfits and send them with good wishes. On your way to work, laugh out loud at every stop light and look around at how many people you can make smile. Ask your work friends to try it on the way home and report back next Monday. This will extend the holiday into next week. Text a picture of you laughing to everyone on your contact list and ask them to do the same. When no one is around, draw a smiley face on any blackboard or whiteboard at work with the words Global Belly Laugh Day.

It is OK to laugh in private, but much better to share. That is why today is not just a local or national holiday, it is a global holiday. Laughter knows no language, age, ethnicity, etc., barriers and can be shared with all.

Today is the day to take the Laughing Oath and paste a copy on your bathroom mirror to remind you every day.

> "I do solemnly swear from this day forward
> To grease my giggling gears each day
> And to wear a grin on my face for no reason at all!
> I promise to tap my funny bone often,
> With children, family, friends, colleagues and clients,
> And to laugh at least fifteen times per day.
>
> I believe that frequent belly laughter
> Cures terminal tightness, cerebral stiffness,
> And hardening of the attitudes,
> And that HA HA often leads to AHA!
> Therefore, I vow, from this day forth,
> To brighten the day of everyone I meet,
> And to laugh long and prosper."
> ~ *The Laughing Classroom, by Diana Loomans and Karen Kolberg*

F is for Fried Chicken - This has been around for a while, but still makes me laugh, so I felt compelled to share.

Our teacher asked what is my favorite animal and I said, "Fried chicken". She told me I am not funny, but she could not have been right because everyone else laughed. My parents told me to always tell the truth. I did. Fried chicken is my favorite animal. I told my dad what happened, and he said my teacher is probably a member of PETA. He said they love animals very much. I do too, especially chicken. Anyway, my teacher sent me to the principal's office. I told him what happened and he laughed too. Then he told me not to do it again.

The next day in class, my teacher asked me what is my favorite live animal. I told her it is chicken. She asked me why, so I told her it is because you can make them into fried chicken. She sent me back to the principal's office. He laughed and told me not to do it again. I don't understand. My parents taught me to be honest, but my teacher does not like it when I am.

Today, my teacher asked me to tell her what famous person I admired most. I told her, "Colonel Sanders". Guess where I am now?

Greatest Clown In History - Britain's Joseph Grimaldi has been known as the "greatest clown in history". Joseph Grimaldi (18 December 1778 – 31 May 1837), is the most celebrated of English clowns. Grimaldi's performances made the 'Joey Clown' character the central character in British harlequinades. He was born in Clare Market, London, the son of an Italian, Signor Joseph 'Iron Legs' Grimaldi, ballet-master at the Drury Lane and Rebecca Brooker, a dancer in the theatre's corps de ballet.

His father died when he was nine, and plunged the family into debt. When less than two years old, he was introduced to the stage at Drury Lane; at the age of three, he began to appear at the Sadler's Wells theatre. As a young man, he fell in love and married the daughter of the principal proprietor of Sadler's Wells. Maria Grimaldi died in childbirth 18 months after their marriage. He found solace in performance, and eventually married again, to Mary Bristow. After he passed away, his burial site and the area around it was later named Joseph Grimaldi Park.

Charles Dickens was invited to edit and improve a clumsily written life of Grimaldi, which had been based on the clown's own notes. The 'Memoirs of Joseph Grimaldi' sold well for Dickens.

Be Positive, Stay Healthy - A recent study analyzed data on 3,199 people, 60 and older, including their attitudes about how much they enjoyed life, problems they had with basic daily functions such as dressing and bathing, and how mobile they were.

About 21 percent were deemed to have a high level of enjoyment about life, 56 percent a medium level and 23 percent a low level of enjoyment. In an eight-year span, problems with day-to-day tasks generally increased and mobility declined. About 4 percent of those most upbeat about life developed two or more new functional impairments, compared with 17 percent of those who enjoyed life the least. People assessed as enjoying life at a medium or low level were about 80 percent more likely than their happier counterparts to have developed mobility and functional problems.

There is growing evidence that optimistic people not only tend to live longer, but may enjoy physical benefits as well. As the song says, "Don't worry. Be Happy!" (Bobby McFerrin with Robin Williams and Bill Irwin)

Power of Smiles - Research from Echnische Universität in Munich Germany shows a 2009 study. Scientists there used fMRI (functional MRI) imaging to measure brain activity in regions of emotional processing in the brain before and after injecting Botox to suppress smiling muscles. The findings showed that facial feedback (such as imitating a smile) actually modifies the neural processing of emotional content in the brain, and concluded that our brain's circuitry of emotion and happiness is activated when we smile.

Smiling stimulates our brain's reward mechanisms in a way that even chocolate, a pleasure inducer, cannot match. In a study conducted in the UK (using an electromagnetic brain scan machine and heart-rate monitor to create "mood-boosting values" for various stimuli), British researchers found that one smile can provide the same level of brain stimulation as up to 2,000 chocolate bars; they also found that smiling can be as stimulating as receiving up to 16,000 Pounds in cash.

And unlike lots of chocolate, lots of smiling can actually make you healthier. Smiling has documented therapeutic effects, and has been associated with: reduced stress hormone levels (like cortisol, adrenaline, and dopamine), increased health and mood enhancing hormone levels (like endorphins), and lowered blood pressure.

Humans intrinsically know that smiling is powerful. This simple act goes a long way toward improving your mood and the mood of those around you, reducing stress, and spreading happiness in a way that is contagious.

Smile whenever you want to look great and competent, improve your marriage, or reduce your stress.

A smile is the least expensive, most thoughtful, and personal gift you can give.

Only the emotionally destitute are too poor to share a smile.

Smile, Be Happy - In one set of studies, depressed participants were invited to take a few minutes once a day to relish something that they usually hurry through, such as eating a meal or taking a shower. When it was over, they were instructed to write down in what ways they had experienced the event differently as well as how that felt compared with the times when they rushed through it.

In another study, healthy students and community members were instructed to savor two pleasurable experiences per day, by reflecting on each for two or three minutes and trying to make the pleasure last as long and as intensely as possible. In all these studies those participants prompted to practice savoring, regularly showed significant increases in happiness and reductions in depression.

Researchers told people to smile and the subjects actually felt happier. More than 26,000 people were randomly assigned to groups and asked to carry out various exercises designed to make them happier. When it came to increasing happiness, those altering their facial expressions came out on top.

Smiles Work - NYU students smiled, on average a little over once a minute when they were with a smiling confederate and averaged only a third of a smile per minute when they were with a confederate who did not smile.

> A smile has a thousand friends, but a frown sleeps alone.

We judge people and objects to be more pleasant when we are smiling in comparison to when we are frowning, so if you want your interviewer to think positively about you, try smiling.

Six Benefits of Laughter - Laughter increases a sense of well being and doctors find that people who have a positive outlook on life tend to fight diseases better than negative people. Laugh a little or laugh a lot, it is all good.

1- Laughing lowers blood pressure, which reduces risk of strokes and heart attacks. 2- It reduces stress hormone levels and cuts the anxiety and stress impacting your body. 3- It tones your abs by expanding and contracting stomach muscles. 4- It improves cardiac health and burns a similar amount of calories per hour as walking at a slow to moderate pace. 5- It boosts T cells to help you fight off sickness. 6- Laughing triggers the release of endorphins, which can help ease chronic pain and make you feel good all over.

Gelotophobia, Gelotophilia, and Katagelasticism - Most people have heard none of these conditions, but they all have to do with laughter. Gelotophobia is a fear of being laughed at, a type of social phobia that makes them feel awkward. Gelotophilia is the joy of being laughed at. Katagelasticism is the joy of laughing at others. None are particularly good to have. *Luckily these are not common, so have a good laugh and enjoy yourself.*

Happiness is Catchy - If you are happy and you know it, thank your friends—and their friends. And while you're at it, their friends' friends. If you are sad, hold the blame. Researchers from Harvard Medical School and the University of California, San Diego have found that "happiness" is not the result solely of a cloistered journey filled with individually tailored self-help techniques. Happiness is also a collective phenomenon that spreads through social networks like an emotional contagion.

In a study that looked at the happiness of nearly 5,000 individuals over a period of twenty years, researchers found that when an individual becomes happy, the network effect can be measured up to three degrees. One person's happiness triggers a chain reaction that benefits not only their friends, but their friends' friends, and their friends' friends' friends. The effect lasts for up to one year.

However, sadness does not spread through social networks as robustly as happiness. Happiness appears to love company more so than misery.

Helpful Happiness Hack - At the end of the day just before you go to bed, write down something good that happened to you, or something that made you happy, or made you smile that day. Put the note where you will find it in the morning as you are getting ready. It also helps if you look in the mirror and smile when you read the note in the morning.

Do this for seven days and you will be at least 20% happier - and it will last for another week, even if you stop doing it.

If you want to stay happy, date the notes and save them. You will be amazed when you go back and look at them, the smallest things keep you happiest the longest.

Ten Different Types of Laughter

Laughter is a social structure, something that connects humans with one another in a profound way. People are about thirty percent more likely to laugh in a social setting that warrants it than when alone with humorous media. In other words, you are more likely to laugh with friends while watching a comedy together than when you are watching the same show by yourself. Laughing for no reason can still produce real, contagious laughter.

Belly Laughter - Belly laughter is considered the most honest type of laughter and it the type where the whole body shakes and you gasp for air. Men are more likely to grunt or snort at something they find funny, while women tend to produce giggles and chuckles.

Canned Laughter - Canned laughter is another term for 'laugh track'. It is real laughter taken completely out of one context and placed in another, such as from a real studio audience to a filmed movie. Canned laughter over a soundtrack to programming increases the chance of an audience finding humor in the material.

Contagious Laughter - Imagine you are out for dinner with a group of friends and someone tells a joke and gets one person laughing, which gets a second person laughing, and so on. Contagious laughter raises the possibility that humans have laugh detectors. People are made to respond with laughter on hearing laughter itself, much like the mystery of spreading a yawn. If it spreads too far, it is called mass hysteria.

> About ninety percent of our laughter is related to jokes or humor.

Cruel Laughter - Cruel laughter has been around for a long time. It often accompanies gruesome acts of cruelty. Laughter has been present at the entertainments of public executions and torture. The killers at Columbine High School in Littleton, Colorado, USA were laughing as they strolled through classrooms murdering their classmates. Slapstick comedy also often induces cruel laughter.

Etiquette Laughter - People rely on laughter to get along with others, so whether we are with a boss or friends, we tend to laugh at things they say or do, to be polite. Laughter could have developed in our ancestors before full speech, so the sound is merely a way to communicate and show agreement.

Nervous Laughter - During times of anxiety, we often laugh in a subconscious attempt to calm down. However, nervous laughter usually just heightens the awkwardness of the situation.

Pigeon Laughter - Pigeon laughter, which is often practiced in laughter therapy or laughter yoga, involves laughing without opening your mouth. By keeping your lips sealed, the laughter produces a humming sound, much like the noises a pigeon makes.

Silent Laughter - Silent laughter can have real benefits, because it involves the same type of deep breathing that comes with belly laughter. One woman who worked as a clown in a children's hospital explained that teaching sick children the art of silent laughter enabled them to go back to sleep after waking up from a bad dream. This type of laughter is also practiced in laughter yoga and laughter therapy, where it is often called joker's laughter.

Stress-relieving Laughter - Stress is an important reason to find something humorous and laughter can be a cure for stress. Stress builds tension in the human body, and that tension has to go somewhere. Stress-relieving laughter can take many forms, but it is usually found in an outburst, much like belly laughing.

Snorting Laughter - About twenty five percent of women and thirty three percent of men laugh through the nose. This is the kind where you might blow milk out your nose when surprised with a humorous situation. A person might either blow air out or suck it in through the nose when laughing. *A well told joke often induces me to experience a few different types of laughter in one bout.*

Five Attributes That Happiness and Sex Share

Here is another way to ease pain. A 2004 study asked 900 American women how various daily activities made them feel and found that "intimate relations" topped the charts for happiness. Both reduce anxiety, reduce stress, boost your immune system, ease pain, and both reduce neuroticism, a trait marked by mood swings and frequent worry. *Not sure who paid for the study to show the obvious.*

Laugh
until
your
belly
hurts
and then
just a
little
bit
more!

Calendar and Holiday Facts

INTERESTING HOLIDAYS

Global Belly Laugh Day

January 24 is Global Belly Laugh Day. According to Belly Laugh Day Founder Elaine Helle, the day is about celebrating with the people in your life, past and present, who laugh with you and help you laugh and smile.

The time for the Global Belly Laugh Bounce is 1:24 pm local time. That is when everyone should throw arms up in the air and laugh out loud. Maybe it can be heard around the world.

According to Jennifer Cline, laughter helps with:
Lowering blood pressure,
Reducing particular stress hormones,
Increasing vascular blood flow and oxygenation of the blood,
Working out the diaphragm, abdomen, respiratory system, face, legs and back,
Increasing alertness, creativity and memory, and
Increasing memory and learning.

Discovered a dubious personal achievement when I Googled images for "Global Belly Laugh Day" and found my picture on the first page. When I clicked on it, the link was to one of my blog posts. The good news is that it made me laugh and that is what the day is for. Go ahead, laugh out loud and pass it on.

National Weatherperson's Day

Every February 5th, the world collectively expresses their appreciation for meteorologists everywhere. There are not many firm traditions around this holiday. In truth few probably notice it is National Weatherman's Day other than weather geeks. It is not even a real holiday and no one really 'honors' them, but everyone should have a holiday for themselves.

National Weatherperson's Day commemorates the birth of John Jeffries in 1744, a Boston physician, scientist, and a military surgeon with the British Army in Nova Scotia and New York during the American Revolution.

Jeffries, one of America's first weather observers, began taking daily weather observations in Boston in 1774 and he took the first balloon observation in 1784. This is a day to recognize the men and women who collectively provide Americans with weather, water, and climate forecasts, and warning services.

Pi Approximation Day

Pi Day was invented by physicist Larry Shaw and the first Pi Day celebration was held at the San Francisco Exploratorium in 1988. In 2009 the US Congress officially recognized March 14 as Pi Day in the United States. *Traditional Pi Day activities include eating pizza, fruit pies, pancakes, and other circular food.*

Texas Independence Day

Texas Independence is March 2. Here are a few interesting facts about the great state of Texas.

- El Paso is closer to California than to Dallas.

- World's first rodeo was in Pecos, Texas, July 4, 1883.

- The Flagship Hotel in Galveston is the only hotel in North America built over water. It was destroyed by Hurricane Ike in 2008.

- Brazoria County, Texas has more species of birds than any other area in North America.

- Aransas Wildlife Refuge is the winter home of North America's only remaining flock of whooping cranes.

- Jalapeno jelly originated in Lake Jackson, Texas in 1978.

- The worst natural disaster in US history was in 1900, caused by a hurricane in which over 8,000 lives were lost on Galveston Island.

- The first word spoken from the moon on July 20, 1969 was "Houston," but the Space Center was actually in Clear Lake City at the time.

- The King Ranch in South Texas is larger than Rhode Island.

- Texas is the only state to enter the US by treaty, (known as the Constitution of 1845 by the Republic of Texas to enter the Union) instead of by annexation. This allows the Texas Flag to fly at the same height as the US Flag, and Texas may choose to divide into five states.

- Dr Pepper was invented in Waco in 1885. There is no period in Dr Pepper.

- The Capitol Dome in Austin is the only dome in the US which is taller than the Capitol Building in Washington, DC (by 7 feet).

- The name 'Texas' comes from the Hasini Indian word 'tejas' meaning 'friends'. Tejas is not Spanish for Texas.

April Fool's Day

On April Fool's Day, April 1, 1974, Oliver Bickar climbed into Mt. Edgecumbe, a volcano that had been dormant for around 9,000 years, and made it look like it was coming back to life. After four years of planning, Bickar doused 100 tires in cooking oil and lit them on fire inside Mt. Edgecumbe. He also spray painted "April Fool" in 50 foot letters around the rim.

Earth Day

April 22 we celebrate Earth Day. I thought it might be interesting to review some of the predictions from past Earth Days.

On the first Earth Day in 1970, here are some profound predictions that were made. "It is already too late to avoid mass starvation," — Denis Hayes, Chief organizer for Earth Day

"We have about five more years at the outside to do something." "The world has been chilling sharply for about twenty years. If present trends continue, the world will be about four degrees colder for the global mean temperature in 1990, but eleven degrees colder in the year 2000. This is about twice what it would take to put us into an ice age." — Kenneth Watt Kenneth Watt, ecologist

"Demographers agree almost unanimously on the following grim timetable: by 1975 widespread famines will begin in India; these will spread by 1990 to include all of India, Pakistan, China and the Near East, Africa. By the year 2000, or conceivably sooner, South and Central America will exist under famine conditions. By the year 2000, thirty years from now, the entire world, with the exception of Western Europe, North America, and Australia, will be in famine." North Texas State University professor Peter Gunter

In 1972, a report was written for the Club of Rome warning the world would run out of gold by 1981, mercury and silver by 1985, tin by 1987 and petroleum, copper, lead and natural gas by 1992. Gordon Taylor, in his 1970 book "The Doomsday Book," said Americans were using 50 percent of the world's resources and "by 2000 they [Americans] will, if permitted, be using all of them." In 1975, the Environmental Fund took out full-page ads warning, "The World as we know it will likely be ruined by the year 2000."

"Civilization will end within 15 or 30 years unless immediate action is taken against problems facing mankind." (1970) George Wald, Harvard Biologist

"We are in an environmental crisis which threatens the survival of this nation, and of the world as a suitable place of human habitation." — (1970) Washington University biologist Barry Commoner

"Population will inevitably and completely outstrip whatever small increases in food supplies we make. The death rate will increase until at least 100-200 million people per year will be starving to death during the next ten years." (1970) Stanford University biologist Paul Ehrlich

"In a decade, urban dwellers will have to wear gas masks to survive air pollution... by 1985 air pollution will have reduced the amount of sunlight reaching earth by one half." — (1970) Life magazine

By 1995 "... somewhere between 75 and 85 percent of all the species of living animals will be extinct." Sen. Gaylord Nelson

"By 1975 some experts feel that food shortages will have escalated the present level of world hunger and starvation into famines of unbelievable proportions. Other experts, more optimistic, think the ultimate food-population collision will not occur until the decade of the 1980s." Paul Ehrlich

Earth Day 2013 - NOAA State of the Climate Report - "All of those things indicate that the climate system as a whole is continuing to warm up – and warm up faster as we go along." ~ Climatologist

"It's hard to read the report and not be led to the conclusion that the task of reducing carbon emissions is now more urgent than ever." another Climatologist

"Sea level rising an average of 3.2mm per year" *(0.125984 inches)*

"The climate system is not quite so simple as people thought." Danish environmental analyst Bjorn Lomborg

At least these folks are consistent with their predictions, in spite of a few facts, such as the earth is not over-populated, with very few countries producing enough children to replace themselves. In addition, we are not running out of resources. *History has proven that Punxsutawney Phil has been more accurate in his predictions than the "human expert climate predictors."*

ANZAC Day

ANZAC Day is the solemn day of remembrance of those Australian and New Zealand Army Corps soldiers who fought and died at Gallipoli in 1915. It is also a day of remembrance for all soldiers who died while fighting for their country.

On 25 April 1915, eight months into the First World War, Allied soldiers landed on the shores of the Gallipoli peninsula. The troops were there as part of a plan to open the Dardanelles Strait to the Allied fleets and force a Turkish surrender. The Allied forces encountered unexpectedly strong resistance from the Turks, and both sides suffered enormous loss of life. The forces from New Zealand and Australia, fighting as part of the ANZAC (Australian and New Zealand Army Corps), played an important part in the Gallipoli campaign.

The day is marked with parades, tributes, and playing Reveille and The Last Post (now used in British Ceremonies and funerals).

Valentine's Day

Saint Valentine's Day is also known as Valentine's Day, or the Feast of Saint Valentine. It is observed on February 14 each year in many countries around the world. It is not an official holiday.

Its origins go back to the ancient Roman celebration of Lupercalia, which honored the gods Lupercus and Faunus, and the legendary founders of Rome, Romulus and Remus. Lupercalia festivities and feasts are purported to have included the pairing of young women and men. Men would draw women's names from a container and each couple would be paired until next year's celebration.

It was not called "Valentine's Day" until a priest named Valentine came along. Emperor Claudius handed down a decree that soldiers remain single, believing that soldiers would be distracted and unable to concentrate on fighting if they were married or engaged.

Valentine converted many guards to Christianity and defied the emperor by secretly performing marriage ceremonies. As a result of his defiance, Valentine was put to death on February 14. As Christianity spread through Rome, priests moved Lupercalia from February 15 to February 14 and renamed it St. Valentine's Day.

Cupid became associated with Valentine's day for another reason. According to Roman mythology, Cupid was the son of Venus, the goddess of love and beauty. He caused people to fall in love by shooting them with his magical arrows. He also fell deeply in love with a mortal maiden named Psyche.

Cupid married Psyche, but his mother, Venus was jealous of Psyche's beauty and forbade her daughter-in-law to look at Cupid. Psyche could not resist temptation and sneaked a peek at her handsome husband. As punishment, Venus demanded that she perform three tasks, the last of which caused Psyche's death. Cupid brought Psyche back to life and the gods, moved by their love, granted Psyche immortality.

Easter

Easter is observed in all Western Christian churches, Easter commemorates the Resurrection of Jesus. It is celebrated on the first Sunday after the full moon that occurs on or next after the vernal equinox (fixed at March 21) and is therefore celebrated between March 22 and April 25 inclusive. This date was fixed by the Council of Nicaea in A.D. 325.

The Orthodox Church uses the Julian calendar when calculating Easter (Pascha), rather than the more contemporary Gregorian calendar. For this reason, Orthodox Easter generally falls on a different date than the Western Christian Easter.

The Easter Bunny - Today's Easter Bunny grew out of religious practices in pre-Christian Germany. Eostra, a goddess of fertility and spring, was associated with the rabbit because of the animal's high reproductive rate. The legend was subsequently merged with the Christian celebration of Jesus' rebirth.

Easter Eggs - Decorated eggs predate Easter and have been found as early as 60,000 years ago. About 3000 BC in Persia, eggs were dyed red given as gifts in celebration of the first day of spring.

The practice of giving red Easter eggs, symbolizing the blood of Christ, became a Christian tradition, with the hatching of an egg symbolizing the resurrection. The Easter egg is also a byproduct of Lent, as many families would give up eggs during those 'fast days', which ended with Easter.

Some of the oldest egg dyes were made from a variety of materials, including onion peels, tree bark, flower petals, and vegetable and fruit juices.

Cadbury sells over 200 million cream eggs each year in the UK. More than three for each person who lives there.

The PAAS Dye Co. launched its product during the 1880s. The first packets contained five colors for 5 cents. The company now claims to sell more than 10 million kits annually including dyes, paints, stickers, glitter, etc.

In some European countries, children go from house to house to collect eggs.

The US White House Easter Egg Roll, an annual tradition on the Monday after Easter, is the only time that tourists are allowed to gather on the White House lawn. The tradition actually started on the lawn of the Capitol, by Dolly Madison during the early 1800s, and was moved to the White House in 1878, when Rutherford B. Hayes was president.

Many Easter eggs are formed from chocolate. In Scotland, a popular treat sold in fish-and-chips shops is deep-fried chocolate eggs.

The most valuable Easter eggs are the jewel-encrusted Fabergé eggs, crafted in the late 1800s and early 1900s as Easter gifts for the families of Russian czars. Only 65 were known to have been made. Most are worth millions of dollars.

The world's largest Easter egg, as recognized by Guinness World Records, was made of chocolate in 2005 in Belgium and weighed 1,200 kilograms or more than 2,600 pounds.

The term for intentional inside joke, hidden message, author's names, or feature in a work such as a computer program, video game, movie, book, or crossword is Easter Egg. The term was coined at Atari after a programmer put his name in a hidden room in the game Adventure, released in 1979. The name evokes an Easter egg hunt.

National Pretzel Day

April 26 is unofficially National Pretzel Day. National Pretzel Day was declared in 2003 by Pennsylvania Governor Ed Rendell.

During the 19th century, southern German and Swiss German immigrants introduced the pretzel to North America. Pennsylvania is the center of American pretzel production for both the hard crispy and the soft bread types of pretzels.

Pretzels are believed to be the world's oldest snack. The commonly held story is that pretzels date back to 610AD. Monks baked thin strips of dough into the shape of a child's arms folded in prayer as a reward for students saying their prayers. The strips of baked dough were called 'pretiola' (little rewards).

During the 17th century, pretzels symbolized the bond of marriage. This is where the phrase "tying the knot" originated.

Helen Hoff is the world-champion pretzel twister, at 57 pretzels a minute.

The annual United States pretzel industry is worth over $550 million. The average American consumes about 1.5 pounds (0.7 kg) of pretzels per year.

Pretzels without salt are called baldies.

Eeyore's Birthday

Also on April 26 is Eeyore's birthday. If you want to attend the biggest birthday party dedicated to a donkey, you need to go to Austin, Texas for Eeyore's Birthday Party. Each April, Austinites and visitors gather in Pease Park for live music, drum circles, outrageous costumes and an extra dose of Austin weirdness, all to celebrate Winnie the Pooh's companion.

National Doughnut Day

Every first Friday in June, doughnut (donut) lovers all rise to celebrate a wonderful circle of sweet, doughy goodness. The day was created by the Salvation Army in 1938 to honor the men and women who served doughnuts to soldiers during World War I. A military doctor, Morgan Pett was sent to a military base and, on his way he stopped at a bakery and picked up eight dozen doughnuts to give to the wounded soldiers. During the Second World War, Red Cross Volunteers also distributed doughnuts.

Three other, less well known doughnut holidays are International Jelly-Filled Doughnut Day, June 8; National Cream-Filled Doughnut Day, September 14; and Buy A Doughnut Day, October 30.

Stop by your favorite donut shop, as many American doughnut stores offer free doughnuts on National Doughnut Day.

German-American Day

It became Public Law 100-104 when President Reagan signed it on August 18, 1987. The US celebrates German-American Day on Oct. 6. It commemorates the date in 1683 when 13 German families from Krefeld, near the Rhine landed in Philadelphia. These families subsequently founded Germantown, Pennsylvania, the first German settlement in the original thirteen American colonies. About 1 in 4 Americans claim part or full German heritage.

Day of German Unity (Tag der Deutschen Einheit) is observed on October 3, when the official German holiday commemorates Germany's reunification in 1990, when East and West Germany once again became one country known as the Federal Republic of Germany die Bundesrepublik Deutschland).

German Pioneers Day is celebrated in Ontario, Canada on the day after Canadian Thanksgiving, second Monday in October. A law passed by the Ontario provincial Legislative Assembly in 2000 proclaimed the annual celebration of the German contributions to Canada on the day after Canadian Thanksgiving.

Columbus Day

Columbus Day is celebrated for most of the US, but Seattle, WA., holds its Indigenous Peoples' Day. It makes little difference as Columbus Day is not an official holiday in Washington. A councilman said it is, "About taking a stand against racism." An opposing lawyer said people of Italian descent are "deeply offended." "By this resolution you say to all Italian-Americans that the city of Seattle no longer deems your heritage or your community worthy of recognition." *Seems like politics never takes a holiday.*

National Peanut Butter Day

Interesting that National Compliment Day and National Peanut Butter Day would be on the same day. January 24.

Peanut butter is a staple in over 90% of US households and the average person consumes more than six pounds of peanut products each year. Women and children prefer creamy peanut butter, while most men go for the chunky variety.

George Bayle, a St. Louis snack food maker, started making peanut butter in the 1890s. For many years, manufacturers struggled with the oil separating from the grainy solids of the peanut butter. In 1923 Heinz became the first company to homogenize the peanuts into the spreadable butter we know and love today.

It takes about 550 peanuts to make a 12 ounce jar of peanut butter. It is the high protein content that causes peanut butter to stick to the roof of your mouth.

Undiscovery Day

It officially passed October 1986 by Ocean Shores city council. Each year on the last Saturday in April, the citizens of Ocean Shores, Washington, celebrate "Undiscovery Day" to commemorate the night in 1792 when British explorer Capt. George Vancouver sailed past Ocean Shores without discovering it. Vancouver was en route to Nootka Sound, on what is now Vancouver Island, to settle a controversy between Spain and Great Britain. He passed the area where Ocean Shores is now located, near the mouth of Grays Harbor, at about midnight on April 27, 1792.

Undiscovery Day is observed at the entrance to a harbor that was finally discovered by a Yankee named Robert Gray. About 75 to 100 people gather at Lumpy's Tavern from noon to 2 p.m.

At midnight they gather on the shore. Preliminary ingestions are deemed necessary before braving the elements and at the stroke of 12 the celebrants wend their way down to the shore, yelling "Hey George, over here" and other appropriate instructions, hoping that Vancouver's ghost will answer and explain his oversight. To date, there has never been a reply.

Alascattalo Day

November 21 is Alascattalo Day. It is described as a day to honor humor in general and Alaskan humor in particular. The day is named after 'alascattalo', said to be the genetic cross between a moose and a walrus. It has been celebrated in Anchorage for over 25 years.

A mild-mannered moose named Morris met a witty walrus named Wanabelle. It was love at first sight, and soon the moose and the walrus were wed in the church down the way. Within sixty weeks, Morris and Wannabelle welcomed into the world a wee little weeble who made their love complete, and the first Alascattalo was born.

Christmas

Merry Christmas in any language sounds as sweet. Happy Christmas, Joyeaux Noel, Froehliche Weihnachten, Mele Kalikimaka, Blithe Yule, Nollaig Shona Dhuit, Buone Feste Natalizie, Buon Natale, Bon Natali, krismas mubarak, Feliz Navidad, Glædelig Jul, Hyvää Joulua, Meri Kirihimete, Maligayang Pasko, Linksmu Kaledu, Craciun fericit, Pozdrevlyayu s prazdnikom Rozhdestva s Novim Godom, Schöni Wiehnachte, Z Rizdvom Khrystovym, Cestitamo Bozic, Vrolijk Kerstfeest.

Xmas vs. Christmas - Some people use Xmas as shorthand for Christmas, the abbreviation is not modern and was not invented for the purpose of being disrespectful to Christians. It is not supposed to eliminate the word "Christ" and the X is not meant to stand for anonymity. The X is actually considered to represent the letter Chi from the Greek alphabet, the first letter in the word Christos. The "-mas" part on the end of Christmas and Xmas comes from the Old English word for "mass".

Xmas is sometimes pronounced xmas, but it and variants such as Xtemass, originated as handwriting abbreviations for the typical pronunciation of Christmas. There is a common misconception that the word Xmas stems from a secular attempt to remove the religious tradition from Christmas by taking the 'Christ' out of 'Christmas', but that was not originally so, as its use dates back to the 16th century.

In the United States, in 1977 New Hampshire Governor Meldrim Thomson sent out a press release saying that he wanted journalists to keep the 'Christ' in Christmas, and not call it Xmas, which he called a pagan spelling of Christmas. Many of those who dislike abbreviating the word are unfamiliar with a long history of Christians using X in place of 'Christ' for various purposes.

The word 'Christ' and its compounds, including 'Christmas', have been abbreviated in English for at least the past 1,000 years, long before the modern "Xmas" was commonly used. Christ was often written as "Xρ" or "Xt" as far back as 1021. This X and P arose as the uppercase forms of the Greek letters χ (Ch) and ρ (R) used in ancient abbreviations for Χριστος (Greek for Christ), and are still widely seen in many Eastern Orthodox icons depicting Jesus Christ.

The two Greek letters shown as ☧, is a symbol often used to represent Christ in Catholic, Protestant, and Orthodox Christian Churches. *Bottom Line; it was once positive to use xmas, but has now become bad form to use anything but Christmas.*

Santa Claus in Canada - Santa Claus has his own postcode in Canada: HOH OHO.

The Yule Lads - Jolasveinar, or Yulemen, or Christmas boys are figures from Icelandic folklore who in modern times have become the Icelandic version of Santa Claus. Their number has varied throughout the ages, but currently is thirteen. They put rewards or punishments into shoes placed by children on window sills during the last thirteen nights before Christmas Eve. Every night, one Yuletide lad visits each child, leaving gifts for good children or rotting potatoes for bad children.

In 1932 the poem "Jólasveinarnir" was published as a part of the popular poetry book "Christmas Arrives" by Icelandic poet Jóhannes úr Kötlum. The poem reintroduced Icelandic society to Icelandic Yuletide folklore and established what is now considered the thirteen Yule Lads, their personalities, and connection to other folkloric characters.

The Icelandic Santas first appeared in the 17th century as the sons of two trolls. Gryla and Leppaludi are frightening creatures, and have a reputation for stealing and eating naughty children. Grýla is a dreadful character, described as part troll, part animal, and the mother of 13 precocious boys (the Yule Lads). Grýla lives in the mountains with her third husband, Leppaludi, her thirteen children, and a black cat. Every Christmas, Grýla and her sons come down from the mountains: Grýla in search of naughty children to boil in her cauldron and the boys in search of mischief. She can only capture children who misbehave, but those who repent must be released.

193

The first Jolasveinar arrives Dec 12 and leaves Dec 25, the second arrives Dec 13 and leaves Dec 26, etc. Below are the names and mischief they cause. They sound like a fun bunch.

Sheep-Cote Clod - Harasses sheep, but is impaired by his stiff peg-legs.

Gully Gawk - Hides in gullies, waiting for an opportunity to sneak into the cowshed and steal milk.

Stubby, abnormally short - Steals pans to eat the crust left on them.

Spoon-Licker - Steals spoons to lick and is extremely thin due to malnutrition.

Pot-Scraper - Steals leftovers from pots.

Bowl-Licker - Hides under beds waiting for someone to put down their bowl, which he then steals.

Door-Slammer - Likes to slam doors, especially during the night.

Skyr-Gobbler - A Yule Lad who loves skyr (like yogurt).

Sausage-Swiper - Hides in the rafters and snatches sausages that are being smoked.

Window-Peeper - A voyeur who looks through windows in search of things to steal.

Doorway-Sniffer - Has an abnormally large nose and an acute sense of smell which he uses to locate laufabrauð (Christmas bread).

Meat-Hook - Uses a hook to steal meat.

Candle-Stealer - Follows children in order to steal their candles, which are made of tallow and thus edible.

Origin of Christmas Stockings - The tradition of Christmas stockings is said to have originated from the actions of a kind noble man named Nicholas, who was born in March, 270 AD, in Patara, at the time Greek, but now Turkey. While still young, his wealthy parents died in an epidemic. Nicholas became a Christian priest and used all his riches to help the poor, the needy, the sick, and the suffering. He was made Bishop of Myra (modern Turkey) at a young age and became known for his kindness and generosity.

He traveled across the country helping people, giving gifts of money and other presents. He had a reputation for secret gift-giving, such as putting coins in the shoes of those who left them out for him, a practice celebrated on his feast day - St Nicholas Day, December 6 in Western Christianity and 19 December in Eastern Christianity. He died December 6, 343 AD. Many still observe December 6 as a St. Nicholas holiday. *I grew up enjoying the candy treats thrown on my porch the evening of December 6.*

Nicholas was so widely revered that thousands of churches were named for him, including three hundred in Belgium, thirty-four in Rome, twenty-three in the Netherlands, and more than four hundred in England.

Through the centuries many stories and legends have been told of Saint Nicholas' life and deeds. One popular account (with many variations) tells us of a poor peasant who lived happily in a small cottage in Saint Nicholas' hometown, with his wife and three daughters. The wife suddenly died of an illness, leaving the poor man and his three daughters in despair. All the burden of household chores now fell upon the daughters.

When the daughters reached a marriage age, the poor father became depressed for he knew he could in no way marry them off to good men. In those days a young woman's father had to offer prospective husbands something of value - a dowry, which he could not afford.

Saint Nicholas found out about the peasant and his daughters and decided to help him. He went to the peasant's house the night before the eldest daughter came of age, with a bag of gold and waited for the family to go to bed. That night, after finishing their washing for the day, the daughters hung their stockings by the fireplace to dry.

As they turned off the lamps and fell asleep, St. Nicholas tiptoed to the cottage window and saw the daughters' stockings hanging close to his reach. He carefully put in his bag of gold in one of the stockings and went away.

When the father found the bag the next morning and opened it, he was delighted to find enough gold in the stocking to pay for the dowry of one daughter. The father was able to provide for his eldest daughter and saw that she got married to a nice groom.

Soon after, Saint Nicholas took another bag of gold, and threw it carefully into another stocking. The next morning the man opened the stocking and found enough gold to marry off his second daughter.

The father had grown eager to discover his mysterious benefactor, and each night he stayed awake. When Saint Nicholas came up with another bag of gold, the man recognized him. He fell on his knees and cried of gratitude and thanked him with all his heart.

This is how the tradition of Christmas stockings is said to have begun.

Origin of Santa Claus - It is believed that Santa Claus is actually an alteration of this same Saint Nicholas, Santa for Saint and Claus for Nicholas. The original Santa Claus (and many current European) outfits resemble a Bishop's clothing, hat, and staff. The modern figure of Santa Claus is derived from the Dutch figure of Sinterklaas, whose name is a dialectal pronunciation of Saint Nicholas.

The 19th century was a time of cultural transition and many wanted to domesticate the Christmas holiday. Through the first half of the 19th century, Presbyterians, Baptists, Quakers, and others continued to regard December 25th as a day without religious significance.

In 1809, Washington Irving published the satirical fiction, Knickerbocker's History of New York, with numerous references to a jolly St. Nicholas character. This was not the saintly bishop, rather an elfin Dutch burgher with a clay pipe. Irving's work was regarded as the "First notable work of imagination in the New World."

In 1810, the New York Historical Society commissioned artist Alexander Anderson to create the first American image of Nicholas for St. Nicholas Day. Nicholas was shown in a gift-giving role with children's treats in stockings hanging at a fireplace.

During 1821, the first lithographed book in America, the 'Children's Friend' described how "Sante (sic) Claus" arrived from the North in a sleigh with a flying reindeer. The anonymous poem and illustrations proved pivotal in shifting imagery away from a saintly bishop. Sante Claus rewarded good behavior and punished bad.

Gifts were safe toys, "pretty doll . . . peg-top, or a ball; no crackers, cannons, squibs, or rockets to blow their eyes up, or their pockets. No drums to stun their Mother's ear, nor swords to make their sisters fear; but pretty books to store their mind with knowledge of each various kind."

The sleigh had a bookshelf for the 'pretty books'. The book also marked Sante Claus' first appearance on Christmas Eve, rather than December 6th. The book may have actually been penned a few years earlier according to some accounts.

In 1823, a poem, "A Visit from St. Nicholas" was written. It is now better known as "The Night Before Christmas."

He was dressed all in fur, from his head to his foot,
And his clothes were all tarnished with ashes and soot;
A bundle of toys he had flung on his back,
And he looked like a peddler just opening his pack.

His eyes - how they twinkled! His dimples how merry!
His cheeks were like roses, his nose like a cherry!
His droll little mouth was drawn up like a bow,
And the beard of his chin was as white as the snow;

The stump of a pipe he held tight in his teeth,
And the smoke it encircled his head like a wreath;
He had a broad face and a little round belly,
That shook, when he laughed like a bowlful of jelly.

He was chubby and plump, a right jolly old elf. . . .

This is how St. Nicholas was transformed into Santa Claus.

Mistletoe - Mistletoe is a partial parasite that grows on the branches or trunk of a tree and sends out roots that penetrate into the tree to take up nutrients. Mistletoe is also capable of growing on its own. Like other plants it can produce its own food by photosynthesis.

There are two types of mistletoe. The mistletoe that is commonly used as a Christmas decoration (Phoradendron flavescens) is native to North America and grows as a parasite on trees in the west and also in a line down the east from New Jersey to Florida.

The other type of mistletoe, Viscum album, is of European origin. The European mistletoe is a green shrub with small, yellow flowers and white, sticky berries which are considered poisonous. It is commonly seen on apple trees, and rarely on oak trees. The rarer oak mistletoe was venerated by the ancient Celts and Germans and used as a ceremonial plant by early Europeans. The Greeks and earlier peoples thought that it had mystical powers and it became associated with many folklore customs.

Mistletoe of the oak was especially sacred to the Druids. On the sixth night of the moon white-robed Druid priests would cut the oak mistletoe with a golden sickle. Two white bulls would be sacrificed amid prayers that the recipients of the mistletoe would prosper. Later, the ritual of cutting the mistletoe from the oak came to symbolize the emasculation of the old King by his successor.

Kissing under mistletoe is first found associated with the Greek festival of Saturnalia and later with primitive marriage rites. They probably originated from two beliefs. One, that it has power to bestow fertility and two, that it possess life-giving power.

In Scandinavia, mistletoe was considered a plant of peace, under which enemies could declare a truce or warring spouses kiss and make-up. In France, the custom linked to mistletoe was reserved for New Year's Day: "Au gui l'An neuf" (Mistletoe for the New Year).

During the eighteenth-century, English created a kissing ball. At Christmas time a young lady standing under a ball of mistletoe, brightly trimmed with evergreens, ribbons, and ornaments, could not refuse to be kissed. Such a kiss could mean deep romance or lasting friendship and goodwill. If the girl remained unkissed, she could not expect to marry the following year.

In some parts of England the Christmas mistletoe is burned on the twelfth night or all the boys and girls who had kissed under it will never marry. The custom of exchanging a kiss under the mistletoe can still be found in many European countries as well as in the US and

Canada. Kisses can be exchanged under the mistletoe any time during the holiday season.

Mistletoe was considered to bestow life, fertility, protection against poison, and act as an aphrodisiac. Mistletoe was long regarded as both a sexual symbol and the "soul" of the oak. It was gathered at both mid-summer and winter solstices. The custom of using mistletoe to decorate houses at Christmas is a survival of the Druid and other pre-Christian traditions. During the Middle Ages and later, branches of mistletoe were hung from ceilings to ward off evil spirits. In Europe they were placed over house and stable doors to prevent the entrance of witches.

Christmas Thought - *Christmas is the day to skip the past, skip the future, and enjoy the present, presents, and presence of family and friends.*

Holiday Boozing

Many equate the holidays with drinking, so I looked up some of the common terms we use, beginning with 'crapulous' (a substitute for hangover), from the 18th century Greek kraipale (drunken headache or nausea). *I love that word.*

Booze first appeared in Middle Dutch as bûsen, which meant 'to drink to excess.' There was also the Old High German word bausen, which meant 'to bulge or billow.'" It took 200 years for English speakers to start using it as both a verb (to booze) and a noun (give me some booze). It is a common misconception that the word was borrowed from a brand of whiskey sold by E.S. Booz in the 1800s, but booze is much older. The 1529 Oxford dictionary defined it as "affected by drinking."

Hooch comes from Alaska. There was a native tribe there called the Hoochinoo that distilled rum made primarily from molasses and introduced it to soldiers from the lower 48.

Spirits are alcohol and both are liquor.

Alcohol began as an Arabic word describing a fine metallic powder used as eye shadow (al-kuhul). The word was broadened to mean 'the pure spirit of anything'. Later it was expanded to include a distilled spirit or liquor. *Alcoholic* meaning 'caused by drunkenness' is attested by the 1800s and meaning 'habitually drunk' by 1910.

Liquor dates back to at least 1200, likur "any matter in a liquid state," and the Latin verb liquere, meaning "to be fluid", from Latin liquorem.

The definition including a fermented or distilled drink followed about a hundred years later. In North America, the term *hard liquor* is used to distinguish distilled beverages from undistilled ones and does not include beverages such as beer, wine, and cider, which are fermented, but not distilled.

Spirits refers to a distilled beverage that contains no added sugar and has at least 20% alcohol by volume. It probably originated with ancient alchemists, who referred to the vapor given off and collected during an alchemical process (like the distillation of alcohol) as the 'spirit' of the original material. Early European Monks believed that the spirit was removed from the mash during the distilling process.

Cocktail refers to any beverage that contains two or more ingredients with at least one of them being alcohol. When a cocktail contains only a distilled spirit and a mixer, it is a *highball*.

The Oxford English dictionary cites the word as originating in the US. The first recorded use of the word cocktail as a beverage was during the early 1800s. Of the many origins, two stand out: an old French recipe for mixed wines, called a coquetel, brought to America by General Lafayette's soldiers in 1777; and New Orleans brandy drink in an egg-cup called a coquetier in French. The latter was a morning drink served at the time the tail of the evening met with the morning cock-a-doodle-do of a rooster.

Bar is an abbreviation of barrier, the counter that separates drinks from the drinkers. Toward the end of the 16th century it expanded to mean the building that housed the barrier. *Barmaid* didn't appear in print until the mid 1700s and *bartender* arrived about fifty years later and *barfly* came about during the early 1900s. *Bottom line, beer, wine, cider, hooch, and alcohol are booze, but only hooch, and alcohol are liquors.*

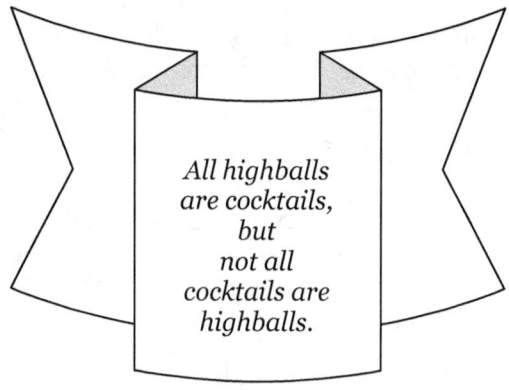

All highballs are cocktails, but not all cocktails are highballs.

TIME AND CALENDAR FACTS

Grand Predictions - Toward the end of any year many pundits either rehash the greatest, best, and worst of the past year or offer predictions for the near and distant future. Here are a few from the 1890s predicting life in the 1990s.

"Three hours will constitute a long day's work by the end of the next century."

"Longevity will be so improved that 150 years will be no unusual age to reach."

"In the 1990s, the United States will be a government of perhaps 60 states, situated in both North and South America."

"In 100 years Denver will be as big as New York and . . . if the republic remains politically compact and doesn't fall apart at the Mississippi River, Canada will be either part of it or an independent sovereignty."

"We shall not only restore the dress of our great-grandfathers before we stop, but run the costumes of Adam and Eve a pretty close shave."

"The waist line will be just below the bosom."

"Politically, there will be far less money expended in electing officials, I fancy. Many of our leading politicians, out of a job, will be living on the island." [in jail].

"There will be no need of a standing army."

"Law will be simplified and brought within the reach of the common people . . . The occupation of 2/3 of the lawyers will be destroyed."

"Transcontinental mail will be forwarded by means of pneumatic tubes."

"By the year 1993, the mechanical work of publishing newspapers may be done entirely by electricity."

"Aluminum will be the shining symbol of that age. The houses and cities of men, built of aluminum, shall flash in the rising sun with surpassing brilliance."

"Long before 1993, the journey from New York to San Francisco, and from New York to London, will be made between the sunrise and sunset of a summer day. The railway and the steamship will be as obsolete as the stagecoach."

"Labor organizations will have disappeared, for there will be no longer a necessity for their existence."

Time and New Year - Ah, the beginning of another New Year and the world awaits what wonderful things we can accomplish this coming year. Time is such an important part of our lives and is so personal to each of us that there are hundreds of ways to describe it. Each of us has our own specious present. This year, do not bide your time. Use this window of time to spend some face time with family and friends and keep them close for all time.

Words from the Rolling Stones (I like the second version) title come to mind <u>LINK</u>. In the nick of time we look at the fresh calendar, sit a spell, adjust our circadian clock, and ponder the current epoch. This is the kairos to begin before we reach our first poronkusema.

Kairos is an ancient Greek word meaning the right or opportune moment (the supreme moment).

The Finnish word poronkusema describes the distance equal to how far a reindeer can travel without taking a comfort break.

The Malaysian word for the time it takes to eat a banana is pisan zapra. To say that someone would arrive in pisan zapra means they could be expected in a few minutes.

The Turkish phrase 'zaman dilimi' means time period as does the Haitian Creole phrase 'peryòd tan'.

A jubilee is 50 years.

A vigil is a period of time, especially at night, when you stay in a place to wait for something or to provide support.

In medieval time, a moment was defined as being 90 seconds.

In the Old Testament, Yom is translated as period of time, such as year, always, and more.

A sidereal time is the measurement of time relative to a distant star. It is used in astronomy to predict when a star will be overhead. A sidereal day is 4 minutes less than a solar day.

Scientist Gilbert Newton Lewis defined a jiffy in the early 1900s as the amount of time it takes light to travel 1 centimeter (0.4 in), which is about one-hundredth of a second.

A Planck is the duration light takes to travel one Planck length, theorized to be the smallest duration measurement that will ever be possible, roughly 10 to the 43rd seconds.

Aging and Time - Time obviously affects our age, but how we feel about our age can make a difference between just getting old and aging gracefully.

JAMA Internal Medicine online published a study that looked at data from 6,489 people with an average age of 65.8 years who reported that they felt a little less than 10 years younger. Most said they felt about three years younger and 4.8%, felt at least a year older than their actual age.

During the next eight years, scientists found just over 14% of those who felt younger than their years had died, while more than 24% of the people who reported feeling older or feeling their age died.

The study concluded that self-perceived age has the potential to change us. This and other research shows that personality can affect our destiny. New research into the link between personality and aging finds that there are two main traits that seem to help people live longer: conscientiousness and optimism. Happiness and a positive attitude can become a self-fulfilling prophecy. *These results certainly make me happy.*

Interesting Time Facts - In 1903 the Wright brothers successfully flew a plane for 59 seconds. Sixty six years later Apollo 11 landed on the moon in 1969.

Teaching started in Oxford in 1096 and by 1249, the University was officially founded. The Aztec civilization, as we know it began with the founding of Tenochtitlán in 1325.

More than ten percent of photos ever taken were taken during the past 12 months.

The Chicago Cubs baseball team last won a world series in 1908, before women were allowed to vote, which came during 1920.

If you were born in 1968, the world population was 3,557,000,000. Today, the world population has more than doubled from then and is over seven billion.

January Tidbits - Using a baby to signify the New Year began in ancient Greece around 600 B.C.

January is named for the Roman god Janus, who had two faces, one looking back, the other forward.

The original New Year's Eve Ball in Times Square was a 700 pound ball of iron and wood covered with 25 watt bulbs.

The modern ball weighs 11,875 pounds, is 12 feet in diameter and is covered with 2,668 Waterford crystals.

Do not eat lobster or chicken in January. Lobsters can move backward and chickens can scratch in reverse, so these foods could bring a reversal of fortune.

By the second week of January, twenty five percent of people have abandoned their resolutions.

Forbes magazine reports that only eight percent of people actually achieve their New Year's resolution.

January 19 is National Popcorn day. January 20 is National Cheese Lover's Day. January 21 is National Hug Day. *In my house, I celebrate them all together and have 'hug some cheese popcorn day'. It is much easier.*

International Year of Light - On 20 December 2013, The United Nations General Assembly 68th Session proclaimed 2015 as the International Year of Light and Light-based Technologies. "An International Year of Light is a tremendous opportunity to ensure that international policymakers and stakeholders are made aware of the problem-solving potential of light technology. We now have a unique opportunity to raise global awareness of this." John Dudley, Chairman of the IYL 2015 Steering Committee

2015 was also the Einstein Centenary. In 1915, the theory of General Relativity developed by Einstein showed how light was at the center of the structure of space and time.

Thought I would toss in a few facts about light, such as lighting represents almost 20% of global electricity consumption.

The first commercially viable incandescent light bulb, patented by Thomas Edison in 1880, used a filament made from burned bamboo.

Other animals can see parts of the spectrum that humans cannot, for example, a large number of insects can see ultraviolet light.

The giant squid, Taningia danae, has the largest light-producing organs of any living creature. The lemon-yellow light organs are called photophores and are found at the tip of the two of the squid's feeding arms and they flash blinding light.

The speed of light in a vacuum is about 186,000 miles per second (300,000 kilometers per second).

Light takes 1.255 seconds to get from the Earth to the Moon.

More than half of the visible sunlight spectrum is absorbed within three feet of the ocean's surface; at a depth of 10 meters, less than 20% of the light that entered at the surface is still visible; by 100 meters, this percentage drops to 0.5%.

Refraction can make things look closer than they really are. The difference in speed between light traveling through water and through air means that, from the surface, a 13ft (4m) pool appears to be just 10ft (3m) deep.

Between 18% and 35% of the human population is estimated to be affected by a so-called 'photic sneeze reflex', a heritable condition that results in sneezing when the person is exposed to bright light.

For ebook readers, here is a link to "Light my Fire" by the Doors, because it fits the topic.

National Hamburger Month - May is national hamburger month and it is also Barbecue month.

The term hamburger originally derives from Hamburg, Germany, from which many people emigrated to the United States. Hamburger, in the German language, is the demonym of Hamburg. A hamburger is typically made with ground beef. White Castle traces the origin of the hamburger to Hamburg, Germany with its invention by Otto Kuase. Many others have claimed to be the first in the US to make hamburgers.

The term "burger" is generic and may refer to sandwiches that have ground meat, chicken, fish, or vegetarian fillings other than a beef patty, but share the characteristic round bun. Other "burgers" are usually referred to as "chicken burgers", "fish burgers", etc. Some fast food places more accurately call them "chicken sandwiches", "fish sandwiches", etc. An infinite number of fillings and toppings can be found in many locations around the world.

A veggie burger, garden burger, or tofu burger uses a meat substitute such as tofu, TVP, wheat gluten, beans, grains, or an assortment of vegetables, ground up and mashed into patties. *This really stretches the definition of 'burger'.*

Another variety of hamburger is the slider, which is a very small hamburger patty served on an equally small bun. This is the kind of hamburger has been popularized by White Castle. The name comes from their size (and sometimes greasiness) and are considered to slide down your throat in one or two bites.

A cheeseburger is a hamburger accompanied with melted cheese. The term itself is a portmanteau of the words "cheese" and "hamburger." The cheese is usually sliced, then added a short time before the hamburger finishes cooking, to allow it to melt.

In the US Upper Midwest, particularly Wisconsin, burgers are often made with a buttered bun, butter as one of the ingredients of the patty, or with a pat of butter on top of the burger patty, and called a "Butter Burger."

In Alberta, Canada a kubie burger is a hamburger made with a pressed Ukrainian garlic sausage, kubasa.

In Toronto the local eatery Dangerous Dan's Diner offers the Colossal Colon Clogger, 24oz burger served with a quarter pound of cheese, a quarter pound of bacon, and 2 fried eggs.

A slugburger is a traditional southern delicacy found in northeast Mississippi, US. It is a patty made from a mixture of meat or pork and an inexpensive extender such as soybeans and deep fried in canola oil.

My favorite is the Bacon Cheese Bomb, a cheeseburger with cheese inside the meat patty rather than on top. A thick chunk of sharp cheddar cheese is surrounded by the meat, which is a mixture of ground beef mixed half and half with finely chopped bacon. *The smoky bacony flavor with a molten core of cheese within the patty is ooey, gooey, heavenly, bacony food for the gods.*

Darwin Beer Can Regatta - Jul 06, 2014, Darwin, Australia. The first Beer Can Regatta was held on 16 June 1974, and was a "festival" developed by Lutz Frankenfeld and Paul Rice-Chapman. Each year contestants handcraft boats out of recycled beer cans and take to the seas. For boats that do not float, there is another chance, to see how fast the team can carry a Henley boat in a straight line in a race down the beach.

Entrance is by a gold coin donation and proceeds go to projects of the combined Lions Clubs of Darwin. There are many festivities along with eating and drinking booths set up.

Rules for the beer can boats - The Ten Can-Mandments

1. Thou shalt enter the event in the right spirit.

2. Thou shalt build the craft of cans.

3. The craft shall float by cans alone.

4. Thou shalt not drown.

5. Thou shalt not take the name of the craft in vain. Any craft bearing signs or lettering that may be offensive will be barred.

6. Thou shalt not drift from the straight and narrow and end up at Mandorah.

7. Thou shalt not protest too much.

8. Thou shall honor thy Committee.

9. Thou shalt not commit adultery – nothing really to do with the Regatta, but it gives us an air of responsibility and respect.

10. Thou shalt go back and read the first can-mandment again.

The Aussies sure know how to have a good time.

National Senior Citizens Day - This is celebrated on August 21 with various events and activities held across the United States, in recognition of National Senior Citizens Day. This day was created as a day to support, honor, and show appreciation to seniors and to recognize their achievements and the contributions they make to their communities.

On August 19, 1988, President Ronald Reagan signed Proclamation 5847 declaring August 21 as National Senior Citizens Day. *Someday I may be forced to grow up and celebrate this day, but for now, every day is a good day to celebrate the achievements of others.*

International Bacon Day - The Saturday before Labor Day is International Bacon Day.

(Homer Simpson: I'll have the smiley face breakfast special. Uhh, but could you add a bacon nose? Plus bacon hair, bacon mustache, five o'clock shadow made of bacon bits and a bacon body.

Waitress: How about I just shove a pig down your throat? (Homer looks excited)

Waitress: I was kidding.

Homer: Fine, but the bacon man lives in a bacon house.) *Enjoy!*

September 19, International Talk Like a Pirate Day - It is a parodic holiday created in 1995 by John Baur (Ol' Chumbucket) and Mark Summers (Cap'n Slappy) of Albany, Oregon, US, who proclaimed September 19 each year as the day when everyone in the world should talk like a pirate.

Pirate Myths Debunked - The rumor that pirates commonly made people walk the plank is not true. Only five documented instances were recorded. Peg legs were not common, because amputated legs usually meant a quick death. Buried treasure was usually found very quickly and no one needed a map. There have only been three well documented instances throughout pirating history where a pirate admitted to burying treasure. The earliest use of "shiver me timbers" came from Captain Frederick Marryat's 1835 book Jacob Faithful, about hundred years after the age of piracy.

Love Your Teeth Day - To increase awareness of the importance of dental care, the Chinese government designated September 20 as national "Love Your Teeth Day." This day involves promotions from dentists to attract clients, as well as information meant to encourage people to see a dentist and take better care to avoid cavities in the future. The campaign has been running for decades and has been successful in getting more people to the dentist.

National Pizza Month - It was first observed in the US during October 1984. The observance was thought up by Gerry Durnell from Santa Claus, Indiana and the founder of Pizza Today magazine. It is also observed throughout much of Canada.

The US has about 63,000 pizzerias and 94% of Americans eat pizza at least once a month. About three billion pizzas are sold in the United States every year, plus an additional one billion frozen pizzas. That works out to about 100 acres of pizza per day, or 350 slices per second.

World Toilet Day - Not a joke. United Nations secretary-general Ban Ki-Moon, along with a coalition from Singapore, introduced a resolution to declare November 19th the first 'World Toilet Day'. The resolution was co-sponsored and adopted by 122 countries at the 67th session of the UN General Assembly in New York. On July 24, 2013, World Toilet Day became an official UN day.

Since its inception in 2001, World Toilet Day is celebrated globally by NGOs, UN agencies, the private sector, civil society organizations and the international community.

> 40% of the world's population does not have access to toilets.

19 November is a special day for the World Toilet Organization. It was founded on 19 November 2001. World Toilet Day was established with the aim to draw global attention to the sanitation crisis. The organization's approach of mixing humor with serious facts resonated with people around the world.

A clean and safe toilet ensures health, dignity and well-being, yet 40% of the world's population does not have access to toilets. Over two billion people do not have access to proper sanitation, including toilets or latrines, with dramatic consequences on human health, dignity and security, the environment, and social and economic development.

Daylight Saving Time - Daylight saving time is often incorrectly referred to as "Daylight savings time." It is difficult to imagine why some still follow this political tradition of messing with our clocks in the vain attempt to change Mother Nature. Nonetheless, the second Sunday in March is the day in the US most move clocks forward one hour (and also to change the batteries on smoke detectors), while some are not required to change their clocks.

United States Congress established the Uniform Time Act of 1966 that stated DST would begin on the last Sunday of April and end on the last Sunday of October. The US Congress extended DST to a period of ten months in 1974, and back to eight months in 1975. The DST schedule period lasted for about seven months from 1987 to 2006. The current schedule began in 2007 and follows the Energy Policy Act of 2005, which extended the period by about one month where DST starts on the second Sunday in March and ends on the first Sunday in November.

Interesting that the vast majority, well over one hundred countries, do not change clocks for DST or any other reason. Those that do observe it have different days, ranging from Mar 9 to April 6, and September in New Zealand, Antarctica, and Namibia. Some of Australia changes on October 5, with other parts of Australia not changing their clocks.

Pro - According to a 2004 Japan Productivity Centre (sic) for Socio-Economic Development report titled, 'Summer Time as a Means to Lifestyle Structural Reform', "lighter evenings could, in the long-term, reduce bag theft by up to 10 percent."

Con - The California Energy Commission published a report, 'The Effect of Early Daylight Saving Time on California Electricity Consumption: A Statistical Analysis'. According to the report, the extension of daylight saving time in March 2007 had little or no effect on energy consumption in California.

No studies have been conducted to prove the heated rhetoric caused by DST discussions that could possibly increase global warming by .1658%.

When told the reason for daylight savings time the Old Indian said, "Only the government would believe that you could cut a foot off the top of a blanket, sew it to the bottom, and have a longer blanket."

Wise words indeed!

Fun Facts and Trivia

A is for Alcohol - A recent study from the Research Society on Alcoholism shows that regular drinkers are less likely to die prematurely than people who have never indulged in alcohol. It concludes that abstaining from alcohol altogether can lead to a shorter life than consistent, moderate drinking.

The controlled study followed 1,824 individuals between ages 55 and 65 over a 20-year period and accounted for variables including socioeconomic status to level of physical activity. It found that mortality rates were highest for those who had never had a sip, lower for heavy drinkers, and lowest for moderate drinkers who enjoyed one to three drinks per day.

Results showed 69 percent of nondrinkers and 60 percent of heavy drinkers died prematurely, while only 41 percent of the moderate drinkers died prematurely. Even with the other heavy drinking mortality factors, such as risks for cirrhosis and cancer, accidents, and poor judgment associated with heavy drinking; those who imbibe are less likely to die prematurely than nondrinkers.

A possible explanation offered is that alcohol can be a social lubricant and strong social networks are essential for maintaining mental and physical health. Also, nondrinkers demonstrate greater signs of depression than drinkers. Another recent study found that moderate alcohol consumption boosts your immune system. In addition, there is potential heart health and circulation benefits of moderate drinking, especially red wine.

The difference between moderate and chronic is defined by the National Institute on Alcohol Abuse and Alcoholism. They define moderate as no more than four drinks on a single day and no more than 14 in a week for men. For women, it is defined as no more than three drinks on a single day and no more than seven in a week.

Perspective - Here is a thought as we ponder our place in the universe. *"Put three grains of sand inside a vast cathedral, and the cathedral will be more closely packed with sand than space is with stars."*

Six Interesting Tidbits - "I have noticed that even people who claim everything is predetermined and that we can do nothing to change it, look before they cross the road." - Steven Hawking

Squirrels are able to lower their body temperature to below freezing while hibernating, and yet no ice crystals form in their blood. No other mammal can do this.

Sheep have a good memory for faces.

Aladdin's face was based on Tom Cruise.

Backpfeifengesicht is German for 'a face that makes you want to hit it'.

Bill Hewlett and Dave Packer flipped a coin to see whose name would be first in the company title.

Drain Fix - Grab some baking soda and sprinkle it in and on the drain. If it just sits on top of the drain, that is okay.

Pour white vinegar down the drain. Add as much vinegar as you can without overflowing the clogged drain. You will immediately be able to see the baking soda and vinegar start to go to work. Together, they will form bubbling carbon dioxide, which will clear away any build-up.

Plug the drain with a stopper.
Allow it to sit for 10 minutes.
Remove the plug and run very hot water through the cleared drain.

Ten Unique Jobs - With so many people out of work, I thought it might be nice to help them expand their job search. Here are some jobs you might not thought of applying for.

Dog Food Taster
Odor Judge (for underarm odors)
Bull Semen Collector
Artificial Inseminator (animals)
Condom Tester
Coin Polisher
Dinosaur Duster
Mount Rushmore Crack Filler
Pollen Collector
Breath Odor Evaluator
Now get out there and expand your horizons.

How Streets Get Named - Real estate and subdivision developers have the privilege of naming new streets in the United States. The name is submitted to the city for review. Police, fire, and the post office, are given the opportunity to veto the name if they feel it creates any confusion.

Building, engineering, and public works departments all comment, but the departments that have the most input and veto power are police and fire. The reason is for the street names to be unique and intelligible enough for them to distinguish and find a street and property in an emergency.

Most cities have guidelines and standards for certain areas that require street names to be of a specific theme. This is why you see a large quantity of streets named after trees in one particular section of a city, or all 50 states represented in street names in Washington D.C.

If you happen to be a developer and want to name a street after yourself, you would have better luck in a newly developing suburb than you would in an established city.

The names of trees and numbers make up the greatest number of street names in the US.

Basketball Quickie - In 1892, the first officially recognized basketball game was played at the YMCA gym in Springfield, Mass., US.

Flying vs. Driving - MIT statistics professor Arnold Barnett reports that in the last five years, the risk of dying on a flight in the United States was one in 45 million. So, you can fly every day for 123,000 years before encountering a crash.

Your chance of being killed in a car accident in a given year is one in 7,000, making flying thousands of times safer.

New Way to Achieve Goals - Came across an interesting idea this week. If you really want to accomplish something, the normal process is to set a goal by making it a TODO item, such as: 'Lose five pounds in one month'.

An alternative idea is to turn that goal into a question, such as, 'How can I lose five pounds in one month'? The ideas quickly come, because our mind needs to solve the puzzle we posed. People have a built in need to come up with an answer to a question. It has less need to accomplish a goal.

That question, "How can I drink more water?" might spark all kinds of follow-up questions and ideas. What if I connect drinking water to certain triggers, e.g. taking a swig of water every time I check my email? What if I put a desired amount of water in a bottle each day? The various what, if, and how questions may help you arrive at a concrete plan, instead of just a goal.

Origin of the Bra - Wearing a specialized garment to support women's breasts dates as far back as the 14th century BC in Greece where women wore a band of wool or linen that was wrapped across the breasts and tied or pinned in the back.

It is not clear who was the first to invent the modern bra, as numerous patents in various nations were filed in the mid-19th to early 20th centuries. However, Caresse Crosby, born Mary Phelps Jacob, invented her design in 1910 and was among the first to patent her 'backless brassiere'. She got the idea for her bra when she was just 19 years old and going to a ball. Her dress for the evening was a sheer gown. She, with the help of her maid, took two handkerchiefs and some ribbon and sewed them together to make something like a modern day bra, so she could have support, but not need to wear a corset.

Frederick Mellinger, founder of Frederick's of Hollywood, introduced a padded bra, a push-up bra, a front hook bra, and more colorful bras. The most expensive bra in history, valued at $15 million, was modeled in 2000 by Gisele Bundchen and made from red satin and hand-cut Thai rubies and diamonds.

Corsets dominated the undergarments of wealthier women in the Western world for centuries, until WWI required quite a bit of metal. In 1917, the US War Industries Board asked American women to help their 'men win the war' by not wearing or buying corsets. *During the war it is estimated that they freed up around 28,000 tons of steel that could be used for the war effort.*

Disposable Diaper Double Duty - Diapers keep baby bottoms dry because they absorb liquids. They can also be used in planters.

Cut strips of unused diapers and place on the bottom of the pot before adding soil. They absorb water and keep plants hydrated longer as they slowly release the water to the soil on top.

Four Useful Household Hacks - Spray nonstick spray on the inside of your votive candle holders. Remaining wax will easily slide out.
Use newspaper to eliminate odors in Tupperware, or the crisper bin of your refrigerator, or in a purse with lingering smells.
Add a few drops of vodka and a teaspoon of sugar to make cut flowers last longer.
Rub the cut edge of cheese with butter or olive oil to keep it from getting moldy.

Jokes Pay - I love reading studies about odd things. For instance, if you are a waitperson you probably are concerned about the tips that you receive from customers. One way to increase tips might be to leave a joke on a card with the bill.

Someone conducted a study about tipping at a bar. Each person in the study was randomly assigned to one of three conditions, no card with the bill, an advertising card with the bill, and a card with a joke on it with the bill.

They found that a higher percentage of customers gave a tip after receiving a joke card than in the other two conditions. In contrast, the difference between the advertisement card and the no card, the percentage of people tipping was not statistically significant.

These findings indicate that humor may increase tips. One possible explanation of the effect of humor on tipping is that it reflects the reciprocity principle, which suggests that we should help someone who helps us.

Providing a joke on a card can be viewed as helping the customer and it may make the person more happy and cheerful. The customer, in turn may wish to reciprocate by providing a tip. *That reminds me of a joke about the waiter and a spoon. . .*

Facts About the Olympics - With the beautiful pictures of the Sochi games in mind, I thought it might be interesting to write about the origin of the Olympics. The Olympics got its name from city named Olympia, Greece, where the original games were held.

The 1936 Olympics were the first to be televised.

Pierre de Frédy, Baron de Coubertin convened a congress in Paris in 1894 with the goal of reviving the ancient Olympic Games. The congress agreed on proposals for a modern Olympics, and the International Olympic Committee was formalized and given the task of planning the 1896 Athens Games.

The first new Olympic Games, featuring athletes from all five inhabited parts of the world were held in Stockholm in 1912. This prompted the design of five interlocked rings. He drew and colored the rings and added them to a letter sent to a colleague. He used his ring design as the emblem of the Committee's 20th anniversary celebration in 1914. A year later, it became the official Olympic symbol.

The rings were to be used on flags and signage at the 1916 Games, but those games were cancelled, because of the ongoing World War, so the rings made the official debut at the 1920 Games in Antwerp, Belgium.

At the end of each Olympic Games, the mayor of the host-city presents the flag to the mayor of the next host-city. It then rests at the town hall of the next host-city for four years until the Opening Ceremony of its Olympic Games.

Coubertin explained his design: "A white background, with five interlaced rings in the centre (sic): blue, yellow, black, green and red is symbolic; it represents the five inhabited continents of the world, united by Olympism, while the six colors are those that appear on all the national flags of the world at the present time." He never said nor wrote that any specific ring represents a specific continent. *It is a myth that the rings were inspired by a similar, ancient design found on a stone at Delphi, Greece. The stone was made as a prop.*

The Olympic motto was also proposed by Pierre, "Citius, Altius, Fortius", which is Latin for "Swifter, Higher, Stronger."

Special Olympics - In 1971, The US Olympic Committee gave the Special Olympics official approval to use the name "Olympics". In 1988, the Special Olympics was officially recognized by the International Olympic Committee. Special Olympics is the world's largest sports organization for children and adults with intellectual disabilities, providing year-round training and competitions to more than 4.2 million athletes in 170 countries. Special Olympics competitions are held every day, all around the world, including local, regional, and national competitions, adding up to more than 70,000 events per year.

The motto for the Special Olympics is, "Let me win, but if I cannot win, let me be brave in the attempt."

I have the honor and privilege to assist in presenting medals to Special Olympians during various Special Olympics of Texas Games.

What Causes Tornadoes - The first four months of the year brings risk for tornadoes in the southern US. From April through June, the biggest tornado threat shifts to the Plains, Upper Midwest, and Great Lakes. The main tornado risk then stays along the northern tier of the country through much of summer, while tropical storms and hurricanes increase back in the South as they move inland. These are followed in November and December with more chances of tornadoes moving back to the South.

About ninety percent of US twisters occur in a 300-mile wide corridor extending from West Texas to Canada. Warm, moist surface winds blow up from the Gulf of Mexico, while cool high-altitude winds blow over the tops of the Rockies. The cool air wants to sink while warm air wants to rise. However, the mountain air causes a temperature inversion, which prevents the warm surface air from rising.

It is like clamping the lid on a pressure cooker. The surface weather systems build up a big head of steam until they break through the inversion and shoot up to towering heights and the violent updrafts and downdrafts lead to form tornadoes. *Tornadoes occur most frequently in the central plains of the US. Australia has the second most tornadoes each year.*

Toothpaste - As far back as 3000-5000 BC, ancient Egyptians were using a tooth cream. This dental cream was comprised of powdered ashes from oxen hooves, myrrh, egg shells, and pumice. They used their fingers, instead of a brush. Greeks and Romans improved on the process. Then China and India began using a powder/paste as well. The Chinese were particularly forward-thinking in adding flavoring, such as Ginseng, herbal mints, and salt.

Doctors, dentists, and chemists in Britain introduced tooth powders (or dentrifice) that included abrasive substances like brick dust and crushed china. Glycerine was added in the early 19th century, transforming the powders into pastes. During 1873 toothpaste was first mass-produced. In 1892, Dr. Washington Sheffield of Connecticut invented Dr. Sheffield's Crème Dentrifice. It was the first time toothpaste was featured in a collapsible tube.

Tom and Kate Chappell sought to create their own toothpaste. They moved from Philadelphia to rural Kennebunk, Maine, and introduced the first natural toothpaste in 1975. It is still called Tom's of Maine.

What the Recycle Symbols Mean - The original recycling symbol was designed in 1970 by Gary Anderson, a senior at the University of Southern California at Los Angeles. It was submitted to the International Design Conference as part of a nationwide contest for high school and college students sponsored by the Container Corporation of America.

The symbols show the various types of materials. If there is an R in front of the letters, that means it was already recycled. A container or package, marked with this symbol was manufactured with at least some materials that have been recycled. Generally, additional information is conveyed with the symbol such as, 'Printed on recycled paper'.

The numbers range from 1 to 7, defining which type of material it is.

Type 1 PolyEthylene TErephthalate is used for pop/soda bottles. Twenty-seven percent of type 1 is recycled, including 41 percent of plastic pop/soda bottles.

Type 2 High-Density PolyEthylene is used for milk and detergent bottles. About 7 percent of type 2 plastic recycled.

Type 3 is used on window cleaner bottles, cooking oil bottles, detergent bottles, shampoo bottles, clear food packaging, wire and cable jackets, medical tubing, and in other household products and building materials, particularly siding, piping, and windows.

Recycling types 3 through 7 are rare, because using virgin material is cheaper. Recycling rates for these materials are about 1-2 percent.

The recycling rate for all plastic packaging is about 4 to 5 percent, compared with 53 percent for aluminum.

There is a symbol for glass, but usually all glass is recyclable. There are many other symbols used for various materials, and different symbols in different countries. *They are all meant to make consumers aware of recycling, even if many of the products are not recycled.*

Who Threw That? - Fans at the University of Pennsylvania throw toast on the football field after the third quarter because the school banned liquor, which was formerly used to toast the team. The students took the toast literally and now throw real toast.

This is much better than the University of New Hampshire fans, who throw a fish on the ice during school hockey games. Also fishy, during 2011, fans of the Nashville Predators threw catfish on the ice.

Speaking of hockey, fans in Detroit have a tradition of throwing an octopus on the ice during Detroit Red Wings home playoff games. It began during the 1952 playoffs, when a National Hockey League team played two best-of-seven series to capture the Stanley Cup. The octopus, with eight arms, symbolized the number of playoff wins necessary for the Red Wings to win the Stanley Cup. Brothers Pete and Jerry Cusimano hurled an octopus into the rink. The team swept the Toronto Maple Leafs and Montreal Canadiens en route to winning the championship.

Florida Panthers fans littered the ice with plastic rats during face-offs and regular play during Game 5 of their 2012 playoff series.

Other tosses, that seem mild by comparison, include throwing flowers for figure skaters, or tossing hats when a hockey player makes a hat trick.

Sliced Bread - Sliced bread was introduced in 1928 by Otto Frederick Rohwedder. Before then, bread was sold in whole loaves as bakers didn't believe sliced bread could stay fresh.

Betty White was born in 1922 and that makes her older than sliced bread.

Also, 1922 was the last year of the Ottoman Empire, when it was taken over by the Turkish government.

1922 was also 14 years after the last time the Chicago Cubs won a World Series, in 1908. *The record still stands at 107 years.*

Dial 311 - The 311 number has been used for years, but many are not aware of it. It was used in the distant past as a number dialed in TV shows and some movies in the same way as the now used 555 prefix.

This number is available in most US and Canadian cities for a wide range of non-emergency services, such as graffiti, high weeds, litter, and garbage cart replacement, aggressive or dead animals, non-working street lights, noise complaints, potholes, etc. Most large cities have made this available and the list of cities continues to grow. When in doubt, try dialing 311 before calling 911 and they can help. *Handy to use when you do not know the phone number for non-emergency police or city services.*

Foiling Garden Pests - Early spring planting tip - cut up small strips of used aluminum foil and mix in with garden soil to keep away aphids and other garden pests.

Burning Snowman - Ah, Spring! Lake Superior State University in Michigan is home to the annual tradition of burning a snowman to signal the beginning of Spring.

LSSU is also the place where you can obtain a license to hunt unicorns and you can find all the regulations. There is a limit of one per month.

This university is also home to the annual banished words list. The word with most nominations for 2014 was "selfie".

In spite of the foregoing Tongue-in-cheek nonsense, it is a real university located in Sault Ste. Marie (pronounced Soo Saint Marie), in Michigan's Upper Peninsula. Undergraduate degrees are offered in 45 areas of study.

Why Grass - Approximately 80% of all homes in the United States have grass lawns. Lawns are a $40 billion per year industry and 3 billion man-hours are spent mowing lawns. A variety of factors caused grass lawns to become more popular.

The Industrial Revolution resulted in the first lawn mower, originally developed by Edwin Budding in 1830. Doing away with scythes and back-breaking labor meant that trimmed grass lawns were more accessible to the average person.

Frederick Law Olmstead, who designed Central Park in New York, also designed suburbs where each house had its own little lawn. This further popularized the idea that houses should have grass lawns.

About that time, the games of golf, lawn bowling, and other sports were becoming popular in North America. As people worked less hours and had more time to themselves, there was time to play golf, or to tend a lush, green lawn.

Next to grass at a major league baseball field is a strip of dirt located in front of the home run fence. This dirt trail is known as the warning track. Outfielders use the warning track as a warning that they are nearing the fence when chasing a fly ball.

Sunglasses Facts - If you get a really good pair of sunglasses it will certainly be to your benefit. Ophthalmologists have explained that if you get a cheap pair that does not protect you from UVA and UVB, you might as well not wear sunglasses. Normally if you are looking toward a bright light, your eyes will squint to protect you, but if you are wearing sunglasses, your eyes will open further to allow in more light. One researcher used a meter to test random sunglasses that he bought from vendors in New York and found that some of them did not live up to the protection claims on the glasses. *Caveat Emptor.*

Boston Marathon History - In the 2013 marathon, over 23,000 runners participated. Lelisa Desisa won the men's division with a time of 2:10:22. Rita Jeptoo won the women's division with a time of 2:26:25. More than $800,000 of prize money was awarded.

On April 19, 1897, John J. McDermott of New York won the first Boston Marathon with a time of 2:55:10. *(During the past 100 plus years, winners have shaved 45 minutes off his original time.)*

The Boston Marathon was created by Boston Athletic Association member and inaugural U.S. Olympic team manager John Graham, who was inspired by the marathon at the first modern Olympic Games in Athens the year before, 1896. A measured distance of 24.5 miles from the Irvington Oval in Boston to Metcalf's Mill in Ashland was eventually selected. Fifteen runners started the race, but only ten finished.

The marathon's distance was changed in 1908 in accordance with Olympic standards to its current length of 26 miles 385 yards.

The Boston Marathon was originally held on Patriot's Day, April 19, a regional holiday that commemorates the beginning of the Revolutionary War. In 1969, Patriots Day was officially moved to the third Monday in April and the race has been held on that Monday ever since.

Women were not allowed to enter the Boston race officially until 1972, but Roberta "Bobbi" Gibb could not wait. In 1966, she became the first woman to run the entire Boston Marathon, but had to hide in the bushes near the start until the race began. In 1967, Kathrine Switzer, who had registered as "K. V. Switzer," was the first woman to run with a race number. Switzer finished even though officials tried to physically remove her from the race after she was identified as a woman.

In 1975, the Boston Marathon became the first major marathon to include a wheelchair division competition. Bob Hall won it in two hours, 58 minutes, just three minutes off of the original winning run.

Great San Francisco Earthquake - On April 18, 1906 at 5:13 a.m., an earthquake estimated at close to 8.0 on the Richter scale struck San Francisco, California, killing hundreds of people as it toppled numerous buildings. The quake was caused by a slip of the San Andreas Fault over a segment about 275 miles long, and shock waves could be felt from southern Oregon down to Los Angeles.

By April 23, most fires were extinguished, and authorities commenced the task of rebuilding the devastated city. It was estimated that 3,000 people died as a result. Almost 30,000 buildings were destroyed, including most of the city's homes and nearly all the central business district.

Origin of Safety Glass - Safety glass is used widely today and has saved millions of people, especially during vehicular mishaps. French chemist Edouard Benedictus in 1901 discovered the unique properties of safety glass by accident.

When he accidentally bumped a flask, causing it to fall and crash, he discovered the flask was broken, but not shattered. After researching, he discovered the glass contained cellulose nitrate, which served as an adhesive and held the broken pieces together.

"Indestructo" safety glass was originally manufactured by British Indestructo Glass Ltd of London. This glass was first used as gas masks during WWI and has become a standard in manufacturing windshields since 1939 and many other items today.

Six Uses for WD40 - If you have tea stains on your counter tops, just spray a little on a damp sponge or cloth, then wipe.

Remove marker and crayon marks by spraying it on upholstered furniture (spray on inconspicuous place first to make sure it does not leave a mark of its own).

Spraying a little WD40 on a zipper then moving it up and down will help lubricate.

Prevent wasps nests tend to build in eaves, so a few sprays in those areas will prevent them.

Also, in early spring, spray into weep holes in bricks to prevent ant, bees, and other little critters.

Spray a bit into your hands to degrease, rub them together, and wash with soap and water.

Statue of Liberty Symbols - The statue's formal name is "Liberty Enlightening the World" and it has many symbols. The crown contains 25 windows that symbolize gemstones and heaven's rays shining through to the world. Chains and shackles at her feet represent America breaking the chains of tyranny and accepting democracy as a form of government. The torch represents enlightenment and the tablet she holds represents a book of law. The seven rays around the head form a halo, showing she is divine and evokes the sun, the seven seas, and the seven continents.

The United States Post Office issued a Statue of Liberty Stamp a few years ago, but used the Las Vegas Liberty statue by mistake. Of course, the artist sued for copyright infringement.

Taming Odor Tips - Leave bar soap in the package and rest it somewhere out of sight. Hide an extra bar near your kitchen garbage can. Soap also lasts longer when it is dried. Open the your new soap bars and place them in closets, under the bed, in your armoire, in clothes drawers, or any place else you want to smell fresh, but not overpowering. Since it does not pick up odors, you can use it to shower after it becomes a bit hard.

Cat litter is good for eliminating cat odors, but can also be used to reduce other odors. Use cat litter in closets to reduce odors or put some in a coffee filter and stick in smelly shoes. If you have cats, be careful, as they might use the litter for their own purpose.

Put a large bowl of vinegar in a smelly room, such as the kitchen to eliminate unwanted odors. Put out a large bowl when you leave for work and when you arrive home at the end of the day, you will be surprised how well it works. Vinegar also works to clean wood furniture. Mix a 50-50 solution with water and wipe down the wooden furniture with a damp (not wet) cloth of the mixture.

I put used dryer sheets in clothes drawers and the pantry. They work for months. You can also put them in shoes to make them fresh. It is a good way to get a second use. They also work well in gym bags and luggage.

Baking soda is great to unstink a clothes hamper. Sprinkle on top of clothes. When ready, toss clothes into washer as usual. The baking soda also helps clean the clothes during washing. In fact, baking soda can replace detergent for washing clothes. Baking soda is also good for carpet stains or furniture odor. Sprinkle on, wait a while, then vacuum. Do not leave on for too long, or it may tend to bleach the fabric.

Coffee is the favorite of airlines to unstink airplane restrooms. Leave a dish of fresh, ground, unused coffee on a table and within hours the room smells better. If you travel, those little hotel room packets of coffee are perfect to use in your bag with dirty laundry and at home for room odors.

Sports Wave Origin - The wave was the brain-child of the longest continuously active professional cheerleader, Krazy George Henderson. It made its national debut on October 15, 1981 in a playoff game between the Oakland Athletics and the New York Yankees, which the Yankees won 4-0.

Krazy George's claim is easily verified by the Major League Baseball archives. As the wave was something not seen before, with nearly all 47,000 in attendance participating, players and the announcers were amazed. Video of this first documented wave, including Krazy George leading it, made it onto the Oakland A's highlight video for the season.

Of this first documented wave, Krazy George states, "I started with three sections and it went about five or six sections down. I did it again and it went 11 and then all the way around. Joe Garigiola was in the broadcast booth yelling at his cameramen to get that thing. Of course, no one knew what it was."

It is generally called the 'Mexican wave' outside of the United States due to the 1986 FIFA World Cup in Mexico, where the rest of the world was first introduced to the wave. Krazy George invented the move, but not 'the wave', or the 'Mexican wave' name.

Socks and Puppets - Socks have been around as a form of footwear for thousands of years. They initially started as matted animal hair shaped to fit inside a shoe or around the foot and ankle. The ancient Greeks were known to have used this technique as far back as 750 BC. The Romans innovated with thick fabrics that were wrapped around the legs to form a shaped sock.

Knitting was invented in Egypt during the 12th century AD by nomadic sheep herders who would create fabric through the simple use of knotting wool yarn using straight twigs. The technique had advantages over traditional weaving and allowed any shepherd and his wife to produce a more valuable product instead of just selling their wool. The practice quickly spread from Egypt throughout the Middle East and into Europe. Muslim knitters in Spain started developing a variety of knitting stitches that allowed them to create shaped fabrics, the sock being one of the first knitted items of clothing to be produced.

In 1589, William Lee of Calverton in England invented the first knitting machine which overnight transformed knitted garments into something almost everyone could afford. Knitting is credited with transforming the textile industry and became the precursor to the industrial age.

In China and Japan during the first millennium BC puppets were being intricately carved from wood. Puppets were being used in India by the 11th century as devices to give morality stories a visual impact that words couldn't convey. Puppets have been used to represent good, evil, jealousy, and greed without running the risk of identifying individuals who might exact revenge against the storyteller. In ancient India puppets were constructed from carved sticks, and were often elaborately decorated. Sock puppets were likely invented when knitted socks became more widely in use.

As the puritan movement in England gained momentum, traditional puppetry was banned along with all other forms of theater. During these years in England and France, radicals would organize secret theater shows and used puppets, as they were easier to transport and conceal than sets, costumes, and large bands of actors. Socks and very basic stages made of suspended fabric hung behind a table became a popular way of getting around the ban. It was about this time that the puppet character Punch was created.

After the return of the monarchy and the end of puritan times, Punch and Judy, puppets became more commonly associated with glove or hand puppets. Children used discarded socks that could be decorated to mimic a hand puppet.

Recently the term sock puppet is also used to describe a fictitious identity used online to promote a particular point of view or defend a person who is seen as controversial.

Sit Straight, Be Confident - In a recent study, participants were asked to think about and write down their best or worse qualities while they were sitting down with their back erect and pushing their chest out in a confident posture, or slouched forward with their back curved. Then, participants completed a number of measures and reported their self-evaluations. Researchers found the effect of the direction of thoughts (positive/negative) on self-related attitudes was significantly greater when participants wrote their thoughts in the confident posture. The postures did not influence the number or quality of thoughts listed, but did have an impact on the confidence with which people held their thoughts.

In the Middle - We all look at records for first and last, top and bottom, largest and smallest, and left and right. Sometimes it is its own reward to be in the middle. Here are a few examples of things that celebrate being in the middle.

July 2, at noon is the exact middle of the year. It has 182 days before it and 182 days following.

There is a obelisk monument located at U.S. Highway 2 and North Dakota Highway 3, in Rugby, North Dakota, United States that claims to be the middle of North America. Rugby was named after the town of Rugby in Warwickshire, England (yes, where rugby football was born).

It is approximately 15 miles (24 km) from the geographic center of North America, but that is close enough according to locals. (The

Geographic Center of the Contiguous United States is located about two miles northwest of Lebanon, Kansas.)

A monument in Ecuador is dedicated to being the center of the globe. It commemorates the 200th anniversary of the French Geodesic Mission which charted the equator and measured the shape of the earth. The San Antonio de Pichincha, Mitad del Mundo also has a painted line on the pavement marked Latitude 0° 0' 0", where visitors take a photo straddling both hemispheres. The original calculations have been proven incorrect by more accurate modern technology and the actual equator line runs about 240 meters north of the monument, but that is close enough for locals.

At exactly 45 degrees latitude, 90 degrees longitude, in the town of Rietbrock, Wisconsin, Untied States is the exact center of the Northern half of the Western Hemisphere. It is here that the 90th Meridian of Longitude bisects the 45th Parallel of Latitude meaning it is exactly halfway between the North Pole and the Equator and is a quarter of the way around Earth from Greenwich, England. The marker is about 1063 feet away from the actual 45x90 spot, but that is close enough for the locals.

The equator monument is at Pontianak on the Indonesian side of the island of Borneo. This monument marks where the exact middle of the world used to be.

Due to constant global shift, the true Equatorial line was recorded a short distance south of the monument and, according to GPS readings, the line continues to move south, but that is close enough for the locals.

Before you ask, there is no middle of the universe. According to standard theories of cosmology, the universe began about 14 thousand million years ago and has been expanding ever since. Expansion is the same everywhere; it is not expanding out from a center into space, but is expanding equally at all places. *This is the end of the middle.*

Saggy Pants - Have often wondered where the style of some youth began with wearing pants sagging much below the waist. Many US towns have banned wearing in public trousers that are slung so low as to expose the wearer's underwear.

This saggy trend appears to have originated in US jails where the combination of a prison diet and vigorous sports leads to a slimmer waist. As prisoners are required to wear the trousers they were issued with at the beginning of their sentences, and because belts are usually banned for various reasons, this led to inadvertent sagging. The 'fashion statement' spread beyond the prison walls and has become a sought-after look among America's disaffected youth.

Negotiating Technique - From a recent study, people who sat in hard chairs were more likely to maintain a hard line in negotiations and were less receptive to their partner's way of thinking.

In a series of studies, scientists found that they could easily manipulate people's feelings and perceptions based on nothing more than what the subjects were touching. Holding heavier objects, for instance, made men think more seriously about things, which in turn made them more likely to donate money to charity if asked. Men holding lighter objects were less likely to donate to charitable causes. People handling rough objects were more likely to see neutral social situations in a bad light, saying that other people were obviously in a bad mood.

What Makes Super Glue Work - Super glue works like a two-part adhesive, the glue in the tube and the hardener is water. Most dry surfaces have microscopic droplets of water adhering to them. When super glue comes in contact with these droplets they create the chemical reaction that causes the super glue to harden.

You can wipe both surfaces with a very slightly damp cloth or breathe on it, like breathing on a mirror to speed the adhesive's setting. It sticks to skin because skin is full of large, medium, small and microscopic grooves and pores that provide the perfect type of roughness for glue to grab. Second, the skin tissues are saturated with water so the super glue can soak in and find water to cause the hardening reaction.

The super glue that doctors use is different than the type available in hardware stores. Surgical super glue contains types of alcohols that are less toxic to human tissue. The type sold in stores uses ethyl of methyl alcohols that can kill cells.

Hot Weather Thoughts - While some of complain about heat, think of this: Lowest temperature recorded was in Vostok, Antartica July 21, 1983, −128.6f or −89.2C.

Record breaking rainfall during 24 hours in Alvin, Texas, July 25–26, 1979 43 inches or 109 centimeters.

The hottest temperature recorded was 134f or 56.7C at Furnace Creek Ranch in Death Valley California, July 10, 1913.

Heaviest hail officially recorded: 2.25 pounds or 1.02 kg; Gopalganj District, Bangladesh, 14 April 1986.

Beer-nails - College students have loved beer for centuries. They are also generally very smart. In one fit of brilliance, students invented biernagels (beer-nails).

These are metal studs placed on the covers of books to keep the leather covers away from wet (spilled beer) pub tables. With biernagels on it, a book cover is raised half a centimeter from the surface of the table, and thus remains mostly dry. *From the name, we can only assume it was some inventive German students.*

National Hobo Convention - August 7-10 was the National Hobo Convention in Britt, Iowa (close to Mason City and Clear Lake). There was a parade on Saturday at 10:00 a.m. "Some in rags, some in tags, some in velvet gowns."

Hobos are migratory workers, some with a special skill or trade, others ready to work at any task, but always willing to work to make his way.

There was marching bands, queens, business floats, children, adults, and hobos all came down the streets in one long line and share the fun that only a Hobo Convention can provide. Following the parade, mulligan stew was available. Other events during the weekend included a 5K & 10K Walk/Run, Hobo King & Queen coronation, Hobo Museum, Hobo Auction, Hobo Memorial Service, Vagabond Craft show, and Outdoor Classic Car Show.

A tramp is a traveling non-worker, moving from town to town, but never willing to work for the handouts he begs for.

A bum is the lowest class, too lazy to roam around and never works.

Social Security Checks - A friend asked me when Social Security checks are mailed, so it sent me to the dot gov site to find out some details. If you were born on the: 1 – 10th of the month, your Social Security check is deposited on the 2nd Wednesday of each month.

11 – 20th of the month, your Social Security check is deposited on the 3rd Wednesday of each month.

21 – 31st of the month, your Social Security check is deposited on the 4th Wednesday of each month.

However, if you started receiving benefits before 1997, or you get SS and SSI payments, then your Social Security check is paid on the third day of the month.

If the day your Social Security check is supposed to be deposited is a holiday, it is deposited the day before. *Very simple formula for very complicated system.*

Wall Plug Tip - Wall plugs or outlets have no top or bottom. Unlike light switches, it does not matter which way is up or down. However, most buildings have switch-controlled outlets mounted upside-down with the center hole on top. Normal position for plugs is to have the center hole below the two prongs. *Very handy info to know when moving into a new place and you want to place a lamp that you want to be controlled by a light switch.*

Short Performance Oscars - The record for shortest Oscar winning performance is held by Beatrice Straight, who won a Best Supporting Actress Oscar for her work in Network (1976), which she appeared in for just one 5 minute and 40 second scene.

Second shortest record for a Best Actor Oscar is held by David Niven, for his work in Separate Tables (1958), which he appeared in for 15 minutes and 38 seconds.

Third shortest record for Best Actor Academy Award is held by Anthony Hopkins, for his work in The Silence of the Lambs (1991), which he appeared in for just over 16 minutes. *All prove that sometimes less is more.*

Bathroom Time Trivia - Normally I do not do this type of trivia, but the numbers staggered me, and not in a good way. This first fact was not a surprise, but the rest were.

Women spend more than twice as long in the bathroom than men. Thirty seven percent of women and fifteen percent of men spend more than one hour in the bathroom per day.

86% of men said the toilet is the place where they did most of their reading.

40 percent of 18 - 24 year olds use social media in the bathroom.

75% of Americans have used their mobile phone in the bathroom. 67% of them read text, 63% answer a call, and 29% do social networking (*Yuck*).

63% of people read books, magazines and newspapers in the bathroom. Magazines are the favored literature (*Author note: many of my books are considered good bathroom reading*). Men's top two reading are erotic magazines and sports. Women's top two are romance novels and interior design magazines.

33% of people read mail and email in the bathroom.

More than 3% of Americans have TVs in their bathroom.

Hangar Hack - If your clothes keep slipping off the end of hangars, wrap a rubber band toward each edge of the hangar and clothes will stay put.

Funeral Celebrants - Funeral Celebrant is an interesting and relatively new profession. They can help plan a festive or somber ceremony, and work with families to develop a eulogy. Some celebrants perform a whole ceremony while some families prefer to perform a ceremony themselves. Celebrant funerals are funeral ceremonies that are a true celebration of the departed one's life.

Many people are choosing to forgo traditional funerals and cremation is growing as an alternative to funerals with half or more people now choosing it. Unlike funerals with the somber process of casket, service, and internment, the cremation process is more personal, less costly, as well as more positive and celebratory. Cremation typically costs less than one fourth the cost of a funeral (if not done by a funeral home). Most states have cremation societies, which can take care of paperwork for insurance, VA, Social Security, obituary, etc., having the body moved to a facility, and assist with all aspects of the process, just as a funeral director traditionally did.

Scattering of ashes is now the most popular thing to do with cremation ashes. Family and friends are having private memorials, scattering ashes, and having a party in the backyard. In fact, you can now buy a "Loved One Launcher", which is a CO2 cartridge filled tube, including confetti that launches ashes into the air. There are also personalized mementos containing bits of ash used in jewelry, lockets, pictures, action figures, and more. You can even get an urn that can be used as a birdhouse after the ashes have been scattered. *Seems like an oxymoron with an action figure made of ashes.*

Nobel Prizes 2014 - The $1.1 million awards were handed out on Dec. 10, the anniversary of prize founder Alfred Nobel's death in 1896.

MEDICINE
U.S.-British scientist John O'Keefe split the Nobel Prize in medicine with Norwegian couple May-Britt Moser and Edvard Moser for breakthroughs in brain cell research that could pave the way for a better understanding of diseases like Alzheimer's.

PHYSICS
Isamu Akasaki and Hiroshi Amano of Japan and Japanese-born U.S. scientist Shuji Nakamura won the Nobel Prize in physics for the invention of blue light-emitting diodes, which promises to revolutionize the way the world lights its homes and offices, and already helps create the glowing screens of mobile phones, computers and TVs.

CHEMISTRY
U.S. researchers Eric Betzig and William Moerner and Stefan Hell of Germany won the Nobel Prize in chemistry for finding ways to make microscopes more powerful than previously thought possible, allowing scientists to see how diseases develop inside the tiniest cells.

Baseball Trading - Harry Chiti was traded for himself. Chiti was a major league catcher who played from 1950 to 1962. On April 25, 1962, before he actually played a game for the Indians, he was acquired by the expansion New York Mets team for a 'player to be named later'. He was sent back to the Indians on June 15, 1962 after 15 games and a .195 batting average.

Since Chiti was the 'player to be named later', he became the first player ever traded for himself. Three other players in history have been traded for themselves: Dickie Noles, Brad Gulden, and John

McDonald. Chiti never played another major league game, spending two more years at Triple-A before retiring in 1964.

Houseplants and Odors - People in office cubicles have put photos of nature up on the walls or brought in green plants to help personalize their space since cubicles were first invented.

The impact turns out to be more than just aesthetic. Adding a plant or two can boost productivity by 38% or more. Scientists at the University of Exeter conducted ninety experiments and found houseplants not only improve creativity (45%) and overall well being (47%), they also provide a boost to focus. As an added bonus, rooms filled with plants have an average of 50% to 60% less bacteria.

Environmental odors appear to impact how productive we are. As the most powerful of our senses, smell might have an impact. One corporation says to chop up some lemons. In studies, workers made 54% less errors when they smelled lemons, 33% fewer mistakes with jasmine, and 20% fewer with lavender.

Sad Presidential Fact - Theodore Roosevelt's wife and mother died in the same house on the same day, Valentine's Day 1884. His wife had just given birth to their daughter Alice, and the pregnancy had hidden her kidney disease. He held her for two hours, had to be torn away to see his mother die of typhoid fever, then returned to his wife, who died in his arms.

Leather Stain Removing – If you have an oil stain on your favorite leather handbag, coat the stain with baby powder and let it stand overnight. By morning, the stain should be gone. If a bit still remains, repeat the process until the stain is completely gone. Also, add a few drops of vinegar in a bowl of water and scrub for water stains on leather shoes or boots.

Holiday Home Hacks - Remove permanent marker by using toothpaste on it.

A lint roller is perfect to dust your lampshades.

Use bread, or a damp paper towel, or play-doh to pick up broken glass or spilled glitter.

Cut a grapefruit and add salt to clean stubborn tub dirt before company arrives.

Wrap your light strings around a hangar to keep them from getting all tangled.

Make a Christmas tree from jello shots to keep the fun going. You can use orange jello for Thanksgiving.

Four Interesting Facts - The FBI call Ted Kaczynski 'The Unabomber', because his early mail bombs were sent to universities (UN) and airlines (A).

Even though most black bears are black, they also come in white, brown, cinnamon, and blue, depending on where in the world they are found.

During the last 3,500 years, it is estimated that the world has had a total of 230 years in which no wars took place.

Rhode Island is the smallest state with the longest name. The official name, used on all state documents, is 'Rhode Island and Providence Plantations'.

Snurfing and Snowboards - Sherman Poppen from Muskegon, Michigan took two 36-inch skis that had a little leather strap over the top of them that kids could slide their shoes into. He added a couple of cross pieces across them about five of six inches apart. The cross pieces were actually molding so you could put your feet up against it. His wife called it the 'snurfer'.

He kept improving the design, patented it as a "surf-type snow ski," and sold it to Brunswick. By 1970, almost a million of the boards had been sold.

Jake Burton Carpenter had a competing product he called the 'Burton Board'. Carpenter's Burton Snowboards would go on to become one of the largest snowboard brands in the world.

Snowboarders might be riding "snurfboards" today, if Poppen hadn't been so possessive of his trademark. When he got started and Burton was calling his board Snurfboards, and his was a Snurfer. He did not like his name being used so he hired an attorney to protect his trademark. The sport became snowboarding because Carpenter could not use the word Snurfer or Snurf.

Pig Squeals - Experts have determined that the average pig squeals at a level of 100-115 decibels. A jet's engine only reaches about 112 decibels at takeoff. *Bacon does not squeal, it sizzles.*

Turquoise Tidbit - The bridle of many horses is decorated with turquoise. This stems from an early European superstition, which continues today, that the wearer of turquoise could never suffer a broken bone, because the turquoise itself would shatter and prevent the accident.

In Europe, this lucky stone was set into horses' bridles to keep the horse from stumbling and falling, protecting the horse and rider. Decorating the bridles with turquoise has continued through the years.

Travel Tip - While traveling, carry-on bags, purses, and wallets can be easily lost or stolen. This is an easy hack to prevent potential headaches, especially for international travel. Scan driver's license, passport, traveler's checks, credit card number, and card help-line phone numbers, or any other important information, then e-mail the information to yourself. Now you can go to any computer in the world and get a copy of your documents and information.

Subway Restaurant Facts - There are currently 42,859 Subway restaurants in 108 countries around the world. Subway has overtaken McDonald's in number of locations. Subway has plans to have 50,000 restaurants around the world by 2018, which means the company will need to open more than six restaurants a day, every day, for the next four years. Subway has opened, on average, more than two restaurants per day since 1965.

Foiling Garden Pests - Cut up small strips of used aluminum foil and mix in with garden soil to keep away aphids and other garden pests.

Canadian Coins - When Canada introduced its 1-dollar coin in 1987 with the queen on front and a loon on back, it became known as the "loonie" for the loon on its back.

When it introduced the 2-dollar coin in 1996 with a picture of the queen on front and a bear on the back, Canadians tried hard to find a nickname. Toonie or twoonie won. Some of the failed suggestions included "doubloonie," "doozie," and, "moonie." Moonie was suggested, because the coin depicts the queen with a bear behind.

Meeting Minutes - Meeting minutes have nothing to do with time, but rather small, as in minute (my-newt). Minutes in this sense first appeared in the early 18th century, possibly directly from the Latin 'minuta scriptura', meaning small notes.

Minutes as in 'meeting notes' references condensing something, such as information down, as in the 'my-newt' pronunciation, not as in 'seconds, minutes, hours'.

Pluto and Naming the Planets - With all the publicity surrounding the recent photos of Pluto, Seems fitting to look at it and the other (real) planets and how they received their names. Pluto is the largest and second-most-massive known dwarf planet in the Solar System and the ninth-largest and tenth-most-massive known object directly orbiting the Sun. It had been discovered many times by astronomers, who did not realize what they found.

Pluto was discovered 'for real' in 1930 by Clyde Tombaugh, and was originally considered the ninth planet from the Sun. After 1992, its status as a planet fell into question following the discovery of several objects of similar size, in particular Eris, which is 27% more massive than Pluto. This led the International Astronomical Union to define the term planet formally for the first time. This definition excluded Pluto and reclassified it as a member of the new "dwarf planet" category. The other dwarf planets are Ceres, Eris, Haumea, and Makemake (sic).

The tradition of naming planets after mythological gods was continued after Roman names for the five extraterrestrial planets they were aware of.

- Earth is the only planet not named for a mythological god.

- Venus is named after the goddess of love. It is thought this planet got its name from the fact that it is pretty to look at as the third most bright object in our solar system in the sky as viewed from Earth (after the Sun and the Moon).

- Mercury is named after the god of thievery, tradesmen or commerce, and travel. It is thought that the planet probably was named such due to how quickly, relatively speaking, it travels across the sky.

- Pluto, although no longer a "real" planet is named after the god of the underworld. The name was proposed by Venetia Burney, a then eleven-year-old schoolgirl in Oxford, England, who was interested in classical mythology.

- Saturn is named after the Roman god of agriculture. It followed the Greek designation for Cronus. In modern Greek, the planet retains its ancient name *Cronus*—Κρόνος: *Kronos*.

- Neptune was named after the god of the sea. It got its name due to its blue color.

- Uranus (modern pronunciation ur uh nus) is named after the very early god of the sky and father to the Titans.

- Mars was named after the Roman god of war. It is thought that it was labeled such based on the reddish hue of the planet, relating to blood.

- Jupiter is named after the god of thunder and the sky, and king of the gods. It is probable that it was named such as it is the largest non-star in our solar system.

Incidentally, many languages have their own name for Earth, such as 'terra' in Portuguese, 'dünya' in Turkish and 'aarde' in Dutch. However, the common thread in all languages is that they were all derived from the same meaning, which is ' ground' or 'soil'. The modern English word and name for our planet Earth likely extends back more than 1,000 years. The name was also found in early English translations from the bible.

Razor Differences - Men and women use different razors, but there is no difference between men's and women's razors. There are differences between brand names. Gillette issued a press release in which it stated that the blades used in its gendered products both use the same 'blade technology'.

Women's razors are generally more expensive than men's, but cost to manufacture different shapes are negligible. The razors for women are usually larger to cut more hair. The heads of men's razors are designed to facilitate more accurate facial grooming with smaller heads around the blades, as well as having the blades more tightly packed. This serves to better cut thicker hair commonly found on men's faces vs. women's legs, and to cut hair closer to the skin.

The blades of men's razors are often put at more of an oblique angle than women's razors, along with a different contour of handle. The difference in angle and handle shape allows women to see better what they are shaving when looking down at their legs vs. men looking straight into a mirror.

Shaving creams are also identical, except for aroma, because women prefer different fragrances than men.

So, the price for women is much higher, because of perception and because women are more inclined to pay more - for any number of non-tangible reasons. Men see shaving as a chore and women tend to think of it as beauty enhancing. *Save some money and use the less expensive alternative razors, creams, and gels, just do not share the same razor.*

Winter Weather - Highest temperature ever for South Pole Dec. 27, 1978 7.5f −14c

----

Snow Driving Tip - Take out your floor mat, tuck it tightly in front of the spinning tires, and slowly drive forward. *I used this back when I lived in the snow belt and it works.*

Why Snow is White - Snowflakes are crystals of frozen water. Water and ice appear clear or slightly blue in large volumes. Snow is white, because of the way light interacts with snowflakes and the air molecules packed between each snowflake.

Water, ice, and an individual snowflake may appear transparent or clear, but water actually is translucent. The difference is that light can pass through a transparent material unchanged, while it is bent when passing through a translucent material. Light hits a snowflake and is bent and scattered across the spectrum by the facets and imperfections in each crystal.

Snowflakes scatter all frequencies of visible light, so the net effect is to produce white light, but deep layers of snow or compacted snow may appear blue. There is little air between crystals in compacted snow or ice, so there is less opportunity for light to be reflected. Thick layers absorb enough red light to cause this snow to appear blue. Snow also can appear blue if it has a layer of ice over it, which can reflect back the blue of the sky.

Ice is the word for the solid form of water, regardless of how or where it formed or how the water molecules are stacked together.

Snow is the word for precipitation that falls as frozen water. If the water forms crystals, you get snowflakes. Other types of snow include rime and graupel, which are ice, but not crystals. *Bottom line, frost is ice, ice cubes are ice, and snow is a form of ice.*

Climate Change - Clothing could reflect 90 percent of body heat by dipping clothes in a solution made of AgNW, also known as silver nanowire. Regular clothing only reflects 20 percent of body heat back at your skin, making nanowire-coated clothing much more energy efficient. The study was conducted by Professor Yi Cui of Stanford University and his team of researchers. Since metal nanowire coating can conduct electricity, all you would need to do is connect a battery to the clothing.

They see metal-coated clothing as a way to combat the rampant energy demands of the winter months. They report that "47 percent of global energy continues to be spent simply on indoor heating." *We are told global warming is caused by energy use. Now we find half of that is caused by trying to keep us warm. Hmmm!*

Cowboy Hats - The cowboy is one of the most iconic images in American history, but that does not mean our understanding of it is not flawed. The iconic Stetson might be what every cowboy wears in Westerns, but it was not what they actually wore in real life until the very end of the Wild West.

The Stetson was not even around until 1865 and in fact, it became really popular at the end of the 19th century. Up until then, the derby, also known as the bowler hat was most popular. The sombrero was also quite popular, but a gentleman might have preferred a top hat.

Rhino Sex - Not much is known about certain rhino ovulation cycles, but it has been confirmed that some do not have set mating seasons and may become sexually active two times per year. Most seem to mate in the summer and fall seasons, likely due to the availability of food.

Female rhinos put on weight and become irritable if they do not reproduce, according to a study. Experts also discovered that, although they are ready and willing to copulate, they show no outward signs, so males do not realize that they are in heat.

Researchers at Chester Zoo teamed up with Manchester and Liverpool universities to carry out the first comprehensive study into reproduction among black rhinos. They performed hormone analysis on animals from eleven European zoos. A total of 9,743 samples were analyzed by Chester Zoo's wildlife endocrinology laboratory. Dr Katie Edwards, from the University of Liverpool, who led the research, said females that had never bred were found to be heavier than those that had. Non-breeding females were also found to have "unpredictable" temperaments. The results were published in the Journal of General and Comparative Endocrinology.

The male Rhinoceros is ready for mating between the ages of 7 and 8 years old. However, if there are other males to compete with, it can be much older before it is able to find females that are receptive to advances. The bigger and stronger males are the ones that have the best success when it comes to mating. For females mating can begin from the ages of 5 and 6.

It is common for fierce fights to occur between males and females, because the male will not take no for an answer when it comes to mating. The male usually does get his way and will leave after mating.

The fact that the mother carries the young in her body for more than one year and she may keep it with her for several years is a problem when it comes to increasing their numbers. The females may take three years to mate again.

Bee Fact - Honey bees, a very small minority of bee species die after stinging, because their stingers have barbs at the ends and get lodged into their target. When the bees fly off, they are basically ripping themselves in half. Most other species of bees have a smooth stinger that can go in and out of the target with no problem.

Superman's Real Name - Comic book character Superman's alter ego, Clark Kent was named after actors Kent Taylor and Clark Gable. He was also the first superhero to wear a cape.

Toilet, Crapper, and Potty Trivia

Toilet Paper Facts - Sixty million rolls of toilet paper are flushed away in Europe every day. The average American uses 57 sheets a day, six times the global average. Although usage in the US has remained stable, third world countries are catching up. China usage has increased 11% in the last ten years.

Environmentalists are concerned and someone actually calculated that TP usage equals 27,000 trees being flushed down the, um, drain. We can't go back to corn cobs or we will deprive cattle of food or fuel for the new eco cars. *So, if we use less toilet tissue, are we being green, or . . .*

Toilet Talk - Had to share this strange, but useful web site for travelers.

http://www.wheredoiputthepaper.com/

It provides a guide to toilet and use of toilet paper habits around the world. Do not expect pictures or fancy text, just a black and white text of what to expect. You will be surprised at how many cities do not have facilities for flushing and how many do not provide paper. For instance, in Greece you should use the bin next to the toilet, because the plumbing system can't handle the paper. *OK, if you are not planning to take a trip, skip it. If you are planning a trip, it could provide some good advice to save a bit of embarrassment.*

Special Gift - We all know someone who has everything and we never know what to buy them. Well, here is a gift for that special person on that special occasion. The Glow Company, a British firm, recently released a new product, 'GlowRoll', which is glow in the dark toilet paper.

It has many practical uses, such as finding your way around a bathroom at night (the website claims it is capable of lighting up an entire bathroom, camping in the wilderness, or even during power outages. All that for only about ten bucks a roll. Its website sells just about anything that glows.

History of TP in the USA - The first product designed specifically to wipe one's behind was invented in 1857 by a New

Yorker named Joseph Gayetty, who sold boxes of individual sheets infused with aloe. It was a difficult sell and he didn't exactly wipe out the competition as Americans still had the free Sears catalog, as well as other free alternatives.

In 1890, the Scott brothers came up with toilet paper on a roll, which they mainly marketed to hotels and drugstores. It was still a difficult sell and many were reluctant to go out and order something so personal. They managed to cling on and are still selling their product today.

As the 1900s began, more homes included inside flush toilets. That is when greater acceptance came for toilet paper. Indoor plumbing did not do well with catalog paper or other heavier alternatives, like leaves, etc.

People required a product that could be flushed away with minimal clogging or damage to the pipes; and catalog paper, corncobs, and moss did not flush well. Toilet paper became an alternative that still works.

The United States spends more than $6 billion a year on toilet tissue, more than any other nation in the world. *Maybe someone can invent a way to turn junk mail into toilet paper so it would at least have some value.*

Of Toilets and Paper

- ✓ India has more cell phones than toilets. About 545 million Indians have cell phones, but only 366 million have access to toilets.

- ✓ Hermann Goering refused to use regulation toilet paper and used soft white handkerchiefs. (*King Richard II invented the handkerchief.*)

- ✓ Over $100,000 dollars was spent on a study to determine whether most people put their toilet paper on the holder with the flap in front or behind. *Three out of four people have the flap in the front.*

- ✓ The Roman army used a water soaked sponge on the end of a stick instead of paper.

- ✓ The toilet is flushed more times during the super bowl halftime than at any time during the year.

- ✓ King George II of Great Britain died falling off a toilet on the 25th of October 1760.

- ✓ King Minos of Crete had the first flushing water closet recorded in history and that was over 2800 years ago.

- ✓ A toilet was discovered in the tomb of a Chinese king of the Western Han Dynasty that dates back to 206 BC - 24 AD.

- ✓ The ancient Romans had a system of sewers. They built simple outhouses or latrines directly over the running waters of sewers that poured into the Tiber River.

- ✓ Chamber pots were used during the Middle Ages. A chamber pot is a special metal or ceramic bowl that you used and then tossed the contents out (often out the window).

- ✓ In 1596, a flush toilet was invented and built for Queen Elizabeth I by her Godson, Sir John Harrington.

- ✓ The first patent for the flushing toilet was issued to Alexander Cummings in 1775.

- ✓ In 1829, the Tremont Hotel of Boston became the first hotel to have indoor plumbing, and had eight water closets built by Isaiah Rogers. Until 1840, indoor plumbing could be found only in the homes of the rich and the better hotels.

- ✓ Beginning in 1910, toilet designs started changing away from the elevated water tank into the modern toilet with a close tank and bowl.

- ✓ *Thomas Crapper did not invent the toilet, but he did have patent improvements for it. His company went out of business in 1966. World War I soldiers passing through England brought together Crapper's name and the toilet. They saw the words T. Crapper-Chelsea printed on the tanks and coined the slang "crapper" meaning toilet.* The word 'crap' was around before Thomas Crapper.

- ✓ Besides being an obstacle an enemy had to cross, water-filled moats also served as a castle's sewer. Castles had rooms called garderobes which were small wardrobes for undressing, and relieving oneself. Garderobes were either built out from the castle wall, suspended over the moat, or built within the wall, and sluices sent the waste cascading into the moat. *While a wide moat was defensive, a stinky putrid moat was offensive too.*

- Plumbum in Latin means lead. In Roman times, anyone who made things from lead was a "plumber." Back then, "plumbers" not only made sewers and drains, but worked on roofs, gutters, and window frames. Also back then, the weight at the end of a string in a "plumb line" was made of lead. To this day, to get something straight and true is to 'plumb it'.

- Sometimes urinals (mostly in England) were adorned with a bee to give a gentleman a target so he would not splash his shoes.

- 90% of pharmaceuticals taken by people are excreted through urination. Therefore our sewer systems contain heavy doses of drugs. A recent study by the EPA has found fish containing trace amounts of estrogen, cholesterol-lowering drugs, pain relievers, antibiotics, caffeine, and anti-depressants.

- In a 1992 survey, British public toilets were voted the worst in the world. Following quickly behind were Thailand, Greece, and France.

- An average person visits the toilet 2500 times a year, about six-eight times a day. You spend about three years of your life at the toilet.

- The first time there were separate male and female toilets were at a posh party in Paris in 1739.

- Here are some words used for the loo: powder room, lavatory, outhouse, ladies, convenience, washroom, men's room, bathroom, dunny, bog, khazi, gents, garderobe, necessary, women's room, restroom, potty, privy, the smallest room, cloakroom, latrine, place of easement, water closet (WC), john, can, little girls' room, little boys' room, sandbox, throne room, facilities, House of Honor (by the ancient Israelites) and the House of the Morning (by the ancient Egyptians).

> There are 333 squares of toilet paper on a roll.

- We use an average of 57 sheets of toilet paper a day.

- Pyscho was the first movie to have the toilet flushing sound

- Car steering wheels carry more than twice as many germs as a toilet seat.

- ✓ The faucet handle in most bathrooms at work have 400 times more germs than the toilet seat.
- ✓ Toilet brushes were manufactured using the same machinery as artificial Christmas trees.
- ✓ The White House has 35 bathrooms.
- ✓ How far to place your outhouse from your home to avoid unwelcome odors - 50 feet.
- ✓ The Roman god of toilets was Crepitus.
- ✓ Cloacina was the goddess of sewers and drains.
- ✓ Stercutius was the god of odor. (Stercutius was one of Saturn's surnames, given to him when he carpeted the earth with dung to make it fertile.)

> *The faucet handle in most bathrooms at work have 400 times more germs than the toilet seat.*

Ten Interesting Tidbits

1. The average child asks over four hundred questions each day. *Makes it easy to understand why they learn so fast.*

2. Of all the people in history that have reached age 65, half are still living.

3. The US is older than Germany. Germany became independent in 1871 and the US in 1776.

4. Two thirds of the people on earth have never seen snow.

5. A hummingbird weighs less than a US penny.

6. There are more empty houses in the US than homeless people.

7. The US FDA allows ten insects and thirty five fly eggs per eight ounces of raisins.

8. One in ten European babies were conceived on an IKEA bed.

9. A giraffe's tongue is twenty one inches long.

10. The Guinness Book of Records holds its own record as the book most stolen from public libraries.

Six Quick Animal Facts

✓ Armadillos found in the US nearly always give birth to identical quadruplets.

✓ The largest bat colony in the world in Bracken Cave, Texas has 20 million bats.

✓ Dolphins can stay active for 15 days or more by sleeping with only one half of their brain at a time.

✓ Elephants are pregnant for almost two years.

✓ Guinea pigs are neither pigs nor from Guinea.

✓ Koala bears are not bears, they are marsupials.

Ten Alcohol Facts

1.) The production of alcohol has been traced back at least 12,000 years.

2.) Sherry was the alcohol of choice for many world travelers; both Magellan and Columbus had it on board during their respective voyages. Magellan liked Sherry so much that he spent more money stockpiling the alcoholic beverage than he spent on weapons.

3.) Frederick the Great, who was the king of Prussia, was so enamored by alcohol that he tried to ban coffee in an attempt to get everyone in Prussia to drink liquor instead.

4.) The Pilgrims made the decision to stop at Plymouth Rock because they were running low on supplies, particularly alcohol.

5.) Winston Churchill's mother was the inventor of the Manhattan cocktail. It is made with whiskey and sweet vermouth.

6.) Until the mid-1600's, wine makers in France used oil soaked rags in lieu of corks.

7.) Vikings enjoyed alcohol, and they preferred to toast to their victories by drinking it from the skulls of their defeated enemies.

8.) Many historians believe that the practice of farming was not started as a means of food production, but in order to produce the necessary ingredients to create alcoholic beverages.

9.) Hangover cures date back almost as far as alcohol itself. Ancient Romans believed that eating a fried canary would take care of their hangover symptoms, and the ancient Greeks were believers in the power of cabbage. People today are still trying to find the perfect cure for a hangover. In France they put salt into a strong cup of coffee, and in Puerto Rico some drinkers lift their drinking arm and rub half a lemon under it. (*None have proven to be effective*).

10.) The term honeymoon traces its roots back to ancient Babylon. It was a tradition for the soon to be father-in-law to supply his daughter's fiancé with a month's supply of mead. This time period was referred to as the honey month, and that phrase eventually morphed into what we now call a honeymoon.

Five Generations

- Silent Generation, people born before 1946. - Current Population: 41 million (declining)
This generation had significant opportunities in jobs and education as the War ended and a post-war economic boom struck America. However, the growth in Cold War tensions, the potential for nuclear war, and other never before seen threats led to levels of discomfort and uncertainty throughout the generation. Members of this group value security, comfort, and familiar, known activities and environments.

- Baby Boomers, people born between 1946 and 1959. - Current Population: 71 million
The first Boomer segment is bounded by the Kennedy and Martin Luther King assassinations, the Civil Rights movements and the Vietnam War.

Boomers I were in or protested the War. They had good economic opportunities and were largely optimistic about the potential for America and their own lives, the Vietnam War notwithstanding. They held optimistic attitudes and had trust in government.

Boomers 2 or the Jones Generation started about 1955 and overlap Generation X to about 1965. They missed the whole thing. This first post-Watergate generation lost much of its trust in government and optimistic views the Boomers I maintained. Economic struggles including the oil embargo of 1979 reinforced a sense of "I'm out for me", and narcissism, and a focus on self-help, and skepticism over media and institutions; all representative of attitudes of this group. They had AIDS as part of their rites of passage.

- Generation X, people born between 1960 and 1979. - Current Population: 41 million
Sometimes referred to as the "lost" generation, this was the first

generation of "latchkey" kids, exposed to much daycare and divorce. Known as the generation with the lowest voting participation rate of any generation, Gen Xers were quoted by Newsweek as "the generation that dropped out without ever turning on the news or tuning in to the social issues around them."

Gen X is often characterized by high levels of skepticism, "what's in it for me" attitudes and a reputation for some of the worst music to ever gain popularity.

- Generation Y, people born between 1980 and 1995. - Current Population: 71 million
The largest cohort since the Baby Boomers, their high numbers reflect their births as that of their parent generation, the last of the Boomers. Gen Y kids are known as incredibly sophisticated, technology wise, and immune to most traditional marketing and sales pitches, as they not only grew up with it all, they have seen it all, and been exposed to it all since early childhood. Gen Y members are much more racially and ethnically diverse and they are much more segmented as an audience aided by the rapid expansion in Cable TV channels, satellite radio, the Internet, e-zines, etc. They are less brand loyal and the speed of the Internet has led them to be similarly flexible and changing in fashion and style consciousness.

- Generation Z, people born between (about) 1996 and 2012. - Current Population: 23 million
While we do not know much about Gen Z, also known as the Millennial Generation yet, we know a lot about the environment they are growing up in. This highly diverse environment will make the grade schools of the next generation the most diverse ever. Higher levels of technology will make significant inroads in academics, allowing for customized instruction, data mining of student histories to enable pinpoint diagnostics, and remediation or accelerated achievement opportunities. They kids will grow up with a highly sophisticated media and computer environment and will be more Internet savvy and expert than their Gen Y forerunners.

Six Interesting Baseball Facts

❖ Two brother pitchers win every World Series game for the winning team: In the 1934 World Series, the St. Louis Cardinals defeated the Detroit Tigers 4 games to 3. Jerome "Dizzy" Dean and his kid brother Paul "Daffy" Dean won two games each, accounting for all four Cardinal wins.

- Pitching a no-hitter and homering twice: On June 23, 1971, Phillies Pitcher Rick Wise pitched a no-hitter against the Cincinnati Reds at Riverfront Stadium and hit two home runs in the same game.

- Making the final out in two no-hitters against the same pitcher: Harvey Kuenn made the final out of two no-hitters, both against Dodgers' Sandy Koufax. On May 11, 1963, Kuenn made the final out of Koufax's no-hitter against the San Francisco Giants. On September 9, 1965, Kuenn struck out to end Koufax's perfect game against the Chicago Cubs.

- Eddie Gaedel was 26 year old, 3 feet, 7 inch tall. He was signed by Bill Veeck to a Major League contract of $15,400 ($100 per game), which was the set minimum one could pay a little person performance act, per event. During his first (and last) game he walked. Eddie took his base, stopping to take a bow twice on his way, and was lifted for a pinch runner, Jim Delsing. Two days later, American League President Will Harridge voided Gaedel's contract and he was out of a job. Further, Harridge officially banned midgets from being able to play in the American League. Although he only made $100 for the one game, it is estimated he earned over $17,000 ($140,000 today) in the few weeks following his lone Major League at bat. Gaedel's uniform had the number 1/8 on the back and it now sits in the MLB Hall of Fame.

- Four more people in the history of Major League Baseball had only one plate appearance and drew a walk. The others were Dutch Schirick on September 17, 1914, with the Browns; Bill Batsch on September 9, 1916, with Pittsburgh; Joe Cobb on April 25, 1918, with Detroit; and Kevin Melillo on June 24, 2007, with the Oakland A's.

- The only man who hit a home run, but did not score on it was former Major League baseball player Benji Molina. He was so slow that he once hit a home run that he never scored on. What happened was Molina hit a home run that initially was ruled a single and a pinch runner, Emmanuel Burris was put in. However, manager Bruce Bochy challenged the call and it was ultimately ruled a home run, but because the pinch runner had already been put in, the umpires ruled that Molina could not go back out to complete the home run. Burris was given credit for scoring the run, while Molina was credited with hitting the home run.

Ten Life Hacks

✓ When traveling, keep a few laundry dryer sheets or a small bar of soap in the bag you use for dirty clothes. It will mitigate some of the odor.

✓ Hide some extra money in a prescription bottle when traveling, just in case you lose your wallet.

✓ Doritos make good kindling to get a charcoal grill going fast, and it smells better than the lighter fluid.

✓ Cut a used toilet paper roll lengthwise to wrap around wrapping paper and keep it from unraveling.

✓ Push a straw through a strawberry from the bottom to remove the stem.

✓ Tie a small knot in one earphone cord to remember which ear it goes into.

✓ The easiest way to clean a blender is to put some soap and water in it and spin for a few seconds.

✓ A frozen sponge in a closed baggie makes a no-drip ice pack.

✓ If your corkscrew is missing, screw a regular screw into the cork and pull it out with a hammer.

✓ Turn on the seat warmer to keep a pizza or other fast food warm during the drive home.

Seven Spring Facts

o The vernal (spring) equinox (equal <u>night</u>) is the day when the center of the Sun is visible for exactly 12 hours. That is not the same as the equilux (equal <u>light</u>) when there are 12 hours of daylight from the Sun's first appearance and going down. Australia and other parts of the Southern Hemisphere begin the first day of autumn at the same time and there is a movement to call this event the March Equinox or Northward Equinox to avoid a North Hemisphere bias.

o Astronomically, spring officially begins on the spring equinox.

o The spring and autumn equinoxes are the only days when the Sun rises directly due east and sets due west in the northern hemisphere.

o The reason there is more daylight during the spring is the earth's axis tilts toward the sun at this time of year.

- We have used the word 'spring' for the season since the 16th century. Before that spring was used for centuries to apply to the source of a river and the spring season was known as Lent or Lenten.

- The Slatina spring in Slovenia is alleged to have been discovered by the mythological winged horse Pegasus.

- The earliest known use of the term 'spring-cleaning' was in 1857.

Eight Strange Things You Can Find in a Library

Erie, Pennsylvania's Blasco Library loans out fishing poles and tackle boxes, while several branches of the Chicago Public Library run a "Rods and Reads" program that provides poles and tackle sets for adults and children.

Many libraries lend out passes for free or discounted admission to museums and other institutions. In Michigan, the Library Network provides "Michigan Activity Passes" for admission or discounts at more than 100 museums, galleries, and other institutions across the state. Georgia libraries have passes for Georgia State Parks and historic sites that provide admission for four people and cover parking fees.

Libraries in Ann Arbor, Minneapolis, Iowa City, Aurora, Ill., and Braddock, Penn. have original artwork, prints, posters, and even sculptures that you can take home and display.

The Chicago Public Library and New York Public Library both loan out mobile hotspots so patrons can have mobile broadband Internet access at home or on the go.

Arizona's Pima County Public Library has seeds for hundreds of types of vegetables, herbs, and flowers that patrons can take home and plant in their gardens. The library encourages borrowers to save and donate seeds from their grown plants.

Berkeley and Oakland public libraries both have a variety of carpentry, masonry, plumbing, electrical, and landscaping tools to lend out. The Ann Arbor library has a tool collection, but focuses on uncommon tools like thermal leak detectors and air quality meters.

The Forbes Library in Northampton, Mass. has banjos, bongos, and ukuleles to lend.

Libraries around the world host "human library" programs where visitors can sit down with human 'books' and learn about their different cultures, backgrounds, and life experiences.

Interesting Trivia

A friend of mine, Bob Davenport passed on these tidbits, some old some new, but all interesting.

- The population of the world could fit into the state of Texas and it would still be less crowded than New York City.

- The surface area of Russia is slightly larger than that of Pluto.

- Lego makes more tires than any company, including tire companies.

- The combined weight of all ants on earth is about equal to the combined weight of all humans.

- Alexander the Great conquered half the known world by age 22.

- Tenth US president John Tyler (born 1790) has two grandsons (born 1924, 1928) still living (as of 2015).

- The last known widow of a civil war veteran died in 2008.

Facts About Money

Cost of Money - As of 2009, it costs the government 9 cents to produce a nickel, 5.65 cents to produce a dime, 11.31 cents to produce a quarter, 30.4 cents to make the 'gold' (manganese/brass) dollar, and 6.4 cents to make a dollar bill.

In 2008 a bill was introduced known as the Coin Modernization and Taxpayer Savings Act of 2008. This bill proposed changing the composition of the cent to steel, although it would be treated to look like copper. The bill would have also provided the Secretary of the Treasury with authority to change the metallic content of the five cent coin. This bill was passed in the House, but never voted on in the Senate.

The 2011 Budget revived the issue and expanded the scope to include the dime, quarter, and half dollar, in addition to the penny and nickel. The Department of the Treasury will have authorization to approve alternative weights and compositions for any of these five denominations. *A penny saved. . .*

Three Interesting Coin Facts - A blind child read Braille on an American coin for the first time, and it was the 2009 Louis Braille Bicentennial Silver Dollar.

The United States Mint produced fewer coins in 2009 due to so many coins being cashed in from savings, because of the bad economy. It was the lowest production in 45 years.

The mint made up for other losses by selling 1.7 billion dollars worth of gold bullion, eighty percent higher than 2008.

Money Fact - If we spent a dollar a second, it would take more than 31,600 years to spend a trillion dollars. A trillion $10 bills, if they were taped end to end, would wrap around the globe more than 380 times.

In 2010, the U.S. government issued almost as much new debt as the rest of the governments of the world combined. The latest budget anticipates trillions in deficits during the next 5 years.

Penny for Your Thoughts - Did you know it costs the government 1.8 cents to make a penny? That is up from .008 cents in 2001. It produces 5.4 billion of them a year.

Do you know why the government needs to keep producing pennies? It is because of sales tax, which makes purchases cost an uneven amount, because tax is a percent of the price. The coin's name derives from the Old English pennige, pronounced, roughly, penny-yuh.

Can you see those initials under Lincoln's right shoulder? They are the initials of the designer.

The government is loosening up its rules for what metals can be used to make coins. Using cheaper metal should help bring the cost of making one penny closer to one penny.

Billionaires - Maybe the old saying about the rich getting richer is no longer true, at least in the US. Brazil, Russia, India, and China produced 108 of the 214 new billionaires in the Forbes list of richest people. These four nations are home to one-in-four members, up from one-in-ten five years ago.

Before 2013, only the US had ever produced more than 100 billionaires. China now has 115 and Russia 101. The US used to have one in two, now it has one in three billionaires and it is down 56 billionaires from 2008 peak. *So sorry, I didn't see your name on the list either.*

Buying Canada for a Penny - Sir William Alexander, the Earl of Sterling, (1567 – 1640) received a grant from James I of all the lands of Canada, Nova Scotia, all the bays, rivers, islands, mines, and forests. The price was one Scottish penny payable on Christmas Day. The Earl died broke, having spent a fortune in an attempt to develop his vast estate.

Nine Porcupine Facts

1. The porcupine is one of the world's largest rodents and can weigh about 12 kg (26 pounds).

2. There are about thirty different species of porcupine.

3. Porcupines have weak eyes and rely entirely on their nose for food search.

4. One of the olfactory signals porcupines use is a pungent odor that lets potential predators know they have raised their quills and are not afraid to use them.

5. Salty is porcupine's favorite flavor, so it will eat anything salty, such as axe handles, canoe paddles, etc.

6. Female porcupines mate once a year, and often the males bring them into estrus by urinating on them.

7. Babies are called porcupettes and they are born with soft quills, which will begin to harden in a few hours to days.

8. Young porcupine will leave its parents after a few months and begin solitary life.

9. Some porcupines have up to 30,000 quills on their body. Porcupines cannot shoot out their quills, but they will be easily released when predators touch the animal.

Ten Fun Facts

1. We eat pizza from the inside out.
2. Denver International Airport is larger than Manhattan.
3. There are more life forms living on your skin than there people living on earth.
4. The craters named Beer on Mars and the Moon were named for German astronomer Wilhelm Beer, not the drink.
5. Russia considered beer as a soft drink and not alcohol until 2011.
6. Pope John Paul II was named an honorary Harlem Globetrotter in 2000.
7. The number of words posted each day on Twitter would fill a ten million page book.
8. The chance of dying on the way to purchase a lottery ticket are greater than the chance of actually winning.
9. *Not True* - The average mattress weight doubles every ten years from mites and mites poop.
10. *True* - There is a mattress sale every day of the year.

Seven German Inventions

✓ Although it has now been replaced by the Celsius temperature scale in almost all countries except for USA and Belize, Fahrenheit (water's freezing point is 32 degrees and boiling point is 212) was the world standard until relatively recently. It was invented by German physicist Daniel Gabriel Fahrenheit in 1724.

✓ Aspirin, made from willow bark was developed by Felix Hoffmann in August 1897 for pharmaceutical giant Bayer, and although a US company claimed a patent for the drug after World War One, 12,000 of the 50,000 tons of Acetylsalicylic acid (Aspirin) produced each year are still made by Bayer.

✓ After using blotting paper from her children's school books to remove unwanted coffee grounds, Dresden housewife Melitta Bentz had the idea to patent her invention in 1908. She then founded a company selling over a thousand coffee filters by the next year.

✓ German clock manufacturer Junghans Uhren Gmbh developed a watch that automatically adjusts itself to an atomic clock using radio signals. It was invented in 1990 and will remain accurate to the second for at least a million years.

✓ The first true working car was invented by Germans Karl Benz and Gottlieb Daimler in 1886, 22 years before the Model T Ford went into production in the USA.

✓ The first true accordion was invented by a German, Christian Friedrich Buschmann. In 1822 he attached bellows to a portable keyboard with vibrating reeds and called it a "hand-aeoline".

✓ In 1977 after nine years of development, German inventors Jürgen Dethloff and Helmut Göttrup created the first card with a built in programmable microprocessor, the ancestor of the chip and PIN cards in our wallets today.

Ten Crazy US Driving Laws

1. In Alaska it is illegal to tie a dog to the roof of your car.

2. In San Francisco it is illegal to dry your car with used underwear.

3. In Florida, if an elephant is tied to a parking meter, the attendant must deposit money in the meter.

4. In Nevada it is illegal to ride a camel on the highway.

5. In Alabama it is illegal for a driver to be blindfolded while operating a vehicle.

6. In Illinois it's illegal to change clothes inside a car, except during a fire.

7. In Montana it is illegal to leave a sheep unescorted in a truck.

8. In Georgia it is illegal to drive through playgrounds.

9. In Oklahoma it is illegal to read a comic book while driving.

10. In Massachusetts it is illegal to drive with a gorilla in the back seat of your car.

Seven More Interesting Facts

1. Coke would be green if coloring was not added.

2. An average hummingbird weighs less than a penny.

3. The total weight of ants on earth is greater than the total weight of humans.

4. The average person is one percent shorter in the evening.

5. Half of all people in history aged 65 or older are still living.

6. Frozen lobsters can come back to life when thawed (they do not squeal when being boiled).

7. Eyes remain the same size from birth, but the nose and ears never stop growing.

Ten More Alcohol Facts

- The phrase, mind your p's and q's traces its roots back to alcohol. In England, pubs serve liquor in pint and quart sizes. If a customer became unruly, it used to be common for a bartender to tell that customer to mind their own pints and quarts. Over time, the saying was shortened.

- In 1964, Congress declared Bourbon to be the official spirit of the United States.

- Abraham Lincoln owned and operated several taverns, and John Hancock was a well-known alcohol dealer. President Van Buren's mother gave birth to him in their family tavern.

- There are 13 minerals that are essential for human life, and all of them can be found in alcohol. The essential minerals include: calcium, chloride, chromium, copper, iodine, iron, magnesium, phosphorus, potassium, selenium, sodium, and zinc.

- Many people believe that there has been a worm in tequila for centuries, but that is not accurate. The drink that started this tradition was actually Mezcal, and instead of a worm, it was a Gusano butterfly caterpillar.

- The word brandy is derived from the Dutch word brandewijn (burnt wine).

- A bottle of Champagne contains approximately 49 million bubbles.

- Drinking a glass of milk can cause a person to blow a .02 on a breathalyzer test, and that is enough to cause legal issues in some states.

- In order to make a bottle of wine, you will need approximately 600 grapes.

- It is so common in some parts of Europe for teenagers to be permitted to drink that they can obtain an alcoholic beverage at the cafeteria of many high schools. Laws about teenage drinking in the US are the strictest in Western civilization.

Twelve Patent Facts

1. On March 19, 1474, Venice passed the world's earliest known law to grant and protect patents.

2. Around 50,000 patent applications were made from UK inventors in 2013. That is about one new British invention every 10 minutes.

3. The Japanese submit more than 470,000 a year.

4. US patents during 2013, 464,573.

5. The second patent in England was for a monopoly on representing an image of the King.

6. Musical fly swatter was patented in the US in 1994. It played one tune when turned on, another when it hit something.

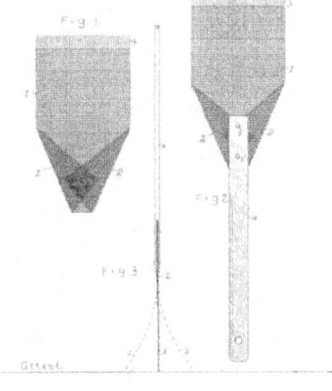

7. IBM has gained more patents than any other company in the US for the past 21 years.

8. US patent number 5528943, issued in 1996, was for a pregnant female crash test dummy.

9. Thomas Edison accumulated 2,332 patents worldwide for his inventions.

10. In 1998, the European patent office reported that the patent visitors most often wanted to see was one for sardine-flavored

ice-cream. This was because nobody believed it until they saw it.

11. Abraham Lincoln was the only US president to hold a patent. It was for a device to lift boats over sandbanks.

12. There are 52,438 US patents for measuring and testing.

Six More Interesting Facts

1. There are over two hundred corpses on Mt. Everest and some are used as way markers for climbers.

2. The tallness of a mountain refers to its length from base to summit. The height refers to the length from sea level to summit. Mount Everest is the highest mountain in the world, but it is not the tallest. At 33,465 ft (10,200 m) Mauna Kea in Hawaii is taller than Everest, which is only 29,029 ft (8,848 m). However, almost two thirds of Mauna Kea is underwater.

3. The US Supreme Court's basketball court is on the fifth floor of the United States Supreme Court Building, higher than the second floor courtroom, so it has been called the highest court in the land.

4. Almost twenty five percent of Los Angeles is covered by automobiles and there are also more cars than people in Los Angeles.

5. John D. Rockefeller's wealth, when adjusted for inflation was ten times greater than Bill Gates.

6. There are over seventy various crafts on the Moon, as well as a few flags, some golf balls, some TV cameras, empty packages and, human waste containers. All total over 400,000 pounds.

World's Top Ten Sports

These are the top ten sports in the world from the lowest to highest, according to number of fans. Seems it is not the age of the sport, but the sport itself that makes it popular.

- American Football, # of fans: 400 million (began 1800s)

- Basketball, # of fans: 400 million (began late 1800s)

- Golf, # of fans: 450 million (began 1400s)

- Baseball, # of fans: 500 million (began late 1800s)

- Table Tennis, # of fans: 850 million (began 1900s)

- Volleyball, # of fans: 900 million (began late 1800s)

- Tennis, # of fans: 1 billion (began in 1300s)

- Field Hockey, # of fans: 2 billion (began 3rd century BC)

- Cricket, # of fans: 2.5 billion (began 1600s)

- Soccer, # of fans: 3.5 billion (began 200s BC)

Biggest, Longest, Tallest Records

➢ The tallest living person is Sultan Kosen from Ankara, Turkey, at 8′ 3″ tall. He also holds the record for the widest hand span at 12 inches. The tallest man in history was Robert Pershing Wadlow, who was 8 feet 11.1 inches (2.72 m) tall. His feet were the largest in history at US Size 37AA, or 18 ½ inches long.

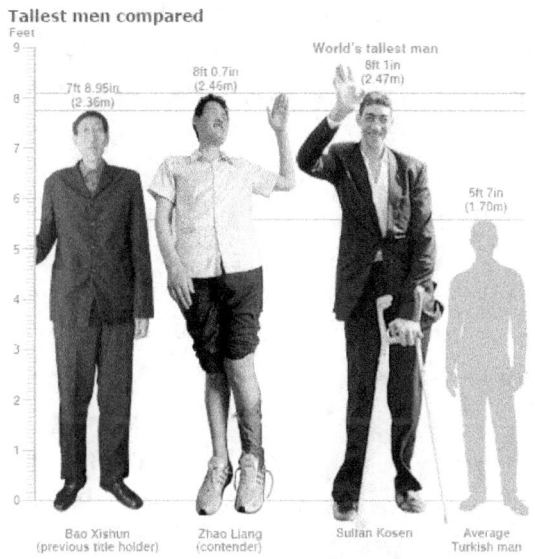

➢ Jyoti Amge, from Nagpur, India, is the world's shortest woman and stands 24.7 inches tall (she was selected to join the cast of American Horror Story season 4). Chandra Bahadur Dangi was declared the shortest human adult ever documented and verified, measuring 21.51 in (54.64 cm).

➢ Matthew McGory had a big toe that was 5 inches long and his little toe was 1.5 inches.

➢ Mehmet Ozyurek from Artuin, Turkey has the longest nose ever at 3.46 inches from the bridge to the tip.

➢ The person born with the most fingers and toes was Akshat Saxena of India. He was born with 14 fingers, 7 on each hand, and 20 toes, 10 on each foot.

➢ The longest tongue belongs to Stephen Taylor from the United Kingdom. From the middle of his closed lip to the tip, it is 3.86 inches long. The longest female tongue belongs to Chanel Tapper of California, at 3.8 inches. The widest tongue belongs to Jay Sloot of San Remo, Australia and is 3.1 inches wide.

➢ The widest mouth belongs to Fransisco Domingos of Angola, at 6.69 inches. The record for the most teeth in a human mouth belongs to two people, Kanchan Rojawat of India and Luca Meriano of Italy, who each have 35 adult teeth.

➢ The longest legs belong to Svetlana Pankratova, who has 51.9 inch legs.

➢ The longest natural head hair belongs to Xie Qiuping of China whose hair measured 18 feet 5.54 inches.

➢ Hans Langseth of Norway had the longest beard ever recorded, at 18 feet 6 inches long.

➢ Mark Lyleate ate 54 Pieces of Bacon in 5 Minutes at the 2010 Beggin' Strips World Bacon Eating Championship. In 2013, Molly Schuyler, Bellevue, Nebraska, was the first person to eat 3 pounds of cooked bacon within less than 5 minutes. Peter Czerwinski of Mississauga, Ontario holds the record for drinking a bacon shake the fastest at 47.72 seconds. It contained five pounds of bacon. *I know, these last facts have nothing to do with body records, but are about bacon and I couldn't resist.*

Nine Squirrel Facts

1. Squirrels can leap ten times their body length?

2. They can turn their ankles 180 degrees to face any direction when climbing.

3. They can learn from copying other animals and humans.

4. Fifty Six cases of bubonic plague (it is now treatable with antibiotics) and seven deaths were recorded in the US between 2000 and 2009, and squirrels harboring the infected fleas were among the main culprits.

5. Squirrels are clever, and can learn to navigate numerous obstacles to find the most efficient route to food.

6. They will find a dead rattlesnake, chew its skin, and then lick themselves. This leaves the squirrels smelling like snakes, and scientists believes this tricks animals into thinking that the squirrels' burrows are actually home to snakes.

7. Squirrels store nuts and acorns for winter, because they do not hibernate. Also, because they bury their acorns, squirrels are partially responsible for oak trees in much of the US.

8. Hungry squirrels have been observed scoring a maple tree's bark with their teeth, letting the sap leak, and returning to lick it later when it dried.

9. Squirrels' tunnels can exceed 9 meters (about 30 ft) in length.

Six Tape Types

Beyond duct tape (Duck tape is a brand name), scotch tape, packing tape, and others are a few relatively unknown to many. Here are a few of the more interesting types of tape.

Speed tape is an aluminized adhesive tape used to do minor repairs on aircraft, and as a temporary repair material until a more permanent repair can be carried out. It has an appearance similar to duct tape, with which it is sometimes mistaken, but its adhesive is capable of sticking on an airplane fuselage or wing at high speeds. It is resistant to water, solvents, and flames, and will reflect heat and UV light. It is also able to expand and contract through a wide range of temperatures.

Bondage tape adheres to itself without using adhesives. Bondage tape is a 2-to-3-inch-wide (51 to 76mm) and 0.0051 inch-thick (0.13mm) strip of thin plastic material, usually latex. It is typically intended to be used for erotic bondage. Since it does not stick to the hair or skin, a person can be tightly bound or gagged without causing harm when the tape is removed

Elastic therapeutic tape, also known as K tape and kinesiology tape, is an elastic-cotton strip backed with acrylic adhesive. It is used for treating various physical disorders. It is claimed to be able to stretch up to 140% of its original length. As a result, if the tape is applied to a patient with a stretch greater than its normal length, it will recoil after being applied and therefore create a pulling force on the skin that it is being applied to. This elastic property allows much greater range of motion compared to traditional white athletic tape and can also be left on for long periods of time.

Gecko tape is being designed with directional adhesion properties, which is the ability to grip a load in one direction and to release its grip when the direction is reversed. The same structures on Scotch tape revealed that this material could support a shear stress of 36N/cm2, nearly four times higher than a gecko foot. This new material can adhere to a wider variety of materials, including glass and Teflon. When pulled parallel to a surface, the tape releases, not because the CNTs lose adhesion from the surface, but because they break, and the tape cannot be reused. It only works for small area (approximately 1 cm2). Researchers are currently working on a number of ways to strengthen the nanotubes used to make it.

Lingerie tape, also called cleavage tape or fashion tape is double-sided adhesive tape used to keep clothing in place. It is used to secure the edges of a strapless dress, or top to the cleavage, or side of the breasts, or on shoulders to secure bra straps from slipping, in order to keep the item of clothing in place. It may also be referred to as toupee tape or wig tape, a similar double-sided tape intended for a different function.

Road marking tape is re-formed polymer tape that can be applied permanently or temporarily on pavement to create road surface markings. It is heavy-grade material with reflective beads embedded in the plastic. It is commonly used to mark crosswalks, stop bars, and traffic guidance, such as turn lanes, HOV lanes, train crossings, pedestrian crossings, taxi lanes, bus lanes, etc.

Colors

Color Me Red - The Proto-Indo-European word for red, reudh, remained largely unchanged for thousands of years, showing up in English red, Spanish rojo, French rouge, German rot, Icelandic rauðr, and Welsh rhudd. Not only did it lead to these words for the color itself, it also led to red-related English words like ruby, rust, and rubeola.

For the ancient Romans, a red flag was a signal for battle.

Because of its visibility, stop signs, stoplights, brake lights, and fire equipment are all painted red.

The ancient Egyptians considered themselves a red race and painted their bodies with red dye for emphasis.

In Russia, red means beautiful. The Bolsheviks used a red flag as their symbol when they overthrew the tsar in 1917. That is how red became the color of communism.

In India, red is the symbol for a soldier.

In South Africa, red is the color of mourning.

In China, red is the color of good luck and is used as a holiday and wedding color. Chinese babies are given their names at a red-egg ceremony.

Superstitious people think red frightens the devil.

A "red-letter day" is one of special importance and good fortune.

In Greece, eggs are dyed red for good luck at Easter time.

To "paint the town red" is to celebrate.

Red is the color most commonly found in national flags.

In the English War of the Roses, red was the color of the House of Lancaster, which defeated the House of York, symbolized by the color white.

The "Redshirts" were the soldiers of the Italian leader Garibaldi, who unified modern Italy in the nineteenth century.

Red is a song by Taylor Swift

To "see red" is to be angry.

A "red herring" is a distraction, which takes attention away from the real issue.

A "red eye" is an overnight airplane flight.

If a business is "in the red," it is losing money.

Color Me Green - The word ghre-, meaning "to grow," is another root which endured the centuries. Grhe- gave us many modern words meaning "green," including English green, German grün, and Icelandic grænn, as well as the English words grow, grass, and graze.

Green Traffic Light means go.

Only one national flag is a solid color: the green flag of Libya.

Ancient Egyptians colored the floors of their temples green.

In ancient Greece, green symbolized victory.

In the highlands of Scotland, people wore green as a mark of honor.

Green is the national color of Ireland.

A "greenback" is slang for a US dollar bill.

Lean green is slang for a US dollar.

The saying "all systems are green," means everything is in order.

The green room of a concert hall or theater is where performers relax before going onstage.

The "green-eyed monster" is jealousy.

A greenhorn is inexperienced, a newcomer, or unsophisticated person.

Green is youthful.

Being "green around the gills" means looking pale and sickly.

"Green with envy" means full of envy or jealousy.

A person with a "green thumb" is good at making plants grow.

Al Green is a great singer.

Green Day group has 13 million viewers of this video

A green, or common, is a town park.

Green is a healing color, the color of nature.

Color Me Blue - The modern English word blue comes from Middle English bleu or blewe, from the Old French bleu, a word of Germanic origin, related to the Old High German word blao. In heraldry, the word azure is used for blue

In Japanese, a novice or inexperienced person is ao-kusai, literally they 'smell of blue'.

In ancient Rome, public servants wore blue. Today, police and other public servants wear blue.

In Iran, blue is the color of mourning.

Blue was used as protection against witches, who supposedly disliked the color.

If you are "true blue," you are loyal and faithful.

Blue stands for love, which is why a bride carries or wears something blue on her wedding day.

A room painted blue is said to be relaxing.

"Feeling blue" is feeling sad.

"Blue devils" are feelings of depression.

Something "out of the blue" is from an unknown source at an unexpected time.

A bluebook is a list of socially prominent people.

The first prize gets a blue ribbon.

A blue blood is a person of noble descent.

"Into the blue" means into the unknown.

A "bluenose" is a strict, puritanical person.

A "bluestocking" used to be a scholarly or highly knowledgeable woman.

The pharaohs of ancient Egypt wore blue for protection against evil.

The "blues" is a style of music derived from southern African-American secular songs. It influenced the development of rock, R&B, and country music.

Am I Blue song by Ray Charles

Blue Bayou is a song in Spanish and English by Linda Ronstadt

"Blue laws" are used to enforce moral standards.

A blue ribbon panel is a group of especially qualified people.

Color Me Yellow - Yellow is the color of gold, butter, and ripe lemons and bananas. In the spectrum of visible light, and in the traditional color wheel used by painters, yellow is found between green and orange. Yellow is commonly associated with gold, wealth, sunshine, reason, happiness, optimism, and pleasure, but also with envy, jealousy and betrayal. It plays an important part in Asian culture, particularly in China, where it is the color of happiness, glory, and wisdom. In China, there are five directions of the compass; north, south, east, west, and the middle, each with a symbolic color. Yellow signifies the middle. China is called the Middle Kingdom; the palace of the Emperor was considered to be in the exact center of the world.

In Egypt and Burma, yellow signifies mourning.

In Spain, executioners once wore yellow.

In India, yellow is the symbol for a merchant or farmer.

In tenth-century France, the doors of traitors and criminals were painted yellow.

Hindus in India wear yellow to celebrate the festival of spring.

If someone is said to have a "yellow streak," that person is considered a coward.

In Japan during the War of Dynasty in 1357, each warrior wore a yellow chrysanthemum as a pledge of courage.

A yellow ribbon is a sign of support for soldiers at the front.

Yellow is a symbol of jealousy and deceit.

In the Middle Ages, actors portraying the dead wore yellow.

To holistic healers, yellow is the color of peace.

Yellow has good visibility and is often used as a color of warning. It is also a symbol for quarantine, an area marked off because of danger.

The Beatles had a song Yellow Submarine

"Yellow journalism" refers to irresponsible and alarmist reporting.

Color Me Purple - Purpura is the Latin name of a particular kind of shellfish which, when ground up, produces a bright purple dye, which in turn was taken from the Greek word porphura to describe the same sea creature. The word purpura later began to refer to the dye, and eventually the color of the dye. This dye was very expensive, and purple was considered a color of royalty throughout Europe. When this dye was exported to England, the word purple was imported into English as well. Today "purpura" is used by doctors to describe purplish discolorations of the skin.

The Egyptian queen Cleopatra loved purple. To obtain one ounce of Tyrian purple dye, she had her servants soak 20,000 Purpura snails for 10 days.

In Thailand, purple is worn by widows mourning husband's death.

A "purple heart" is a U.S. military decoration for soldiers wounded or killed in battle.

Purple is a royal color.

Purple robes are an emblem of authority and rank.

"Purple speech" is profane talk.

"Purple prose" is writing that is full of exaggerated literary effects and ornamentation.

Leonardo da Vinci believed that the power of meditation increases 10 times when done in a purple light, as in the purple light of stained glass.

Purple in a child's room is said to help develop the imagination, according to color theory.

Richard Wagner composed his operas in a room with shades of violet, his color of inspiration.

White and Black - The Proto-Indo-European word bhel evolved into many modern words meaning "white," including Spanish blanco, French blanc, Italian bianco, and Portuguese branco, as well as white-related words such as bleach and blank. Bhel also referred to anything bright, like fire, and the result of fire is blackened, charred remains. Hence, black. Symbols and sayings about white and black:

White
A white flag is the universal symbol for truce.

White means mourning in China and Japan.

Angels are usually depicted wearing white robes.

The ancient Greeks wore white to bed to ensure pleasant dreams.

The Egyptian pharaohs wore white crowns.

The ancient Persians believed all gods wore white.

A "white elephant" is a rare, pale elephant considered sacred to the people of India, Thailand, Burma, and in Sri Lanka it is either a possession that costs more than it is worth to keep or an item that the owner does not want, but cannot get rid of.

It is considered good luck to be married in a white garment.

White heat is a state of intense enthusiasm, anger, devotion, or passion.

To whitewash is to gloss over defects or make something seem presentable that is not.

A white knight is a rescuer.

A white list contains favored items.

A whiteout occurs when there is zero visibility during a blizzard.

A white sale is a sale of sheets, towels, and other bed and bath items.

A whited sepulcher is a person who is evil inside, but appears good on the outside.

White lightning is slang for moonshine, a home brewed alcohol.

A white room is a clean room as well as a temperature-controlled, dust-free room for precision instruments.

White water is the foamy, frothy water in rapids and waterfalls.

Black
The ancient Egyptians and Romans used black for mourning, as do most Europeans and Americans today.

The Blackshirts were the security troops in Hitler's German army, also known as the S.S.

Black humor is morbid or unhealthy and gloomy humor.

A blackhearted person is evil.

If a business is "in the black," it is making money.

A "blacklist" is a list of persons or organizations to be boycotted or punished.

Black is associated with sophistication and elegance. A "black tie" event is formal.

A black belt in karate identifies an expert.

A black flag in a car race is the signal for a driver to go to the pits.

A blackguard is a scoundrel.

The ancient Egyptians believed that black cats had divine powers.

Black lung is a coal miner's disease caused by the frequent inhaling of coal dust.

Blackmail is asking for things by using threat.

Black market is illegal trade in goods or money.

A black sheep is an outcast.

A blackout is a period of darkness from the loss of electricity, for protection against nighttime air raids, or, in the theater, to separate scenes in a play.

When you "black out," you temporarily lose consciousness.

Inventions by Women

Martha Coston decided to peruse through her deceased husband's notebooks. She managed to find some plans he made for a flare system in which ships could use to interact after dark. She devoted the next ten years of her life to redesign and master her late husband's layout for a colored flare system.

One night Martha took her children to see a fireworks show. It was then the concept of implementing a pyrotechnic know-how to her flare system originated. She put it all together, it worked, and the United States Navy bought the rights to it. The Civil War was the first theater for the Coston colored flare system to be used on a grand scale.

She was unable to support her family even though she had 1,200,000 flares produced. The Navy promised her $120,000, but only paid her $15,000. She wrote in her autobiography about the Navy refusing to pay her what was owed.

* * *

Mary Anderson went to New York City for the first time. There were no taxis and there were not countless vehicles contending for a place to drive in the afternoon traffic. The automobile was rare then and had not yet grabbed the curiosity of the American people.

While riding a tram she observed how every few minutes the tram needed to have its front window wiped down to get rid of the accumulated snow.

When Anderson went home, she created a squeegee placed on a spindle that had a handle affixed on the inside of a vehicle. The driver would yank on the handle and a wiping action from the squeegee could clean the windshield. By 1903, Anderson obtained a patent and ten years later, many Americans were using her windshield wipers on their vehicles.

* * *

A Shaker community in Massachusetts had a woman named *Tabitha Babbitt* who worked as a weaver. She would regularly witness the men cutting the wood with a pit saw (a two-handled saw that needed two individuals to operate). Although the saw needed to be pulled in two directions to cut the wood, there was only cutting going on when the saw was being pulled in a forward direction, making the backward motion useless. In 1810 Babbitt developed her own draft of a saw that was circular in shape. It was the first circular saw used in a saw mill in 1813. This has been contested, but not disproven. It is also claimed that she invented a process for the manufacture of false teeth and an improved spinning wheel head.

* * *

Admiral Grace Murray Hopper joined the military during 1943 and was stationed at Harvard University where she was employed using IBM's Harvard Mark I computer, which was the first large-scale computer in the US. She was the third individual programming the machine and she wrote a handbook of operations that led the way for many that would follow her. During the 1950s, the Admiral came out with the compiler, which converted English instructions into a computer code. This meant that computer code could be developed by programmers with less errors and complications. Hopper then created the Flow-Matic, which was utilized to program the UNIVAC I and II computers. Hopper had also been overseeing the advancements of Common Business-Oriented Language or (COBOL), which was one of the very first computer languages. She went on to obtain various awards for her work and even had a US warship named after her. *Heard her speak one time and she used a length of wire 11.8 inches long as a prop. She described how light traveled that distance in one nanosecond.*

* * *

Barbara Askins was a teacher, and once her children were in school she returned to college. After receiving her bachelor's and master's degree in chemistry, she was hired by NASA.

Pictures from space often came back too blurry to decipher and Barbara's invention used radioactivity to enhance negatives, thus resulting in clearer pictures. She also found that this process could be used to enhance pictures even after they had been developed.

After patenting her invention in 1978, NASA put it to use with great success. It was found so useful that it was adopted outside of the agency for things such as x-rays and restoring old photographs.

In 1979 Barbara was awarded the title Inventor of the Year by the Association for the Advancement of Innovations and Inventions. She is the first woman to receive this honor as a sole patent holder.

* * *

Stephanie Kwolek took a temporary position for DuPont during 1946. Her goal was to save enough money to pay for medical school. By 1964 Stephanie was still working there and doing research on how to change polymers into higher strength synthetic fibers. She was working with polymers that possessed rod-like molecules that were all lining up in a single direction.

In contrast to the molecules that had been forming in bunches, Stephanie believed that uniform lines would render the resulting material more powerful, although such polymers had been quite challenging to break down into a testable solution. She finally developed the correct solution that had rod-like molecules and at the same time looked dissimilar to every other molecular solution she had yet made.

The next step was to put it through a spinneret, a device that could generate the fibers. The operator for the spinneret initially refused to allow Kwolek to operate the machine, because her new solution was so different than any other before it, and he believed it would ruin the machine.

Kwolek refused to give up and made a fiber, which was as tough as steel. The material was then named, Kevlar and since that time it has been utilized for radial tires, brake pads, drums, skis, helmets, camping gear as well as suspension bridge cables.

The most widely known use for Kevlar is bulletproof vests. Kevlar was a brand name, but has become generic term. In July 1995, Kwolek was inducted into the National Inventors Hall of Fame. *Perseverance counts.*

GEOGRAPHY FACTS

Island in a Lake - The world's largest island on a lake which is on an island in a lake is eighty two acre Treasure Island (Ontario, Canada) in Lake Mindemoya, which is on Manitoulin Island in Lake Huron.

Manitoulin Island contains two more, Lake Manitou and Lake Kegawong. Each of these lakes also has islands within them.

- - - - - - -

PL Peace Tower - Japan - July 6 fireworks are a tribute to all the fallen souls of war. This six hundred foot tower is located at the Church of Perfect Liberty headquarters in Tondabayashi, Japan. The tower stands as a monument to all the perished souls of war throughout all time. Within the tower is a shrine in which all known

names of the lives claimed in human conflict have been recorded on microfilm and stored in a golden container.

The structure was built in 1970. Once a year, the Church of Perfect Liberty headquarters is the site of one of the world's largest fireworks shows. Every July 6th, the members celebrate the passing of their first founder with what they call the "PL Art of Fireworks." Unlike most fireworks shows, which fire around 5,000 shells, the PL show consists of around 25,000 shells fired. During the finale about 7,000 shells are shot off in unison, almost completely lighting the night sky.

- - - - - - -

Annual Rainfall - While checking a city and looking at annual rainfall can be interesting, it may not be informative. For instance, Houston, Texas gets 49 inches of rain annually, which is more rain than Seattle, which gets only 38 inches of annual rainfall. The key difference is Seattle has a relatively high amount of days per year with relatively light rain, 158 vs. Houston with 104 rainy days. Seattle also has 226 cloudy days per year.

- - - - - - -

Our Globe - Forests cover 30% of earth's land surface, land covers 29.22% of earth surface, water covers 70.78% of earth surface (total 326 million trillion gallons of water) 98% of that is in the oceans, 1.6% in ice caps, .36% under land wells aquifers, .036 lakes and rivers.

Groundwater represents about 30 percent of the available fresh water on the planet and surface water accounts for less than one percent. The rest is in glaciers or the polar ice caps.

Between 780 million to one billion people do not have basic and reliable water supplies and more than two billion people lack the requirements for basic sanitation.

80% of atmosphere is nitrogen most of the rest is oxygen.

People occupy less than 2% of land mass - *It mathematically does not seem possible we create pollution that changes the whole earth and the atmosphere above the earth.*

- - - - - - -

How Big is the United States - The US is about half the size of Russia, three-tenths the size of Africa, half the size of South America, slightly larger than Brazil, slightly larger than China, and more than twice the size of the European Union. 90% of the continental United States is still open space or farmland.

- - - - - - -

Did You Know - Australia has no official national animal, but the red kangaroo is the unofficial, along with the Emu. Both are on the national coat of arms.

They represent moving forward, because neither can walk backward easily. About 95% of the world's opals are mined in Australia.

- - - - - - -

San Diego Border - The border station is now the busiest on earth. It has 24 lanes of northbound traffic for those traveling through from Tijuana to San Diego and 6 southbound lanes for those going the other way. Every day up to 50,000 vehicles pass through this gate, plus another 25,000 people on foot, and that's just <u>into</u> the United States. Plus it is in the process of expansion.

- - - - - - -

North America has more Wilderness than Africa - Percentage of Africa that is wilderness: 28% - Percentage of North America that is wilderness: 38%.

- - - - - - -

Arkansas Tattoo Tax - Since 2005, anyone in Arkansas wanting to get a tattoo or a nose ring has to pay an additional 6 percent, as the state included tattooing and body piercing in its list of services subject to sales taxes.

- - - - - - -

Fifteen Detroit Facts

Detroit, Michigan might not be the city it once was, but it does have a prestigious history and a few firsts attributed to it.

➤ The first news broadcast came out of Detroit on WWJ.

➤ Detroit was the first city to assign individual phone numbers, in 1879.

➤ It is potato chip capital of the world... per consumption. (*Love those Better Made chips*)

➤ Ice cream soda was invented in Detroit.

➤ Pizza deliveryman Richard Davis invented the bulletproof vest, after being attacked by three armed robbers during a delivery. (DuPont chemist Stephanie Kwolek, who recently passed away, discovered Kevlar in 1965).

➤ Detroit has more registered bowlers than any other city.

➤ The salt mines beneath Detroit could keep food flavored for over seventy thousand years.

- Elijay J. McCoy invented the best lubrication system for locomotives and other machinery in 1872. Manufacturers wanted the best, "the real McCoy." (That is also where the saying came from).

- The first four-way traffic light was in Detroit, at the intersection of Woodward and Fort St.

- A one-mile stretch of Detroit road was paved with concrete in 1908, making it the world's first concrete-paved road.

- Vernor's Ginger Ale was invented in Detroit.

- The first air-conditioned car was manufactured in 1939 by Detroit's Packard Motor Car Company.

- The J.W. Westcott II, Detroit, is the world's only floating post office, as it delivers mail to ships as they pass under the Ambassador Bridge (I once rode on it during a mail pickup).

- The first tunnel connecting two countries in the world is the Detroit Windsor Tunnel, connecting Detroit and Windsor, Ontario, Canada.

- Belle Isle, in Detroit is the largest island park in the US.

- - - - - - -

Sixteen Facts about Alaska

Home of Polar Bears, gold, oil, Eskimos, and Sarah Palin.

- Outsiders first discovered Alaska in 1741 when Danish explorer Vitus Jonassen Bering sighted it on a voyage from Siberia.

- In spring, the melting dome of an igloo is replaced with a covering of animal skins to form a between-season dwelling called a 'qarmaq'.

- Alaska has about 640,000 residents.

- The word 'igloo' comes from the inuit 'iglu', meaning 'house'.

- Russian whalers and fur traders on Kodiak Island established the first settlement in Alaska in 1784.

- In 1867 United States Secretary of State William H. Seward offered Russia $7,200,000, or two cents per acre, for Alaska. *Remember Sewards Folly from Geography lessons?*

- On October 18, 1867 Alaska officially became the property of the United States.

- Joe Juneau's 1880 discovery of gold ushered in the gold rush era.

- In 1943, Japan invaded the Aleutian Islands, which started the One Thousand Mile War.

- The Alaska Highway was originally built as a military supply road during World War II.

- Alaska officially became the 49th state on January 3, 1959.

- Alaska historically accounted for 25% of the oil produced in the United States.

- Alaska is the United State's largest state and is over twice the size of Texas (*ouch*). Measuring from north to south the state is approximately 1,400 miles long and measuring from east to west it is 2,700 miles wide. It covers 570,374 square miles.

- The state of Rhode Island could fit into Alaska 425 times.

- The Trans-Alaska Pipeline moves up to 88,000 barrels of oil per hour on its 800 mile journey to Valdez.

- Dog mushing is the official state sport for Alaska.

- - - - - - -

Eleven Facts about Canada

Fun facts about our friends and neighbors in the great white north.

- Canada is the second largest country in the world.

- The Statute of Westminster (1931) confirmed Canada's status as an independent nation within the Commonwealth. It meant that the UK could no longer pass laws affecting the dominions, including Canada, without their request and consent.

- Ottawa is the capital and Montreal the largest city (1 million plus).

- Canada Population: 31,600,000.

- Toronto is the second largest city in Canada.

- The word "canada" comes from the Huron word "kanata" which means village.

- The border between the United States and Canada is the longest unguarded border in the world.

- Canada's life expectancy is the world's highest at 79 years.

- A helicopter installed the world's largest Olympic torch on top of the Calgary tower. The flame was visible for 15-20kms (about 12 miles) and required 30,000 cubic feet of natural gas/hour.

- The elevation of Lake Louise is 1,536m (5,039 feet), the highest permanent settlement in Canada.

- *Last, but not least* - There are more donut shops per capita in Canada than in any other country. *I love Tim Horton's, (larger than McDonald's in Canada and once owned by Wendy's, spun off on its own, then purchased by Burger King in 2014.)*

- - - - - - -

Seven Facts about China

China's economy grew 316% vs. 43% in the US, during the past ten years.

85% of artificial Christmas trees in the US are made in China.

80% of Christmas toys in the US are made in China.

China raises more pigs than the next 43 pig growing countries combined.

US fastest high speed train is half fast compared to China's, 150 to 302mph. (Japan has one that goes 374mph or 603kph)

During the next 15 years, China will build enough new skyscrapers to fill ten New York size cities.

More people study English in China than speak it in the United States.

- - - - - - -

22 *Newest Countries and Political Independence Dates*

We usually do not think of new countries being formed, but some are not as old as you might think.

Bahrain - 15 August 1971 (from UK)

United Arab Emirates - 2 December 1971 (from UK)

Bangladesh -16 December 1971 (from West Pakistan)

Bahamas - 10 July 1973 (from UK)

Iran -1 April 1979 (Islamic Republic of Iran proclaimed)

Belize - 21 September 1981 (from UK)

Antigua and Barbuda - 1 November 1981 (from UK)

Brunei -1 January 1984 (from UK)

Marshall Islands - 21 October 1986 (from US-admin. UN trusteeship)

Federated States of Micronesia - 3 November 1986 (from the US-admin. UN Trusteeship)

Lithuania - 11 March 1990 (from Soviet Union)

Namibia - 21 March 1990 (from South African mandate)

Armenia, Azerbaijan, Belarus, Estonia, Georgia, Kazakhstan, Latvia, Moldova, Russia, Turkmenistan, Ukraine, Uzbekistan - 1991 (from Soviet Union)

Croatia and Slovenia - 25 June 1991 (from Yugoslavia)

Macedonia - 17 September 1991 (from Yugoslavia)

Bosnia and Herzegovina -1 March 1992 (from Yugoslavia)

Cuba became independent from US on 20 May 1902.

Czech Republic and Slovakia -1 January 1993 (Czechoslovakia split)

Palau - 1 October 1994 (from the US-administered UN Trusteeship)

East Timor - 20 May 2002 (from Indonesia)

Serbia - May 2006 (after Montenegro declared independence from Yugoslavia)

- - - - - - -

Debunking Myths

Scientific Proof Isn't

There is no such thing as scientific proof. Scientific evidence is evidence which serves to either support or counter a scientific theory or hypothesis.

Proof is incompatible with science which, by its nature should be provisional and self-correcting. Karl Popper (generally regarded as one of the greatest philosophers of science in the 20th century) once wrote that "In the empirical sciences, which alone can furnish us with information about the world we live in, proofs do not occur, if we mean by 'proof' an argument which establishes once and for ever the truth of a theory." Only Math has proofs.

Coffee and Tea Dehydration Myth Debunked

Caffeinated drinks may send you to the loo quite often, but liquid in the coffee or tea still counts toward your hydration goal, because it is mostly water.

Caffeinated beverages do not dehydrate you when consumed in moderation of about five cups or less per day. In fact, any fluids you ingest will help keep your cells saturated, including coffee, juice, tea, or soda.

High Fructose Corn Syrup Myths Debunked

High fructose corn syrup (HFCS) is basically the same as sugar, both in terms of composition and in the number of calories it contains. HFCS is produced by milling corn (maize) to produce corn starch, then processing that starch to yield corn syrup, which is almost entirely glucose, and then adding enzymes that change some of the glucose into fructose.

High fructose corn syrup contains no artificial or synthetic ingredients or color additives.

High fructose corn syrup and sugar have almost the same level of sweetness.

It has either 42% or 55% fructose, which is comparable to sugar with 50% fructose. Studies found no differences in the metabolic effects of high fructose corn syrup as compared to sugar. Since high fructose corn syrup and sugar are so similar, the human body absorbs them the same way.

There is no scientific evidence that high fructose corn syrup is to blame for obesity and diabetes. In fact, the US Department of

Agriculture data shows that consumption of high fructose corn syrup has actually been declining while obesity and diabetes rates continue to rise.

Studies have shown that the body does not recognize a difference between high fructose corn syrup and regular sugar. They both contain the same ingredients, in the same quantities. The only difference is in how they are extracted and combined.

"After studying current research, the American Medical Association concluded that high fructose syrup does not appear to contribute to obesity more than other caloric sweeteners..."

Fabricated Animal Facts

Rabbits eat carrots, but as any bunny owner will attest, rabbits prefer leafy green vegetables. The image of the rabbit enjoying a carrot was made iconic by the cartoon character Bugs Bunny. However, when Bugs first did it, he was actually parodying a then famous scene from another movie called *It Happened One Night*. In the movie, Clark Gable is munching away on the carrot while talking and, when Bugs did it, he was merely referencing a scene which was quite well-known at the time, but became less so over the years.

Old cartoons tell us elephants love peanuts and they were constantly fed peanuts at circuses and zoos. This is now not a common practice. In the wild, peanuts are not a part of an elephant's diet and most elephants who have been fed peanuts in captivity do not like them. They prefer hay and other grains along with fruits and vegetables.

An elephant's nose is a regular nose. Since it is very long and dexterous, an elephant can use it to grab things, but its primary role is to breathe air, just like any other nose. Something an elephant definitely cannot do is drink water through it like a straw. It might appear that way, because elephants do suck in water through their trunks, but only to carry it into their mouths.

Ostriches been never been observed sticking their head in a hole, except in cartoons. When an ostrich is in danger, it will either 'fight or flight' like most other animals. It is equipped to do both quite well. It can reach speeds of up to 40 mph. In a fight, an ostrich has big, sharp claws and a kick powerful enough to take down a lion.

Vitamin C Myth Debunked

Thought it might be worth replaying this one. Hundreds of studies have now concluded that vitamin C does not treat the common cold.

The results of many studies of various types, involving hundreds of thousands of people from around the world have all arrived at the same conclusion - vitamin C has no effect to prevent or cure colds or cancer.

The FDA, the American Academy of Pediatrics, the American Medical Association, the American Dietetic Association, the Center for Human Nutrition at the Johns Hopkins Bloomberg School of Public Health, and the Department of Health and Human Services do not recommend supplemental vitamin C for the prevention or treatment of colds. Vitamin C does have other benefits and the studies did not say vitamin C is bad for you, it just does not provide the cancer and common cold remedies claimed.

Sweet Potato vs. White Potato Myth Debunked

The differences are much less than some experts would have us believe. These two tubers are very similar. The myth seems to stem from the fact that people tend to eat sweet potatoes baked or boiled, not fried, while more than a third of all white potatoes are consumed as either chips or French fries, so the sweet potato would appear to be less fattening by cooking style, not nutritional fact.

In a 100-gram portion, the white potato has 92 calories, 21 grams of carbs, 2.3 grams of fiber, 2.3 grams of protein and 17% of the recommended daily value of vitamin C. White potatoes are higher in essential minerals, such as iron, magnesium, and potassium.

In a 100-gram portion, the sweet potato has 90 calories, 21 grams of carbs, 3 grams of fiber, 2 grams of protein, 35% of the recommended daily value of vitamin C and 380% of the daily recommended value of vitamin A.

Another difference is that sweet potatoes have a lower glycemic index than regular potatoes. The glycemic index is a measure of how quickly blood glucose levels rise after eating. Foods that have a low glycemic index do not cause a quick spike in blood sugar. As a result, people do not experience the same sugar highs and lows, which can lead to hunger and the consumption of extra calories. In other words, foods with lower glycemic indexes, like sweet potatoes and brown rice, make you feel full longer. However, baked white potatoes typically are eaten with cheese, sour cream, or butter. These toppings all contain fat, which also lowers the glycemic index of a meal.

Bottom line, the form in which you consume a potato, such as baked vs. fries is a more important difference than the type of potato.

Incidentally, *Yams and sweet potatoes are not the same, but they are cousins and come from a different plant family.*

Four Rum Myths Dispelled

Rum is <u>not</u> always sweet. All rum is made from sugar. No, that does not mean it is sweet. Yeast converts sugar to alcohol and carbon dioxide before it goes into the still. A white rum can be as dry as any liquor. And aging in oak adds tannins and other wood flavorings that can produce dark rum as flavorful as Scotch.

Rum is <u>not</u> only best mixed with fruit juices. Rum has traditionally been a cheap spirit, and so was often mixed with cheap juices for frat parties. A good rum holds its own in classic cocktails like a rum Manhattan or a rum Old Fashioned. The finest aged rums are best appreciated neat.

Rum is <u>not</u> just a Caribbean/West Indian spirit. Rum's commercial birthplace may have been the sugar cane fields of the islands and the tropics, but prior to the American Revolution, dozens of rum distilleries existed in New England. Today, rum is a North American product, with craft distillers making distinctive rums from Boston to Hawaii.

Pirates did <u>not</u> always drink rum. Pirates drank whatever they could plunder, and in the early days, that was chiefly Spanish wine. Contemporary accounts of the dreaded Captain Morgan do not even mention rum. It was not until the late 17th and early 18th centuries that pirates started to drink rum, concurrent with the rise of the West Indian rum trade.

Gluten Free Fracas

The FDA finally passed a rule about what it means to be 'gluten free'. "A gluten-free claim means the food contains less than 20 parts per million of gluten, the protein found in grains such as wheat, barley and rye."

The three million, roughly .008% of Americans diagnosed with celiac disease are at risk of nutritional deficiencies, infertility, and intestinal cancer if they do not follow a strict gluten-free diet.

The rules do not apply to restaurants, although the FDA was urging them to comply. The agency also warned consumers that some products labeled gluten-free that do not meet the new standards may still be on the shelves.

Recently, gluten-free products accounted for more than $10.5 billion in sales in what has become an overblown fad for many people, for which gluten free may actually be more harmful to them.

Peter H.R. Green, MD, director of the Celiac Disease Center at Columbia University says for people with celiac disease, a gluten-free diet is essential. But for others, "unless people are very careful, a gluten-free diet can lack vitamins, minerals, and fiber."

Lisa Cimperman, a clinical dietitian at the University Hospitals Case Medical Center in Cleveland, OH, and a spokesperson for the Academy of Nutrition and Dietetics, "There is no research to support gluten-free diets for anyone other than those affected by celiac disease."

According to the Mayo Clinic, a gluten-free diet may lead to lower levels of iron, calcium, fiber, folate, thiamin, riboflavin, and niacin.

Loch Ness Nessie Debunked

British surgeon Robert Kenneth Wilson claimed he took the well known photograph while driving along the northern shore of Loch Ness. He said he noticed something moving in the water and stopped his car to take a photo. For decades the photo was considered to be the best evidence of the existence of a sea monster in the Loch. It came to be known as "The Surgeon's Photo."

It wasn't until 1994 that the secret of the image was revealed, when a man named Christian Spurling, shortly before his death at the age of 90, made a confession. He described a plot involving Wilson, himself, and big-game hunter Marmaduke Wetherell (his stepfather).

Wetherell dreamed up the hoax. He asked Spurling to make a model of a serpent. Spurling did this by attaching a serpent's head and neck to a toy submarine.

This model was then photographed in Loch Ness, and the picture given to Wilson, whose job it was to serve as a credible front-man for the hoax. The image given to the media was cropped to hide perspective, making the fake monster appear larger than it actually was.

Smile and Frown Myth Debunked

One myth which has been spread for years is that it takes many more muscles to frown than to smile. However, it actually takes only one more muscle to smile than it does to frown. Of the 53 facial muscles, 12 are needed for a genuine smile (zygomatic smile) and 11 are needed to frown.

A genuine smile takes two muscles to crinkle the eyes, two to pull up the lip corners and nose, two to elevate the mouth angle, and two to pull the mouth corners sideways.

A frown takes two muscles to pull down the lips in the lower face, three to furrow the brow, one to purse the lips, one to depress the lower lip, and two to pull the mouth corners down.

However, to create a fake smile, a person only needs to tighten the two risorius muscles, which draw back the corners of the mouth. Thus it uses the least amount of muscles to smile.

Four Vaccine Myths Debunked

- *They cause autism*: The origin of the myth was from a study by Dr. Andrew Wakefield. Most of Dr. Andrew Wakefield's co-authors withdrew their names from the study in 2004 after learning he had been paid by a law firm that intended to sue vaccine manufacturers. The same year, the Institute of Medicine reviewed evidence from the US, Denmark, Sweden, and the UK and found no connection between vaccines and autism. Around 2010, another British medical journal concluded Wakefield's study misrepresented or altered the medical histories of all 12 of the patients whose cases formed the basis of his study. The Lancet retracted Wakefield's paper in 2010 and he lost his medical license.

> *The Lancet retracted Wakefield's paper in 2010 and he lost his medical license.*

- *They contain poison*: The cause was from a preservative and Thimerosal is no longer used in vaccines. In 2001, the FDA stopped issuing licenses for children's vaccines containing it. The preservative has been used for decades and still is in adult vaccines.

There have been many studies and none of them show a correlation with autism or other serious side effects, the FDA says.

- *Doctors and insurance companies promote vaccinations to drive profits*: Some insurers pay the cost of vaccinations to prevent paying more later, when a patient gets sick. A 2009 study found that up to a third of doctors actually lose money when giving vaccines.

- *The diseases they help prevent are long gone*: One example of this effect is before the measles vaccine was introduced in the 1960s, there were between 3 to 4 million cases a year, resulting in 400 to 500 US deaths. Measles vaccination in the US has reduced the rate of infection in the population by 99% when compared to times when no vaccine was available. Measles has recently been on an uptick, because so many children have not been vaccinated against it.

Seasonal and Sugar Myths Debunked

Sugar - While parents may be convinced that sugary drinks, sweets and chocolate make their children hyperactive at least 12 studies have shown that there is no evidence to support this belief. Yet parents are so convinced about this myth that when they think their children have been given a drink containing sugar (when it is actually sugar-free) they rate their children's behavior as more hyperactive. In fact, the difference in behavior is all in the parents' mind.

Hats - As the cold weather approaches many people start wearing hats because of the strongly held belief that we lose most of our body heat through our head. The origins of the hat-wearing advice goes back to a US army survival manual from 1950s which strongly recommended covering the head when it is cold, since "40 to 45 percent of body heat" is lost from the head. In those studies, volunteers were dressed in Arctic survival suits and exposed to bitter cold conditions. Because it was the only part of their bodies left uncovered, most of their heat was lost through their heads.

The British Medical Journal, which argues that there is nothing special about the head and heat loss and "if this were true, humans would be just as cold if they went without trousers as if they went without a hat". If it is cold outside it makes sense to wrap up warm, but covering your head does not make a big difference.

Night Snacks - Some people swear by the rule that if you don't eat at night you won't get fat. One Swedish study seemed, at first glance, to support this theory as obese women reported eating more at night than non-obese women. In reality the women were not just night eaters but were generally eating more meals. The simple truth is that people put on weight because they consume more calories than they burn.

> The simple truth is that people put on weight, because they consume more calories than they burn.

Holiday Hangovers, Suicides and Poinsettias - Much research reveals that suicides do not increase over the holidays, poinsettias are not toxic, and that hangover cures do not work. The only way to avoid a hangover over Christmas is to drink moderately or not at all.

Microwave and Plastic Myth Debunked

The dangers of plastic in microwaves appears to have originated with a TV station in Honolulu that ran a segment in 2002 featuring Dr. Edward Fujimoto, who explained how microwaving plastic wrap and containers can release potentially deadly toxins into our food. A short news segment from Hawaii that few actually saw became huge when someone made it into an email that went viral.

The email claimed to be a media release from Johns Hopkins University, has the common urge to "pass this on to your family and friends" as do most untrue or politically incorrect emails. Johns Hopkins has formally debunked the email as originating from it.

Scientists do admit that it is possible heating plastic in a microwave might leach some substances into foods, but nowhere near the amount that would cause harm.

Another myth about chemicals in plastic water bottles getting into our bodies, while a boon for the metal water bottle industry, scientists say that cold temperatures actually inhibit the ability of chemicals to leak out of plastics.

Climate Change Facts and Myths

Global Warming Comments

- Buzz Aldrin, Astronaut "I absolutely do not feel that we as humans are threatening the survival of the world. The world's been here a very long time. We're inhabitants. We make use of the resources here and the world is changing, and it has been changing because of the position of the sun in the Milky Way galaxy; and the perturbations, the changes in the orbital parameters, are always going through cycles, and the world will recover from whatever cycle it has to be going through.

We can be very concerned about what's changing and say, "Wouldn't it be nice if it just stayed just the way it is?" Well, as other people — this is not original with me — but as other people have observed, what right do we have to say that whatever exists right now should be the way it should be forever and ever? It may get much, much better for a number of people; it may get much, much worse. And we can expend all sorts of energies trying to maintain a stable condition at great cost."

Another Comment

- The General Motors exec behind the Chevrolet Volt electric car hands environmentalists another stick to beat GM with when he reportedly calls global warming "a crock of shit." Bob Lutz, GM's vice chairman for product development, later addresses the uproar on his own blog: "General Motors is dedicated to the removal of cars and trucks from the environmental equation, period."

Global Warming Wrong, Again

- The recent acceleration of glacier melt-off in Greenland, which some scientists fear could dramatically raise sea levels, may only be a temporary phenomenon, according to a recently published study.

Researchers in Britain and the United States devised computer models to test three scenarios that could account for rapid (by the standards applied to glaciers) melting of the Helheim Glacier, one of Greenland's largest.

Two were based on changes caused directly by global warming: an increase in the flow of water that greases the underside of the glacier as it slides toward the sea, and a general thinning due to melting.

A team led by Faezeh Nick of Durham University in Britain found that neither of these scenarios matched the data. "They simply don't fit what we have observed," said co-author Andreas Vieli in an interview. "The third computer model, which hypothesized that melt-off was triggered by changing conditions in the confined area where the glacier meets the sea fit like a glove. You cannot maintain these very high rates of peak mass loss for very long. The glaciers start to retreat and settle into a new and relatively stable state," he said. The Helheim Glacier, along with several others in Greenland, started to slow down in 2007."

Global Warming Effect on Polar Bears Penis Bones

- Now I've heard it all. Polar bear penis bones are shrinking in Eastern Greenland, according to the University of Aarhus in Denmark. It found that polar bears living in the Eastern Greenland are somewhat less well endowed than their cousins in Svalbard and the Canadian Arctic. They say this could be due to the high prevalence of pollutants such as PCBs and DDT in Eastern Greenland - pollutants which records show are less prevalent in Svalbard and the Canadian Arctic.

The study showed that carnivores living in snowy environments, close to the poles, tend to have longer penis bones to help them be more competitive. The group concludes that human pollution, combined with the difficulty of finding food in warming climates, may spell disaster for Eastern Greenland polar bears. *I wonder how they get close enough to measure them.*

Alaska Icefield Buildup

- Two hundred years of glacial shrinkage in Alaska, and then came the winter and summer of 2007-2008 when unusually large amounts of winter snow were followed by unusually chill temperatures in June, July, and August.

"Never before, in the history of a research project dating back to 1946 had the Juneau Icefield witnessed the kind of snow buildup that came this year. It was similar on a lot of other glaciers too." said U.S. Geological Survey glaciologist Bruce Molnia.

Melting Icebergs

- We read a lot about melting icebergs and rising ocean levels, but the real story is that this has nothing to do with global warming or cooling. That is another argument for another day. This is about the facts regarding ice and water.

Archimedes' principal states that a floating object displaces its own weight of fluid and should not add more water when it melts. Also, the weight of the displaced fluid is directly proportional to the volume of the displaced fluid. Of course there is some land based ice that is also melting, and it would raise the level of water if it is not absorbed by the land on which it sits.

> If all the floating ice was to melt, sea levels would rise by only 4cm (less than 2 inches).

Melting icebergs cause sea levels spread evenly across the globe to rise by just 49 micrometers a year, about the width of a human hair.

At that rate, it would take 200 years for the oceans to rise by a centimeter (an inch is 2.54 centimeters).

If all the floating ice was to melt, sea levels would rise by only 4cm (less than 2 inches), according to scientists published in the journal of Geophysical Research Letter, April 2010. *So, if the climate folks are correct, it will take a bit less than 800 years to raise the sea levels by a bit less than two inches. Hmmm. . .*

Global Warming Explained

- Finally we have a simple explanation of a global warming cause. The following is from then US Department of State Report - 'Key Uncertainties Affecting Projected Greenhouse Gas Emissions'.

"Any projection of future emissions is subject to considerable uncertainty. In the short term (less than 5 years), the key factors that can increase or decrease estimated net emissions include unexpected changes in retail energy prices, shifts in the competitive relationship between natural gas and coal in electricity generation markets, changes in economic growth, abnormal winter or summer temperatures, and imperfect forecasting methods. Additional factors may influence emission rates over the longer term, notably technology developments, shifts in the composition of economic activity, and changes in government policies."

> "If the Kyoto agreement were fully obeyed through 2099, it would cut temperatures by only 0.3 degrees Fahrenheit."

- *New York Times April 24, 2009 by Bjorn Lomborg, director of the Copenhagen Consensus Center at Copenhagen Business School* - "If the Kyoto agreement were fully obeyed through 2099, it would cut temperatures by only 0.3 degrees Fahrenheit."

Trees are Good? Bad?

- Good - By most accounts, deforestation in tropical rainforests adds more carbon dioxide to the atmosphere than the sum total of cars and trucks on the world's roads. According to the World Carfree Network, cars and trucks account for about 14 percent of global carbon emissions, while most analysts attribute upwards of 15 percent to deforestation.

"Any realistic plan to reduce global warming pollution sufficiently, and in time, to avoid dangerous consequences must rely in part on preserving tropical forests," reports Environmental Defense Fund.

- Bad - "Although temperatures have risen throughout the globe, they've gone up most dramatically in the Arctic. Past warm periods indicate that deciduous tree (deciduous trees lose their leaves in the winter) expansion into the Arctic is a common occurrence when the region warms up, so a new study has looked into the impact trees could have on the regional climate.

As expected, the increase of the leafy trees would result in less reflective ground, but the study suggests they could also induce more cloud cover and an increasingly warm surface and ocean that have more turbulent weather patterns.

The simulation indicated that the expansion of leafy trees, by their ability to increase water vapor and absorb light, would result in an increase of the surface temperature in the Arctic region of about a Kelvin (1K is about 1.8 degrees Fahrenheit) over the next 20 years." From ARS Technica Dec, 30, 2009.

Aspen to the Rescue

- Good - The rising level of atmospheric carbon dioxide is making some trees grow by 50% is a finding of a new study of natural stands of quaking aspen, one of North America's most important and widespread deciduous trees. The study, by scientists from the University of Wisconsin-Madison and the University of Minnesota at Morris and published Dec. 4, 2009 in the journal Global Change Biology, shows that elevated levels of atmospheric carbon dioxide during the past 50 years have boosted aspen growth rates by an astonishing 50 percent.

"We can't forecast ecological change. It's a complicated business."

The findings are important as the world's forests, which cover about thirty percent of the Earth's land surface, play an important role in regulating climate and sequestering greenhouses gases. The forests of the Northern Hemisphere, in particular, act as sinks for carbon dioxide, helping to offset increased levels of carbon dioxide.

Aspen is a dominant tree in mountainous and northern forested regions of North America, including 42 million acres of Canadian forest and up to 6.5 million acres in Wisconsin and Minnesota.

"We can't forecast ecological change. It's a complicated business," explains Waller, a UW-Madison professor of botany. Carbon dioxide is food for plants, which extract it from the air and through photosynthesis convert it to sugar, plant food.

Whether the Weather

- According to the US Department of State - "Energy use for heating and cooling is directly responsive to weather variation. The AEO forecast of Co2 emissions assumes 30-year average values for population-weighted heating and cooling degree-days. Unlike other sources of uncertainty, for which deviations between assumed and actual trends may follow a persistent course over time, the effect of weather on energy use and emissions in any particular year is largely independent from year to year."

Going Green

- How is your carbon footprint?

Plastic bags are only about 1,000th of the carbon footprint of what is in the bags - 10g carbon dioxide equivalent.

Electric hand driers only use 20g CO2e.

Watching TV for an hour in front of a 42-inch plasma screen is about equal to a one-mile drive in a very efficient car - 220g CO2e.

Keeping your old car is better than buying a new one, because making a car creates about half the footprint of the fuel it burns. It takes a long time to recover the fifty percent CO2e cost of building the new car.

> *From a woman's point of view - she can go shopping for an hour and take home 22 bags of goodies to equal one hour of her mate watching TV.*

> *From a man's point of view - he needs to drive his sleek new car fast and far, to quickly make up for the carbon wasted in building it.*

Greenland Ice Loss Not so Bad

- Estimates of the rate of ice loss from Greenland and West Antarctica should be halved, according to Dutch and US scientists.

Several teams have estimated Greenland and West Antarctica are shedding billions of tons of ice per year. However, according to the new study, published in the September issue of the journal Nature Geoscience, those ice estimates fail to correct for a phenomenon known as glacial isostatic adjustment.

"We have concluded that the Greenland and West Antarctica ice caps are melting at approximately half the speed originally predicted. If the figures for overall sea level rise are accurate, ice sheet loss would contribute about 30 percent, rather than roughly half." The rest would come mainly from thermal expansion, meaning that as the sea warms it rises.

Sea Level Rises

- The gist of the study is that very simple, physical considerations show some of the very large predictions of sea level rise are unlikely, because there is simply no way to move the ice or the water into the ocean that fast. A team began the study by postulating future sea level rise at about 2 meters by 2100 produced only by Greenland. Since rapid, unstable ice discharge into the ocean is restricted to Greenland glacier beds based below sea level, they identified and mapped all of the so-called outlet glacier "gates" on Greenland's perimeter.

"For Greenland alone to raise sea level by two meters by 2100, all of the outlet glaciers involved would need to move more 70 times faster than they presently move, and they would have to start moving that fast today, not 10 years from now. It is a simple argument with no fancy physics. In my opinion, some of the research out there calling for 20 or 30 feet of sea rise by the end of the century is not backed up by solid glaciological evidence," said Tad Pfeffer, a fellow of CU-Boulder's Institute of Arctic and Alpine Research. "If we plan for 6 feet and only get 2 feet, for example, or visa versa, we could spend billions of dollars of resources solving the wrong problems."

One last quote

- "With future CO_2 levels expected by the year 2100 to approach levels not seen in the last 25 million years. . ." Climatologist Robert DeConto, Geosciences Department University of Massachusetts.

From Science vol. 332 p 430, 22 April 2011, dealing with past climate variations makes the following statement about the Eocene period (allegedly 34-56 million years ago): "Although the global physiography of the Eocene was broadly similar to that of the modern Earth, the climate was vastly different. Polar regions lacked major ice sheets and were home to cold-intolerant plants and animals, and tropical oceans steamed away at temperatures approaching 40°C. These differences were driven at least in part by atmospheric CO_2 concentrations about five times the preindustrial value." *It happened before and yet mankind is still here to write about it.*

Soil and Carbon Dioxide

- A Cornell study in November 2008, published online in Nature Geosciences, quantified the amount of black carbon in Australian soils and found that there was far more than expected, said Johannes

Lehmann, the paper's lead author and a Cornell professor of biogeochemistry. The survey was the largest of black carbon ever published.

"As a result of global warming, soils are expected to release more carbon dioxide, the major greenhouse gas, into the atmosphere, which, in turn, creates more warming. It takes a few years for organic carbon to decompose, as microbes eat it and convert it to carbon dioxide, but black carbon can take 1,000-2,000 years, on average to convert to carbon dioxide."

Soils produce 10 times more carbon dioxide each year than all the carbon dioxide emissions from human activities combined.

The study quantified the amount of black carbon in 452 Australian soils across two savannas. Black carbon content varied widely, between zero and more than eighty percent. By entering realistic estimates of stocks of black carbon in soil from those Australian savannas into a computer model that calculates carbon dioxide release from soil, the researchers found that carbon dioxide emissions from soils were reduced by about 20 percent over 100 years, as compared with simulations that did not take black carbon's long shelf life into account. The findings are significant because soils are by far the world's largest source of carbon dioxide, producing 10 times more carbon dioxide each year than all the carbon dioxide emissions from human activities combined.

Seven ECO Myths Debunked

Myth: The Earth is warmer than it was 100 years ago.
Truth: At most it has risen by 0.3 Celsius, less than 0.003 degrees annually.

Myth: Global Warming must be happening; it's warmer here in Small Town.
Truth: It is global averages that matter. (see above)

Myth: Carbon dioxide levels and average global temperatures are at a record high.
Truth: No, they are among the lowest determined over the last few million years.

Myth: Rising carbon dioxide levels are directly linked to rising global temperatures.
Truth: Not necessarily, there is a 400-4000 year timelag

Myth: Receding ice sheets prove anthropogenic (man made) Global Warming is happening
Truth: Some ice is melting, other areas are actually growing

Myth: Carbon dioxide is the most potent greenhouse gas
Truth: No, that is water vapor of which there is an abundance in the atmosphere, then there is methane, and nitrogen trifluoride used in the manufacture of flat screen TVs.

Myth: If we accept it as real, we can do something about it.
Truth: We cannot even control local weather, what makes us think carbon sequestration and seeding the oceans, etc. will allow us to affect the climate. (Spliced feed for The Science Network)

Carbon Dioxide Facts

Carbon Dioxide gets a bad rap from the press, but it is natural and essential to life. CO_2 is a colorless, odorless, non-toxic gas and it is not a pollutant. Trying to control CO_2 by regulation is trying to regulate and control nature. Without CO_2, plants die off and without plant life the earth's biological food chain would be terminally broken.

Plants require carbon dioxide to conduct photosynthesis. Greenhouses enrich their atmospheres with additional CO_2 to sustain and increase plant growth. Plants can grow as much as 50 percent faster in concentrations of 1,000 ppm CO_2 when compared with ambient conditions. If carbon dioxide is increasing so much around the globe, it would be logical that plants and trees would be growing faster than they previously did, but they are not.

CO_2 is reduced by photosynthesis of plants. A photosynthesis-related drop (by a factor less than two) in carbon dioxide concentration in a greenhouse compartment would kill green plants, or completely stop their growth. Increased atmospheric CO_2 concentrations result in fewer stomata developing on plants, which leads to reduced water usage and increased water-use efficiency.

Deforestation for agriculture is just replacing one type of vegetation with another. Both trees and plants reduce CO_2.

Photosynthesis by phytoplankton consumes dissolved CO_2 in the upper ocean and promotes the absorption of CO_2 from the atmosphere. Photosynthesis uses carbon dioxide and water to produce sugars from which other organic compounds can be constructed, and oxygen is produced as a by-product. Sea urchins convert carbon dioxide into raw material for their shells.

Carbon dioxide dissolves in the ocean to form carbonic acid (H_2CO_3), bicarbonate (HCO_3) and carbonate (CO_32). There is about fifty times as much carbon dissolved in the sea water of the oceans as exists in the atmosphere. The oceans act as an enormous carbon sink, and take up about 30% of the total released into the atmosphere.

In medicine, up to 5% carbon dioxide (130 times atmospheric concentration) is added to oxygen for stimulation of breathing after apnea and to stabilize the O_2/CO_2 balance in blood.

Liquid and solid carbon dioxide are important refrigerants, especially in the food industry, where they are employed during the transportation and storage of frozen foods. Solid carbon dioxide, dry ice is used for small shipments where refrigeration equipment is not practical.

Carbon dioxide is used in enhanced oil recovery where it is injected into or adjacent to producing oil wells, when it becomes miscible (mixed) with the oil. It acts as both a pressurizing agent and, when dissolved into the underground crude oil, significantly reduces its viscosity, and changes surface chemistry enabling the oil to flow faster.

Carbon dioxide is used to keep the pH level from rising in swimming pools.

Atmospheric concentrations of carbon dioxide fluctuate slightly with the change of the seasons. Concentrations of carbon dioxide fall during the Northern Hemisphere spring and summer as plants consume it, and rise during the northern autumn and winter as plants go dormant or die.

Up to 40% of the gas emitted by some volcanoes during eruptions is carbon dioxide.

Various proxies and modeling suggests larger variations in past times. 500 million years ago CO_2 levels were likely 10 times higher than now.

Incidentally, during 2009, energy-related CO_2 emissions in the US had their largest absolute and percentage decline, seven percent (which followed a three percent drop in 2008), since the start of US Energy Information Administration comprehensive record of annual energy data that began in 1949.

Last Thoughts

FIVE COMMON REGRETS

While derping around the net seeking some more happy thoughts, I came across the following. It brings into focus that way too many people fail to cultivate relationships and be happy until it is too late. This is not meant to be morose, but rather as a heads up to celebrate, have fun, and laugh so you do not have these regrets.

A nurse, Bronnie Ware, on her blog, inspirationandchai relates some things shared by her patients, who were within the last few weeks and months of their life. The most common five regrets her patients related were:

1. **I wish I'd had the courage to live a life true to myself, not the life others expected of me**. This was the most common regret of all.

2. **I wish I didn't work so hard.** Mostly men said this, but also women. They regretted missing so much time with family.

3. **I wish I had the courage to express my feelings.** They regretted not saying how they really felt, just to keep peace with others.

4. **I wish I had stayed in touch with my friends.** After family, they most regretted letting friendships lapse by not taking the time to stay in touch.

5. **I wish that I had let myself be happier.** Too many people forget that happiness is a choice and they waste time on old comfortable habits. They longed to laugh properly and have silliness in their life again.

FAMOUS LAST WORDS

"You can get more with a kind word and a gun than you can get with a kind word alone" — Al Capone

"Money can't buy life" — Bob Marley

"I'm bored with it all" — Winston Churchill

"I finally get to see Marilyn" — Joe DiMaggio

"My God, what's happened?" — Princess Diana

"One never knows the ending. One has to die to know exactly what happens after death, although Catholics have their hopes" — Alfred Hitchcock

"I'm going away tonight" - James Brown

"Is everyone else alright?" -Robert F. Kennedy

"This is absurd, this is absurd." -Sigmund Freud

"Lord help my poor soul." -Edgar Allan Poe

"Am I dying or is this my birthday?" -Lady Nancy Astor

"Now I shall go to sleep. Goodnight." -Lord George Byron

"Don't let it end like this. Tell them I said something." -Pancho Villa

"God damn the whole friggin' world and everyone in it but you, Carlotta." -W.C. Fields

"Just don't leave me alone." -John Belushi

"Please don't leave me. Please don't leave me." -Chris Farley

"I'm going to heaven." -Bo Diddley

"I'll sleep well tonight." -Henry Ford

"Yes, it's tough, but not as tough as doing comedy." -Edmund Gwenn

"Either that wallpaper goes, or I do." -Oscar Wilde

Index

INDEX

www.ingramcontent.com/pod-product-compliance
Lightning Source LLC
Chambersburg PA
CBHW062126280526
45788CB00001B/73